Understanding the Dynamics of a Knowledge Economy

STUDIES IN EVOLUTIONARY POLITICAL ECONOMY

Series Editor: Albert Jolink
RSM Erasmus University, Erasmus University Rotterdam, The Netherlands

Studies in Evolutionary Political Economy is a new series sponsored by the European Association for Evolutionary Political Economy. The series contains original, thematic works that challenge existing perspectives in economics, offering new and exciting views on topical issues. It will undoubtedly promote a better understanding of new developments in economics.

Understanding the Dynamics of a Knowledge Economy

Edited by

Wilfred Dolfsma

Erasmus University Rotterdam and 2005/6 NIAS Fellow, The Netherlands

Luc Soete

Joint Director, United Nations University-Institute for New Technologies (UNU-INTECH) and the Maastricht Economic Research Institute on Innovation and Technology (MERIT) and Professor of International Economics, Maastricht University, The Netherlands

STUDIES IN EVOLUTIONARY POLITICAL ECONOMY

Edward Elgar
Cheltenham, UK • Northampton, MA, USA

Published by
Edward Elgar Publishing Limited
Glensanda House
Montpellier Parade
Cheltenham
Glos GL50 1UA
UK

Edward Elgar Publishing, Inc.
136 West Street
Suite 202
Northampton
Massachusetts 01060
USA

A catalogue record for this book
is available from the British Library

Library of Congress Cataloguing in Publication Data

Understanding the dynamics of a knowledge economy/edited by Wilfred
    Dolfsma, Luc Soete.
        p. cm. — (Studies in evolutionary political economy)
    Includes bibliographical references and index.
    1. Information technology—Economic aspects. 2. Technological
innovations—Economic aspects. 3. Knowledge management. I. Dolfsma,
Wilfred. II. Soete, Luc. III. Series.
HC79.I55.U575 2006
303.48'33–dc22

                                                        2005056791

ISBN-13: 978 1 84542 307 0
ISBN-10: 1 84542 307 0

Printed and bound in Great Britain by MPG Books Ltd, Bodmin, Cornwall

Contents

Figures

Tables

Contributors

Jorge Bateira, ESRC Centre for Research on Innovation and Competition (CRIC) The University of Manchester, UK

Wilfred Dolfsma, Erasmus University Rotterdam and Maastricht University, corresponding editor of the *Review of Social Economy* and 2005/6 NIAS Fellow, The Netherlands

Theo Dunnewijk, Maastricht Economic Research Institute on Innovation and Technology, (MERIT), Maastricht University, The Netherlands

Elizabeth Garnsey, Centre for Technology Management, Institute for Manufacturing, and Judge Institute of Management, University of Cambridge, UK

Nathalie Lazaric, CNRS–GREDEG, University of Nice–Sophia-Antipolis, France

Loet Leydesdorff, Amsterdam School of Communications Research (ASCoR), University of Amsterdam, The Netherlands

Joel Mokyr, Departments of Economics and History, Northwestern University, USA

Paul Muller, BETA, Pôle Européen de Gestion et d'Economie, Université Louis Pasteur, France

Isabel Salavisa, Economics Department, Dinâmia/ISCTE, Portugal

Luc Soete, Joint Director, United Nations University-Institute for New Technologies (UNU-INTECH) and the Maastricht Economic Research Institute on Innovation and Technology (MERIT) and Professor of International Economics, Maastricht University, The Netherlands

Erik Stam, ERIM, Rotterdam School of Management, Erasmus University Rotterdam and Department of Economic Geography, University of Utrecht, The Netherlands

Catherine Thomas, CNRS–GREDEG, University of Nice–Sophia-Antipolis, France

René Wintjes, Maastricht Economic Research Institute on Innovation and Technology (MERIT), Maastricht University, The Netherlands

Source: DaDA. Courtesy of © Gilia van Dijk Pictures, 1994.

Dynamics of a knowledge economy: introduction

Wilfred Dolfsma and Luc Soete

Some commentators believe the term knowledge economy to be too elusive to be useful. Others have found the idea of knowledge, information and abilities as being prime resources for economies to be very valuable. It is fair to say that any assessment of the contemporary role of knowledge must recognize that most economic activity rests on knowledge, not only in present society but in all forms of human society. Palaeolithic society was by any standards 'knowledge-based', and palaeontologists have demonstrated the existence of well-formed bodies of knowledge with respect to animal behaviour, materials, mining, symbolic communication and even medicine. In the more recent past, the industrial economy of the nineteenth century was intensively knowledge-based. At first sight many claims about the current 'knowledge economy' could plausibly have been made a hundred years ago. It is of course true that knowledge accumulates over time, that it changes the quality and quantity of output. Hence that today the knowledge intensity of production is likely to be much higher than ever before. But does this obvious point mean we are entering some new form of society, which is qualitatively different in terms of the use of knowledge?

There is obviously a clear impression that rates of change seem to have increased in the last three decades, at least as appears from the discussions among economists and social scientists. Since Foray and Lundvall (1996), Cowan et al. (2000) and Cooke (2002), much has been said about the knowledge economy or the knowledge base of the economy. Foray (2004) presents a recent overview. As a typical measure of just how much has been said about the term, entering it in the quintessential Internet search engine Google provides one with some 637 000 hits (22 August 2005). This web search only took 0.19 seconds.

A DYNAMIC KNOWLEDGE ECONOMY

Much previous research can perhaps be reinterpreted as analysing the role of knowledge in the economy, and the knowledge economy. The economic development of regions was perceived by Alfred Marshall as dependent on knowledge and ideas that are 'in the air'. Later scholars have called such phenomena externalities or knowledge externalities. Romer (1986, 1993) and more recently Baumol (2002) have both made this case. Attention has focused on, for instance in the field of economic geography, growth poles (Perroux, 1955), learning regions (Morgan, 1997), national or regional innovation systems (Nelson, 1993; Bradzych et al., 1998), and innovative milieu (Camagni, 1995). Diffusion of knowledge and information in geographically restricted areas is relatively fast: circulation, imitation and cooperation is enhanced (compare Saxenian, 1994). There is debate about the nature of the knowledge and information that should be circulating within the bounds analysed: should it be of a highly specialized or of a more diverse nature (van der Panne, 2004)? Sometimes it seems as if the terms in which the discussion is phrased are recast in terms of the knowledge economy (for example, Werker and Athreye, 2004). Turning to a discussion of knowledge's role in the economy is, thus, not new. ICT as both source and medium for knowledge to accumulate and diffuse at the micro level of firms, groups or communities, as well as at the macro level within countries and at a global level did, however, add a particularly acute sense of urgency to the discussion (compare Ter Weel and Soete, 2005).

Whatever one may think of the term, it is clear that developments in our current economy are related to 'knowledge' and noteworthy for their dynamics. Not only do developments seem to have speeded up over recent years and decades, but the complexity of their dynamics seems to have increased. Discussing the role of knowledge in the economy poses fundamental theoretical problems. The conceptualization of information, the individual and how he/she acquires knowledge, as well as his/her interaction with other agents are implicated (Davis, 2003; Dolfsma, 2001). Such a discussion also impacts views on how society is to be institutionally furnished – a realization that first dawned, perhaps, with Hayek (1945).

THIS VOLUME

This volume does not offer ready-made answers to whatever questions one might have about the knowledge economy, as an academic, as someone responsible for making (government) policy, as an entrepreneur, or as a citizen. That is a strong point of this volume, we believe, as it would seriously jeopardize the tenability of what is offered here had we succumbed to the temptation of attempting to offer such answers. The dynamics of the knowledge economy would soon render obsolete whatever concrete answers would be offered that would be readily usable. Instead, what is offered here are views of the knowledge economy that contribute to a better understanding of what is going on. These views allow us to 'read', so to speak, the knowledge economy. The views may be views on macro themes such as the ones offered by Mokyr and Leydesdorff, but others are of a more micro nature. Joel Mokyr, in Chapter 1, extends his previous work on the Industrial Revolution, answering the questions of why it arose, when and where it arose, by turning to the role of ideas and practices one associates with the Enlightenment. According to him, these offer an important element that is needed to explain the extraordinary events of the Industrial Revolution. For all that is said about the knowledge economy, at least by some, the comparison would seem to be appropriate. Even if the two are incomparable phenomena, the act of comparing would allow one to realize that ideas play a powerful role in the economy; their relatively unencumbered circulation is ultimately likely to be beneficial to the economy as well. Circulation of ideas just for the sake of circulation does not make much sense, and there should thus be institutions that not only help circulate ideas, but also sift them (compare Mokyr, 2002).

Loet Leydesdorff offers the theoretical foundations to rebut all those who have criticized the term 'knowledge economy' as elusive, or worse. He draws on information theory, systems theory, and scientometrics to argue that the knowledge base of an economy can be grasped theoretically. In subsequent work (Leydesdorff et al., 2006) the knowledge base was grasped empirically as well, with some noteworthy findings as to the origins of contributions to it. Leydesdorff argues that knowledge and information are exchanged when players in a relatively confined context interact, thereby shaping each others expectations. Coming from a different theoretical background, but nevertheless focusing on that same theme, Nathalie Lazaric and Catherine Thomas present their analysis of just such interactions for a specific region in France that is noteworthy for its economic dynamics: the Sophipolitan telecom cluster. Needless to say, the theoretical framework is much more focused on the micro level, relying on concepts such as routines, rules and knowledge (codification). Specific actors can and do have an influence on the development of a region (see also, for example, Lawson, 2003). Erik Stam and Elizabeth Garnsey, much in line with the theoretical approach adopted by Lazaric and Thomas, study a different phenomenon. Their focus is on the trajectories that newly established firms may go through, trying to establish regularities. Using Edith Penrose's (1995) concept of an opportunity environment, they claim that the growth of firms needs a closer look than tends to be done usually in order to find out what might facilitate or hinder it. At an even more micro level of interactions between individuals, yet at the same time concerning a phenomenon that stretches across the boundaries of organizations and firms, Paul Muller analyses the dynamics within groups informally cooperating, in this case, to develop open source software. He shows what explains the informal structures establishing reputation and leadership that emerge in such groups, and how that influences both the process as well as the outcome of cooperative efforts.

Both Theo Dunnewijk and René Wintjes (Chapter 6) and Isabel Salavisa (Chapter 7) zoom in on the state. Wintjes and Dunnewijk make a more down to earth case about the role of the state in Flanders (Belgium). Here, the state has played a much more active role than is sometimes suggested is appropriate for a state in a globalized, ICT-driven knowledge economy. Such an active involvement it is often argued, is doomed to fail. Wintjes and Dunnewijk show that this need not be the case – there is rather a need for sustained commitment from the state, but, obviously, no guarantee for ultimate success. Isabel Salavisa takes the discussion about the role of the state to a more general level. She argues that one should not expect a reduced role of the state in a complex knowledge economy. Indeed, as society and the economy have become increasingly complex over the last century and more, the state has only grown, despite efforts, on and off, to diminish its role. However, when contemplating measures, a government is in need of some framework that might help it decide in which areas to institute, change or remove what kind of regulations. Chapter 8, by Wilfred Dolfsma, suggests that due to the nature of knowledge and knowledge development, this cannot be the usual measuring rod of Paretian welfare theory provided by economists. He argues that at least the Paretian framework should be complemented with consideration from what he calls a dynamic welfare theory. From such a dynamic (Schumpeterian) welfare perspective, Dolfsma evaluates current developments of an institution that is crucial for the knowledge economy: intellectual property rights.

Rather than starting this volume on the knowledge economy with a contribution about the concept of knowledge itself, the editors have decided to postpone the extensive exploration of that concept to the end of the book. Jorge Bateira offers a profound conceptual analysis of the concept of knowledge. One that is not the common position to take in economics (compare Dolfsma, 2001), but one which finds much support in other social sciences besides economics, and one to which at least the more sensible economists are moving (Nelson and Nelson, 2002). Had the editors started the volume with a contribution defining, or at least extensively discussing, the concept of knowledge, there would be a need to indicate the extents to which the subsequent contributions adhere to such a view. That might have distracted from the main argument of the book – to offer a range of views to read the knowledge economy – and might even have prevented us from offering a wide range of possible readings of the knowledge economy as the focus of chapters. A discussion in each chapter of the extent to which the views on knowledge assumed align with those of others might prevent contributors from arguing their case.

This last consideration has also made the editors decide not to offer concluding remarks. We are under no illusion that the different understandings provided can be synthesized easily and concisely. What is more, and even if that would entail a prolonged discussion, we believe we would be doing the readers of this volume a disservice by attempting to offer such concluding remarks.

REFERENCES

Baumol, W.J. (2002), *The Free-market Innovation Machine: Analyzing the Growth Miracle of Capitalism*, Princeton, NJ: Princeton University Press.

Bradzych, H.J., P. Cooke and M. Heidenreich (eds) (1998), *Regional Innovation Systems*, London: UCL Press.

Camagni, R.P. (1995), 'The Concept of *Innovative Milieu* and its Relevance for Public Policies in European Lagging Regions', *Papers in Regional Science*, **74**(4): 317–40.

Cooke, P. (2002), *Knowledge Economies*, London: Routledge.

Cowan, R., P. David and D. Foray (2000), 'The Explicit Economics of Knowledge Codification and Tacitness', *Industrial Change and Corporate Change*, **9**(2): 211–53.

Davis, J. (2003), *The Theory of the Individual in Economics*, London: Routledge.

Dolfsma, W. (2001), 'Metaphors of Knowledge in Economics', *Review of Social Economy*, **59**(1): 71–91.

Foray, D. (2004), *The Economics of Knowledge*, Cambridge, MA: MIT Press.

Foray, D., and B.-A. Lundvall (1996), 'The Knowledge-based Economy: From the Economics of Knowledge to the Learning Economy', in *OECD Documents: Employment and Growth in the Knowledge-based Economy*, Paris: OECD, pp. 11–32.

Hayek, F. (1945), 'The Use of Knowledge in Society', *American Economic Review*, **35**(4): 519–30.

Lawson, C. (2003), 'Technical Consultancies and Regional Competences', in W. Dolfsma and C. Dannreuther (eds), *Globalization, Social Capital and Inequality*, Cheltenham, UK and Northampton, MA, USA: Edward Elgar, pp. 75–92.

Leydesdorff, L., W. Dolfsma and G. van der Panne (2006), 'Measuring the Knowledge Base of an Economy in terms of Triple-helix Relations among "Technology, Organization, and Territory"', *Research Policy*, **35**(2).

Mokyr, J. (2002), *The Gifts of Athena – Historical Origins of the Knowledge Economy*, Princeton, NJ: Princeton University Press.

Morgan, K. (1997), 'The Learning Region: Institutions, Innovation and Regional Renewal', *Regional Studies*, **31**(5): 491–503.

Nelson, R.R. (ed.) (1993), *National Innovation Systems: A Comparative Study*, Oxford and New York: Oxford University Press.

Nelson, K. and R.R. Nelson (2002), 'On the Nature and Evolution of Human Know-how', *Research Policy*, **31**: 719–33.

Van der Panne, G. (2004), 'Agglomeration Externalities: Marshall versus Jacobs', *Journal of Evolutionary Economics*, **14**(5): 593–604.

Penrose, E.T. (1995), *The Theory of the Growth of the Firm* (first published 1959), Oxford: Oxford University Press.

Perroux, F. (1955), 'Note sure le Notion de Pôle de Croissance', *Economie Appliqué*, **7**: 307–20.

Romer, P. (1986), 'Increasing Returns and Long-run Growth', *Journal of Political Economy*, **94**: 1002–37.

Romer, P. (1993), 'Two Strategies for Economic Development: Using Ideas and Producing Ideas', Proceedings of the World Bank Annual Conference on Development Economics 1992, IBRD/World Bank.

Saxenian, A. (1994), *Regional Advantage*, Cambridge, MA: Harvard University Press.

Ter Weel, B. and L. Soete (eds) (2005), *The Economy of the Digital Society*, Cheltenham, UK and Northampton, MA, USA: Edward Elgar.

Werker, C. and S. Athreye (eds) (2004), *Knowledge and Innovation Driving Regional Economic Development and Growth*, special issue of the *Journal of Evolutionary Economics*, **14**(5).

1. The great synergy: the European Enlightenment as a factor in modern economic growth*

Joel Mokyr

INTRODUCTION

In this chapter I propose to summarize and extend an argument made in a number of other papers (Mokyr, 2005a, 2005b, 2005c). The issue at stake is a variant of the 'European Miracle' question. Despite the resentment in certain circles against the questions concerning the 'Rise of the West' as a valid historical inquiry, the question will not go away; because it is good history even if it is politically controversial. It is perhaps ironic that the problem is now more central to economists and so-called 'world historians' than to the rest of the history profession. Indeed, to paraphrase Robert Lucas (1988), the more we look at the problem of modern growth the harder it is to think of anything else that matters.

The consensus is that modern economic growth started with the British Industrial Revolution. As is well known, during the Industrial Revolution itself growth was in fact fairly modest, but the sudden take-off of GDP per capita after 1825 or thereabouts could not have happened without a long period of laying the foundations.[1] The transformation was tantamount to a 'phase transition', a sea change in the mechanics of economic growth, with technological progress gradually coming to dominate the process, accounting for its novel features. But what were these foundations, exactly? It is this issue that this chapter seeks to address.

Before doing so, two central points have to be understood. The first is that events like the cluster of macro-inventions that came about in the first decades of the Industrial Revolution are not altogether unique in history, either in Europe or elsewhere. Moreover, growth, as Jones (1988) and many others have noted, was not a new phenomenon in nineteenth-century Europe either. Many regions or groups had managed over the centuries to accumulate wealth, to produce surpluses beyond subsistence, as works of art, architecture, and science amply indicate. Yet none of these processes had

7

persistence; growth was always checked and eventually fizzled out. Often it was reversed, and societies declined and in a few cases entirely lost their former wealth. The telling characteristic of modern growth is its sustainability, indeed its inextinguishability. Despite the best efforts of European rulers, growth was not stopped in the twentieth century and indeed on average accelerated and brought much of Europe unimagined riches by the closing decades of the twentieth century. When did this phase transition really happen? The critical watershed was perhaps during the decades after Waterloo. It is quite conceivable that growth would have fizzled out after the inventions in cotton, steam, and iron of the late eighteenth century, and that would have been it. But that is *not* what happened. Indeed, the closing decades of the nineteenth century were a period of unprecedented technological advance, preparing much for the ground for both twentieth-century growth and destruction (Smil, 2005).

The second point is that the idea that the Industrial Revolution was 'British' and that Europe was just a 'follower' seems overstated and in some sense wrong. Some areas of Continental Europe such as Flanders, Alsace, and Switzerland were able to follow Britain fairly quickly, and while a sense of inadequacy among contemporary Continental Europeans in the first half of the nineteenth century when comparing their industrial achievements to Britain can be perceived, modern economic historians have been more cautious about this 'backwardness'. It is necessary to take into account the high toll that the political turmoil between 1789 and 1815 took on the economies of the Continent. Although these upheavals can be regarded as the price that it had to pay to 'catch up', the gap between the Continent and Britain was never on the order of magnitude of the gap between the West and, say, China or Africa.

What, then, was behind this transformation? Historians have engaged the issue now for a century, and little consensus has emerged. Two significant recent contributions, Landes (1998) and Pomeranz (2000) have divided the causal factors between culture and geography. Earlier, Jones (1981) provided a veritable smorgasbord of explanations, including the ingenious idea of the European 'States System' which likened the fragmented political power in Europe to a competitive market, limiting the damage that rulers could inflict on their economies. Others have focused on 'Western Science' as the crucial variable (for example, Rostow, 1975; Cohen, 2004; Lipsey et al., 2006). Still others blamed European imperialism, itself due to accident, and dismissed the entire event as epiphenomenal.[2] These explanations have been vigorously criticized and vigorously defended.

It is odd that the European Enlightenment plays such a minor role in that literature. In recent decades, the European Enlightenment has not fared well in the views of historians. The Enlightenment has been held responsible for the horrors of the twentieth-century by Horkheimer and Adorno and their modern-day postmodern epigones such as John Gray. Some of the oddest phenomena in modern historiography, indeed, are the vitriolic and nasty attacks on the Enlightenment, which is perversely being blamed for modern-day Barbarism but never credited for bringing about modern-day prosperity.[3] On the contrary, it would seem to be a natural candidate in explaining the great divergence. After all, it took place approximately in the century before the beginning of modern growth in Europe, and it was clearly a Western phenomenon, its success more or less confined to the countries that by 1914 constituted the so-called convergence club of rich industrialized countries. Yet economic historians must have felt uncomfortable with the Enlightenment as an explanatory factor, perhaps because it is a relatively amorphous and hard-to-define intellectual movement, perhaps because the Enlightenment was believed to be primarily 'French' whereas the Industrial Revolution was 'British', and perhaps because the connections between beliefs and intellectual conventions and economic events are poorly understood, Keynes's protestations to the contrary notwithstanding.[4] Yet cultural beliefs are increasingly becoming an object of interest to economists, because they tend to be the result of persuasion and diffusion, and because they can be understood as 'conventions' and 'norms' underlying changes in social institutions and behaviour.

In what follows, I will argue that the Enlightenment played an important, perhaps crucial, role in the emergence of modern economic growth. This is not to denigrate other factors altogether. Thus, international trade was critical if only because the cotton industry, one of the mainstays of the Industrial Revolution, could not have emerged without access to the sources of raw cotton. Monetary and financial elements in the story are obscured, as are demographic and other factors. But the Enlightenment had two major effects that I should like to emphasize. First, it transformed the motivation and dynamics of technological progress. Second, it altered the institutional mechanism through which technological change affected the economy. These two formed a synergy that was the very foundation of the 'European Miracle'.

THE ENLIGHTENMENT AND THE GROWTH OF USEFUL KNOWLEDGE

The European Enlightenment was a multifaceted phenomenon, much of it concerned with the natural rights of humankind, concepts of religious and racial tolerance, political freedom, legal reform, and much else. At the deepest level, the common denominator was the belief in the possibility and desirability of human progress and perfectability through reason and knowledge. The material aspect of this belief followed in the footsteps of Francis Bacon's idea of understanding nature in order to control it. Useful knowledge became the buzzword of the eighteenth century. This term should not be associated simply with either 'science' or 'technology'.[5] It meant the combination of different kinds of knowledge supporting one another. Not all of it was abstract science: the taxonomic work of Linnaeus and the descriptive writings of Arthur Young increased useful knowledge just as much as the abstract mathematics of Laplace and the experiments of Priestley and Lavoisier.[6]

The eighteenth century marked both an acceleration of the pace of research and a growing bias toward subject matter that, at least in principle, had some practical value. Indeed, Peter Burke (2000: 44) has argued that the eighteenth century saw the rise of 'the idea of research' and the sense that this knowledge could contribute to economic and social reform. The change in the pace of progress of knowledge after 1680 was indebted to the triumph of Newtonianism in the first half of the eighteenth century. The achievement of Newton did more than anything else to establish the prestige of formal science in the world of learning (Jacob and Stewart, 2004). It was widely believed that the growth of useful knowledge would sooner or later open the doors of prosperity, to some extent with more hope than experience. But it was also clear that this growth could only be carried out collectively, through a 'division of labour' in which specialization and promotion of expertize were carried out at a level far higher than before.[7] The way useful knowledge increased in the eighteenth century was a far cry from the processes of R&D (corporate and government) of today. It might be better to say that much of it was by way of exploration and discovery, trial and error processes minimally informed by an understanding of the natural processes at work, inspired tinkering, and a great deal of serendipity and good fortune, albeit favoured by prepared and eager minds. Over the eighteenth century these search processes became more systematic, careful, and rigorous. New technological methodologies were invented, such as the great engineer John Smeaton's development of the method of parameter variation through experimentation, which is a systematic way of making local improvements in a technique without necessarily understanding the underlying science (Cardwell, 1994: 195). To be sure, there were no truly fundamental scientific breakthroughs in the century between Newton and Lavoisier, but it was an age of consolidation, refinement, and organization of knowledge, the honing and sharpening of mathematical and experimental methods, and an age of observation, classification, and the jettisoning of doomed searches and projects (Porter, 2003).[8]

The hopes for a quick technological pay-off to scientific research were, on the whole, disappointed in the eighteenth century. The 'customary chasm' between science and the mundane details of production could not be closed in a few decades or even a century.[9] One can, of course, find examples in which scientific insights did enrich the knowledge of key actors in the Industrial Revolution. Dexterity and mechanical intuition were in many cases complementary to certain critical pieces of scientific knowledge which guided and inspired the work. The scientific milieu of Glasgow in which James Watt lived contributed to his technical abilities. He maintained direct contact with the Scottish scientists Joseph Black and John Robison, and as Dickinson and Jenkins note in their memorial volume, 'one can only say that Black gave, Robison gave, and Watt received'.[10] The introduction of chlorine bleaching and the solution of the longitude problem depended, to some extent, on advances in science and formal hydraulics which contributed to advances in water power (Reynolds, 1983: esp. 233–48). Yet when all is said and done it is clear that much of the progress we associate with the first Industrial Revolution needed little more than a mechanics that Galileo knew, and that the innovation in manufacturing and agriculture before 1800 advanced without science providing indispensable inputs. William Cullen, the leading chemist of the mid-eighteenth century, was retained by Scottish manufacturers to help them solve a variety of problems. His self-serving prediction that chemical theory would yield the principles that would direct innovations in the practical arts remained, in the words of the leading expert on eighteenth-century chemistry, 'more in the nature of a promissory note than a cashed-in achievement' (Golinski, 1992: 29). Manufacturers needed to know why colours faded, why certain fabrics took dyes more readily than others, and so on, but as late as 1790 best-practice chemistry was incapable of helping them much (Keyser, 1990: 222). In medicine, in metallurgy, and in agriculture, to name a few areas, the situation before 1800 was no different. The world turned out to be more messy and complex than the early and hopeful proponents of the Baconian 'programme' realized, as Cohen has suggested (2004: 123). Scientists did not know enough and lacked the tools to learn quickly. Tacit artisanal knowledge, such as mechanical dexterity, intuition, experience-driven insights, and similar abilities drove many of the early inventions, although dismissing the input of science altogether is unwarranted.

And yet, the belief that somehow useful knowledge was key to economic development did not only endure in the face of such disappointments; it kept expanding on both sides of the Channel. The Baconian programme was built on the belief that the expansion of useful knowledge would solve technological problems and that the dissemination of existing knowledge to more and more people would have substantial efficiency gains. These two notions formed the core of Denis Diderot's beliefs, and his admiration for Bacon – the first philosopher to clearly lay out a technological programme for economic expansion – permeates his writing as it does that of many other eighteenth-century *philosophes* and scientists. In Britain, of course, this belief was not only widespread, but formed the explicit motive for the foundation of organizations and societies that were designed to advance it.[11]

Progress was limited simply by what people knew. The Age of Enlightenment, for instance, never had a good concept of what 'heat' really was. Its chemistry was, until the 1780s, anchored in phlogiston theory, and its understanding of biology and disease, despite some significant local advances, had progressed little beyond Galen. Newton's great insights, much as they supported the belief that rational argument and observation could help people understand the universe, was of limited practical value. Yet it was also readily recognized that intelligent people, schooled in experimental science and mathematics, could make substantive contributions to technology even if they were not always quite sure why and how new techniques worked. Thus mathematicians were asked to solve – and at times succeeded solving – mundane and practical problems.[12] Other examples are easy to find.[13] From the measurement of longitude (perhaps the best-defined single problem that the Age of Enlightenment solved) to the improvement of water-power by applying mathematics to the growing science of hydraulics, the knowledge of various 'applied philosophers' was brought to bear on matters of technology.[14] The same is true for knowledge of plants and animals.[15] Many scientists were concerned with the properties of steel: René Reaumur and Torbern Bergman wrote about it at length, recognizing its economic significance, and in 1786 three of France's most learned men published a paper establishing once and for all the differences between wrought-iron, cast-iron, and steel – even if the full effects of this insight were still decades in the future.[16]

Many men of science applied themselves to invention. Most of them applied the notions of 'open science' to their invention, and placed the knowledge in the public realm. Benjamin Franklin, Humphry Davy, Joseph Priestley, and Benjamin Thompson (Count Rumford), four of the leading scientists of the later decades of the Age of Enlightenment, made numerous inventions and yet refused to take out any patents, arguing that their efforts were made for the benefit of mankind and not for private profit. Such hybrid careers became very common in the nineteenth century. Michael Faraday, besides his pathbreaking research on electricity, worked on various problems in materials, especially steel and glass (Bowers, 1991). Eda Kranakis (1992) emphasizes the work of the French engineer and mathematician Claude-Louis Navier (1785–1836), who used the recently developed Fourier analysis to analyse the vibration in suspension bridges and did pioneering work in fluid dynamics for which he is still famous. His work, and that of other *polytechniciens*, was highly abstract and mathematical, and of long-term rather than immediate applicability. Not so that of Lord Kelvin, a prolific inventor, who owned seventy patents in electromagnetic telegraphy, marine navigation equipment, and electric instruments.

One of the key innovations of this Industrial Enlightenment, as I have called it (Mokyr, 2002: ch. 2) is the building of bridges between the spheres of knowledge and of production, between *savants* and *fabricants*. Diderot expressed this need strongly in his celebrated essay on 'Art' in his Encyclo-pedia. This idea dates from the earliest stages of the Enlightenment,[17] and whether or not it had already led to technological progress already in the age of the Renaissance, as argued by Zilsel (1942), the movement was slow and gradual. William Thompson, Count Rumford, still sighed wistfully in 1799 that 'there are no two classes of men in society that are more distinct, or that are more separated from each other by a more marked line, than philoso-phers and those who are engaged in arts and manufactures' and that this pre-vented 'all connection and intercourse between them'. He expressed hope that the Royal Institution he helped found in 1799 would 'facilitate and con-solidate' the union between science and art and direct 'their united efforts to the improvement of agriculture, manufactures, and commerce, and to the increase of domestic comfort' (see Thompson ([1799] 1876): 743–5).

In Enlightenment Europe a class of people emerged who made it their business to build such bridges, by arbitrating as it were between the spheres of natural philosophy and useful arts. Especially significant was William Nicholson, the founder and editor of the first truly scientific journal, namely the *Journal of Natural Philosophy, Chemistry, and the Arts* (more generally known at the time as *Nicholson's Journal*), which commenced publication in 1797.[18] It published the works of most of the leading scientists of the time, and functioned much like today's *Nature* or *Science*, that is, announcing important discoveries in short communications.[19] Or consider the career of Joseph Banks, one of the most distinguished and respected botanists of his time, whose life was more or less coincident with the Industrial Revolution. Wealthy and politically well-connected, Banks was a co-founder (with Rumford) of the Royal Institution in 1799, a friend and scientific consultant to George III, and president of the Royal Society for forty-two years. While not a pioneering scientist himself, for most of his life Banks laboured tire-lessly to help bring about the social and economic improvement the Baconian programme advocated. He corresponded with many people, sup-ported every innovative branch of manufacturing and agriculture, and was the dominant political figure in Britain's world of science for much of his life.[20] He was every inch an Enlightenment figure, devoting his time and wealth to advance learning and to use that learning to create wealth: 'an awfully English *philosophe*' in Roy Porter's (2000: 149) memorable phrase. These men had counterparts in France such as Henri-Louis Duhamel de Monceau, a noted *agronome* and the chief editor of the massive *Descriptions des Arts et Métiers*, and François Rozier (1734–93), another *agronome* and scientific entrepreneur, 'a clergyman whose vocation was the enlightenment' in Gillispie's succinct characterization, publisher of the *Observations sur la Physique, sur l'Histoire Naturelle, et sur les Arts* (first published in 1771), widely regarded as the first independent periodical to be concerned wholly with advances in cutting-edge science (Bourde, 1967: 253–76, 313–68; Gillispie, 1980: 188, 338).

The connection between the spheres of learning and production has always been a sensitive spot in the history of economic growth. In the Classical world, there seems a deep consensus about this weakness. Similarly in China, the real work in engineering was 'always done by illiterate or semi-literate artisans and master craftsmen who could never rise across that sharp gap which separated them from the "white collar literati"' (Needham, 1969: 27). To be sure, medieval China saw the famed *Nong Shu* (Books of agriculture), such as Wang Chen's famous 1313 opus, but these were books written by and for Mandarins.

The narrowing of this gap was perhaps the crowning achievement of the Industrial Enlightenment. Part of the contact between the two spheres took place through books and periodicals, and part of it through direct contact and transfer of knowledge through teaching, imitation, and espionage. The document most widely associated with the Enlightenment, Diderot and d'Alembert's *Encyclopédie*, contained numerous articles on technical matters lavishly illustrated by highly-skilled artists who, in most cases, were experts in their fields.[21] Encyclopedias and indexes to 'compendia' and 'dictionaries' were the search engines of the eighteenth century. In order to be of practical use, knowledge had to be organized so that it could be selected from. Alphabetization was one way to do this, the organization of science into categories another (Yeo, 2003).

To be sure, in some ways the *Encyclopédie* was a conservative document, and the readership of the many encyclopedias that came out in Europe in the eighteenth century was varied. Most readers, as Darnton (1979) has argued, were probably not in a position to find much direct use for these essays, but the useful knowledge contained in them doubtless found its way to persons for whom just knowing what was possible must have been significant. As Arthur Young (1772: v), himself an assiduous collector of facts, remarked, 'before a thing can be *improved* it must be *known*, hence the utility of those publications that abound in fact either in the offer of new or the elucidation of old ones' (original emphasis). It might be easy to dismiss this remark as self-serving, and it is no doubt exaggerated. The limitations in expressing technical matters in language and diagrams were no doubt severe, even if they differed from area to area. They may have been most serious in relation to the industrial use of coal where knowledge of correct temperatures and the little tricks in operating furnaces were still largely tacit (Epstein, 2004).[22]

The eighteenth century, however, also witnessed the improvement of the codification of formerly tacit knowledge. Part of it was simply the improvement of the language of technology: mathematical symbols, standardized measures, the adoption of universal scales and notation all added a great deal to the ease of communication. Post-Lavoisier chemical nomenclature proposed by the Swedish chemist Berzelius in 1813, after some hesitation, was agreed upon. When new measures were needed, they were proposed and accepted. Thus, as is well known, James Watt proposed in 1784 the total amount of energy necessary to raise 33 000 pounds one foot in one minute as the fundamental unit of work, the horsepower.[23] Visual means of communication, above all diagrams and models, were vastly improved.[24] In addition, between 1768 and 1780, the French mathematician Gaspard Monge developed descriptive geometry (Alder, 1997: 136–46), which made graphical presentations of buildings and machine design mathematically rigorous.[25] Travel became faster and more comfortable during the eighteenth century, and the idea of the travelling expert or consultant was exploited by Boulton and Watt, whose patent-based monopoly on steam power extended to consulting on energy and mechanics. John Smeaton was perhaps the greatest consultant of all, founding the society of civil engineers, but others followed his example.[26]

Knowledge was also transferred through personal contacts and lectures. The years after 1660 witnessed the founding of many state-sponsored, official academies such as the Royal Society, but these were always complemented by private initiatives. Early in the eighteenth century, many of those lectures were informal and ad hoc, in pubs and coffeehouses.[27] In the years after 1750, many of those informal meeting places crystallized into more formal organizations and societies, some of them with official imprimaturs. Of those, the Lunar Society of Birmingham is the best documented (Schofield, 1963; Uglow, 2002), but the Chapter Coffeehouse in London was equally successful as a clearinghouse for useful knowledge (Levere and Turner, 2002). Other organizations were more formal. One such was the Society of Arts, founded in 1754, which encouraged invention by awarding prizes, publicizing new ideas, and facilitating communication between those who possessed useful knowledge and those who could use it. The Royal Institution, founded by Count Rumford and Joseph Banks in 1799, provided public lectures on scientific and technological topics. Its stated purpose in its charter summarizes what the Industrial Enlightenment was about: it was established for 'diffusing the knowledge, and facilitating the general introduction, of useful mechanical inventions and improvements; and for teaching, by courses of philosophical lectures and experiments, the application of science to the common purposes of life'.[28] As McClellan (2003: 92) notes, the reason for all this institutional innovation was simple. They were perceived as useful.

The role of formal educational institutions and human capital in this story is quite different from the roles that they play in the standard stories told for the twentieth century. While the Scottish universities did play an active role in the growth of useful knowledge in Britain, the English universities were a more minor factor, although some of the scorn heaped on Oxbridge by contemporaries and historians is exaggerated. Universities provided some of the most creative scientists of the age with a stable livelihood and often with the experimental tools they needed (such as Alessandro Volta in Pavia) or botanical gardens (Linnaeus's at Uppsala), and most of the members of the scientific communities were first exposed to science in the universities (Brockliss, 2003; Fox, 2003). Yet, in the eighteenth century, alternatives to the universities emerged. The most dynamic element in the English education system were the dissenting academies, which taught experimental science, mathematics, and botany, among other subjects.[29] On the Continent, new institutions training technical experts came into being, many of them under government sponsorship. Two of the famous French *grandes écoles* were founded in the eighteenth century, the *Ponts et Chauseés* in 1747 and the *Mines* in 1783. In Germany, the famous mining academy of Freiberg (Saxony) was founded in 1765, followed by others in the 1770s. Although these institutions reached only a small elite, apparently that was enough. In general, the idea that the role of educational institutions was to create *new* knowledge rather than merely to transmit existing knowledge to the young took a long time to mature. The belief that the Industrial Revolution in its early stages required mass education and literacy has long been abandoned. The British apprenticeship system, with the educational institutions mentioned, was more than enough to supply the skills and craftsmanship that industry needed. The Industrial Revolution was an elite phenomenon: not, of course, just a handful of heroic inventors as Victorian writers in the Smiles tradition would have it, but a few tens of thousands of clever and dexterous mechanics and skilled craftsmen who could read blueprints, knew the properties of the materials they used, built parts according to specification within reasonable tolerance, had respect for precision, and had the experience to understand friction, torque, resistance, and similar concepts. For the rest of the labour force, education and literacy may not have mattered much, and British workers had no advantage in this respect.

THE ENLIGHTENMENT AND INSTITUTIONAL PROGRESS

Economists have lately realized what economic historians have known all along, namely that 'good institutions' are essential to successful economic growth. In recent years, an avalanche of empirical work has pointed to the centrality of property rights, incentives to innovation, the absence of arbitrary rule, and effective contract enforcement, to name but a few of the often-mentioned institutional elements.[30] Yet these studies tend to exploit cross-sectional variation and do not bother much as to how Europe 'acquired' these good institutions. North (1981: 166) noted that:

> the most convincing explanation for the Industrial Revolution as an acceleration in the rate of innovation is one . . . in which a combination of better specified and enforced property rights and increasingly efficient and expanding markets directed resources into new channels . . . more was involved than simply removing restrictions on the mobility of capital and labor – important as those changes were. Private and parliamentary enclosures in agriculture, the Statute of Monopolies establishing a patent law, and the immense development of a body of common law to better specify and enforce contracts are also part of the story.

In subsequent work, North and Weingast (1989) dated this institutional change to the British Glorious Revolution of 1688 and the subsequent reforms.

Regardless of the details of the timing (which has been effectively criticized), the Northian view of the Industrial Revolution raises further doubts that go beyond specific tests. Perhaps the deepest one is that there is now abundant evidence that eighteenth-century China was much as North describes Britain, a large integrated economy, heavily commercialized, entrepreneurial, competitive, with good property rights, law and order, contract enforcement and a government that taxed relatively lightly. If innovation was entirely endogenous to institutional and commercial development, the argument needs to explain China. Even within Europe, however, the argument seems incomplete. Britain's formal law enforcement system was woefully incomplete – it did not even have a police force until deep into the nineteenth century – and its patent system was expensive and notoriously hard to enforce. Moreover, what is really needed is an explanation of the success of the West, not specifically Britain. After all, by 1914 in the 'convergence club' Britain was at best a *primus inter pares*. France, Germany, and the smaller European countries were all part of the modern growth process. What explains these European institutions and where did they come from?

The economic significance of the political and institutional reforms of the late eighteenth and early nineteenth centuries has not been fully realized in part because of the undue focus on the *security* of property rights without much attention to the exact *content* of these property rights. It overlooks that *ancien régime* Europe was overgrown with secure and well-enforced local privileges, tax exemptions, monopolies, exclusionary rights, regulations, entry barriers, freedom of occupation, and similar arrangements that hampered markets, impeded technological progress, and threatened economic growth wherever it was attempted. In other words, what needed to be done was the elimination of *bad* rights and contracts.

Mercantilism, the organizing principle of the *ancien régime* economy, was based on the assumption that economic activity was zero-sum.[31] Both at the aggregate level and at the level of the firm and the individual, the ruling economic paradigm was one of a fixed-size pie, and the more one player got, the less there was for others. The idea that production and commerce could actually expand as the result of free exchange ripened slowly in the Age of Enlightenment, rising to a crashing crescendo with the Scottish enlightenment of Hume and Smith and the French *économistes* of the physiocratic school. As observed persuasively by Ekelund and Tollison (1981, 1997), the mercantilist economy was to a great extent a rent-seeking economy, in which the incentive structure was largely designed for redistributive purposes. As Baumol (1993, 2002), Shleifer and Vishny (1998) and others have argued at length, rent-seeking can be harmful and even lethal to economic growth. This is not so much because of static deadweight losses (since these probably were not all that large) as much as because of the negative interaction that rent-seeking has with technological progress. First, much of mercantilist rent-seeking took the form of protective tariffs, which are widely agreed to be detrimental to technological progress and the international diffusion of best-practice techniques. To make things worse, many of the destructive wars in the eighteenth century were fought over real estate and colonial trade, at times damaging or destroying the sources of revenue. Secondly, rent-seeking activities tend to channel efforts and talents to non-productive activities such as lobbying and litigation and military careers. Finally, in a rent-seeking society, collective bodies will defend the technological status quo against the encroachment of new technology – technological change often renders human skills and physical capital obsolete. It was the demolition of this structure which was the true mark of institutional progress.

It is possible to regard the Age of Enlightenment as in part a reaction against the economic *ancien régime*. This is less far-fetched than it may sound. Enlightenment thought increasingly railed against the institutions that perpetuated rent-seeking. It should be noted that many of those institutions had not originally been designed as rent-seeking institutions, but eventually evolved into them. A paradigmatic example is the craft guild.

Craft guilds in the eighteenth century, as Adam Smith ([1776] 1976: 139–44) argued forcefully, were costly to economic progress. They erected artificial barriers to entry in order to reap exclusionary rents, and on the whole were hostile to new technology.[32] The success of Britain, where guilds had been relatively weak since the mid-seventeenth century, seemed to confirm this belief. The literature on this matter has in recent years been subject to some serious revisionism, especially by Epstein (1998). Guilds were not *invariably* hostile to innovation, this literature argued, and in many ways helped in the formation and intergenerational transmission of human capital. In a recent paper, Sheilagh Ogilvie (2004) has cast doubt on this revisionist literature and shown that at least for Württemberg, the negative view of craft guilds is supported by a great deal of historical evidence. The overall evidence is more mixed: some guilds were more powerful than others, and it seems that over time their actual functions changed. By 1750, they had become in most places conservative and exclusionary, and it seems hard to imagine that radical innovation would have had much of a chance had they been still in control. Whenever guilds tried to maintain product-market monopolies, their incentives to innovate were lower than in a competitive market, and their incentives to protect their knowledge through secrecy and limitations on the mobility of skilled labour were higher. These actions had significant economic costs.

Abolishing or weakening craft guilds was a high priority for Enlightenment reformers, precisely because guilds were viewed as impeding efficiency and economic growth. Attempts to carry out such programmes were, in fact, made before 1789 by reform-minded politicians such as Turgot in France, Sonnenfels in Austria, and Campomanes in Spain. In a forthcoming book, Horn (2006: ch. 2) points out that the reformist elements in the *ancien régime* in France needed to overcome the collective action of both masters and employees in French manufacturing to create an environment more conducive to technological advance and productivity growth. But all these attempts ran into stiff resistance, in part from the vested interests (by both employees and industrialists alike) that were threatened by such reforms, but also in part because the rents that guilds collected were partially dissipated to the government and the fiscal consequences were often serious. Nothing but shock treatment could work, and on 16 February 1791 the French guilds were abolished by fiat of the National Assembly. As the French armies advanced into the Low Countries, Italy, and Germany, this reform was invariably imposed. While suppression of the guilds did not lead to completely free labour markets, and resistance to new technology in France could still be strong on occasion, by the time the dust settled on the Continent in 1815, this vestige of the economic *ancien régime* had been fatally weakened. By itself, the suppression of the guilds cannot be regarded as a necessary condition for economic growth: long before 1791, manufacturers were able in many cases to move out of towns controlled by guilds, employ women and children, and find other ways around guild restrictions. But as a symptom of a general change in the attitude toward rent-seeking, the history of craft guilds is illustrative.

A similar point can be made about the regulation of the grain trade. The original idea may have been for the government to try to help bring about a 'moral economy', that is price stability through regulation and price control. However, through much of the eighteenth century the system evolved into a mechanism in which the rural sector subsidized would-be urban food rioters (Kaplan, 1976; Root, 1994; Persson, 2000).[33] Regulation took many forms beside price controls, including quality and weight control of bread, government sponsored granaries and export and import regulation. In the second half of the eighteenth century, influenced by Enlightenment thought, the pressure for the liberalization of grain markets became increasingly strong. Physiocrat doctrine, much like Scottish political economy, was diametrically opposed to government regulation of the grain trade.[34] Under their influence regulation and price controls were gradually eliminated, although the movement was full of reversals: if the markets happened to have been liberalized in a year that was followed by scarcity, political pressures to bring it back could be too strong to withstand. The reforms introduced under Joseph II of Austria in the 1780s had to be reversed due to the dearth of 1788, and even Napoleon had to reintroduce maximum prices in 1812, though by 1815 liberal policies had triumphed.

Much as in the case of guilds, it can be argued that the liberalization of the grain trade was due to 'real' factors. Specifically, Persson has maintained that improvements in transportation and long-distance trade made controls less necessary, as trade served as an alternative price stabilizer. In the longer run, this may well be correct, but it seems odd that liberalization would happen during the turbulent decades of the Revolutionary and Napoleonic wars when trade disruptions and blockades were frequent. As in the case of the guilds, changes in ideology and a growing trust in the wisdom of free markets played an autonomous role beyond economic interests. Enlightenment economists were no less concerned with poverty than were their mercantilist predecessors, but their idea of alleviating poverty was that free markets would raise overall prosperity, a rising tide that would raise all ships (Norberg, 2003).

Commercial policy was at centre stage of the Enlightenment anti-mercantilist policy. Here, too, there was ambiguity. Not all Enlightenment writers were unambiguously pro free-trade.[35] Yet the theme of trade being a positive-sum game, so eloquently expounded by Adam Smith, had been advocated since the late seventeenth century and was becoming dominant in political economy by 1800. It is ironic, of course, that the wars of 1793–1815, caused by the French Revolution and its aftermath, seriously disrupted international trade, causing the greatest mind of early nineteenth-century political economy (an offshoot of the Enlightenment) to devote an entire chapter to this phenomenon.[36] With the exception of a brief interlude following the 1786 Eden treaty, free trade was not to be seriously considered as a policy option until the 1820s. Smith himself (1976: 493) was not optimistic about free trade being established in Britain any more than 'that Oceana or Utopia be even established in it'. Yet the *pax Britannica* and the slow turn toward freer trade between 1820 and 1880 cannot be seen as the outcome of economic interests alone; persuasion on logical grounds was very much part of the story (Kindleberger, 1975). While the *Wealth of Nations* may not have killed mercantilism by a single blow, it clearly pushed it into a defensive corner.

What is not always realized, however, is that the main triumph of the free trade doctrine was in the establishment of free *internal* trade. Internal tariffs were seen by Enlightenment thinkers as the rent-seeking abomination they were, and the elimination of the French internal tariff barriers followed the abolition of the guilds. The US commerce clause had been passed a few years earlier. Internal trade in Sweden was liberalized in the late 1770s (Persson, 2000: 139). In Germany, the matter was more complex, but the post-1815 movement toward a German *Zollverein* reflected the same sentiment.[37] The system of tolls and duties on Germany's magnificent river system that had hampered trade in the eighteenth century was dismantled. Arguably, the lion's share of gains from trade were secured through internal rather than external trade.

The sentiments against what we call 'rent-seeking' are most eloquently reflected in the Enlightenment's aversion to monopolies, a widely shared view that must be explained by the historical fact that before the introduction of railroads it is very difficult to think of almost any eighteenth-century monopoly that had economic justification in terms of a high fixed cost component, lower transaction costs, or learning effects.[38] Barriers to entry were regarded as imposed by authorities, to create exclusionary rents. This repugnance was extended to the patent system, where even Adam Smith could see some justification to it. The Society of Arts, established in 1754, explicitly ruled out making any awards to inventors who had patented their inventions.

Did these ideological changes have an effect? It is hard, in the end, to be sure that Enlightenment thought was any more than St Exupéry's king who commanded the sun to rise every morning. Mill's statement that a good cause seldom triumphs unless someone's interest is bound up with it does not imply that at times such good causes do not fail. Enlightenment-inspired reforms in the West came in four different waves. First, there were the post-1750 reforms introduced by so-called enlightened despots, which were often inspired by the writings of the *philosophes* but rarely had much staying power since they often ran up against deeply entrenched interests. Secondly, there were the 'natural reforms' introduced in countries that had meta-institutions such as a parliament with sufficient political adaptiveness to bring about induced institutional change, primarily Britain, which was able to pass such 'rational' legislation as the Turnpike Act, the East India Acts of 1784 and 1813, the abolition of the Statute of Apprentices and Artificers (1809), the repeal of the law prohibiting the emigration of artisans (1824), and the elimination of the Navigation Acts (1849). Third, in some countries, violent revolution, whether indigenous or imported, was necessary. Finally, there were 'reactive' reforms in countries such as Prussia as a result of reforms in nations viewed as competitors. The Enlightenment's influence on the French and American revolutions needs no elaboration. Equally well documented is the enormous influence that the *Wealth of Nations* had on policy-makers, especially after Dugald Stewart, Smith's successor at Edinburgh, turned the book into a fountainhead of wisdom (Herman, 2001: 229–30; see also Rothschild, 2001). Among Stewart's pupils were two future prime ministers, Palmerston and John Russell, as well as other senior officials, such as William Huskisson, the prime mover in British liberal reforms of the 1820s. His programme was to remove all state support and protection for manufacturing and agriculture. Huskisson 'zealously and consistently subscribed to the theories of Adam Smith. Smith's teaching, reflected in practically every reform in the twenties' (Brady, 1967: 133). In Germany, the influence of 'the Divine Smith' on Prussian reformers has been thoroughly documented.

In economic history, scholars often write of technological *progress* but rarely of institutional *change*, and for good reason. It is far more difficult to discern any trend toward improvement in the development of institutions. In the century after 1750, however, there was something we might think of in those terms, because this is the age in which rent-seeking in Europe was losing ground to productive commerce and production, in which markets became a little freer of regulation, and in which taxation and economic policy became less distributive. That it did not produce laissez-faire economies, even in Victorian Britain, and that the movement was full of reversals and ambiguities requires no repetition. Britain's technological successes prompted a very *un*enlightened set of laws prohibiting the exportation of machinery and emigration of skilled artisans (which, however, did little to stop the flow of useful knowledge). The French Revolution, despite its overall commitment to Enlightenment values, triggered a serious reactionary backlash in Britain, and in France itself the Academy of Sciences was closed in 1793 by the Jacobins who felt that 'the Republic does not need *savants*'. But 'progress' there was all the same. The quarter century between the Bastille and Waterloo was, in some ways, a *réculer pour mieux sauter* kind of interlude. By the late 1820s mercantilism had retreated and serious growth could occur.

The long-run historical significance of this advance is that it eliminated the negative institutional feedback that before 1700 had impeded economic growth. It is easy to see a counterfactual scenario in which the economic gains of the mule, the Watt engine, and the puddling and rolling process were swallowed up by tax-collectors, wars, protectionists, and distributive coalitions of various kinds. It is not hard to imagine the newly-entrenched technological status quo becoming increasingly more conservative and resisting further technological advances through political action. That this did *not* happen is the result of the double action of the Enlightenment: while it increased useful knowledge and its effectiveness, it at the same time improved the incentives for its implementation and weakened the forces that would set it back. In that sense, Enlightenment-inspired technological progress and institutional change created a powerful synergy, that ultimately was responsible for the sustainability of what started in Britain in the last third of the eighteenth century, and for its diffusion to the societies that shared the Enlightenment.

THE ROOTS OF THE EUROPEAN ENLIGHTENMENT

Attributing the emergence of modern growth in the West to the Enlightenment in Europe leaves the question of the roots of the Enlightenment itself unanswered. To put it bluntly, we need to ask why Europe had an Enlightenment and other cultures such as the Islamic Middle East or China did not. Answering this question satisfactorily would be a huge undertaking. Linking it to previous events such as the emergence of humanism in Renaissance Europe or the Reformation only pushes the question further back. An alternative approach is not to ask why Europe had an Enlightenment, but to postulate that 'enlightened' ideas occurred in all societies, but that only in the 'West' was this movement successful in the fashion described above. The victory of the Enlightenment was not just the attainment of a growing cumulative store of knowledge, but was the triumph of open and public knowledge over secret 'arcane' knowledge, the victory of 'mechanical' philosophy (for example, verifiable knowledge about natural regularities) over 'occult philosophy' and its mystical and unobservable entities. How, then, did the good guys win?

Europe's uniqueness was obviously *not* that it was monetized, commercialized, and enjoyed 'good' governance. 'Capitalism' – whatever may exactly be meant by that term in the context of early eighteenth-century Europe – seems too vague a concept to be of much help. What seems unique to Europe in the period leading up to and including the Enlightenment is the growing opportunity for critics, sceptics, and innovators to try their new notions out in a marketplace for ideas and to survive the experience. The notion that Europe was deeply hostile to 'heretics', based on the tragic experience of such figures as Giordano Bruno and Miguel Servetus, is fundamentally mistaken. The picture of Europe in the period 1500–1750 is one in which innovative, often radical, intellectuals are able to play one political authority against one another: different polities against each other, and when necessary also central against local power, the private against the public sphere, and spiritual against secular authority. By moving from one place to another when the environment became too hostile, the members of the intellectual class ('clerisy' as they are sometimes called) could remain active in the transnational community of scholars, the 'Republic of letters'. Iconoclastic scholars who had brought upon themselves the ire of the local establishment usually went elsewhere. Martin Luther and Paracelsus are the most famous rebels who successfully played this game.[39] For the West as a whole, the salutory effects of this pluralism cannot be overestimated. David Hume, for one, felt that this was the main reason why the sciences in China 'made so slow a progress'. In China, he argued, 'none had the courage to resist the torrent of popular opinion, and posterity was not bold enough to dispute what had been universally received by their ancestors' (Hume ([1742] 1985: 122).

The fragmentation of power and the competitive 'states system' (Jones's, 1981, term is slightly anachronistic for the principalities and bishoprics that enjoyed considerable political autonomy in the seventeenth and eighteenth centuries) has been argued as assisting Europe in another way. Paul David (2004) has argued that rulers competed to attract reputable scientists to their courts, in part because some skills could come in handy, but largely as a signalling device (that, is to show off). The competition for the 'best' scientists between European rulers required open science as a solution to the asymmetric information problem that rulers faced, namely to identify the truly leading scientists of their generation. Only within communities ('invisible colleges') in which full disclosure was exercised, he argues, could credible reputations be established that would allow wealthy patrons to recognize truly distinguished scientists among fraudulent ones. Open science then emerged as a best strategy for scientists competing for patronage.[40] The competition of different institutions for the superstars of science meant that at least the very best could set their own research agendas and appropriate the benefits of research, such as they were, and that few governments had the power to suppress views they considered heretical or subversive.

We may also point to specific institutional changes that encouraged both the growth of intellectual innovation and its growing bias toward 'usefulness' – though the latter term needs to be treated with caution. Perhaps the central development was a change in the relation between the world of production – farmers, merchants and manufacturers, as well as government agencies engaged in military and infrastructural projects – and the world of intellectuals. The idea that *ars sine scientia nihil est* (practice is worthless without theory), first enunciated in Renaissance Italy, slowly won ground. Natural philosophers were increasingly retained and engaged in practical matters where, it was believed, they could bring to bear their knowledge of nature to solve problems and increase efficiency. The growing conviction that this knowledge had (at least in expectation) a positive social marginal product meant of course that the demand for useful knowledge increased. This created the standard problem of intellectual property rights to useful knowledge. The interesting way in which this was solved was by taking advantage of the fact that the creators of propositional knowledge sought credit rather than profit from their work. Such credit, and the enhanced prestige that came with it, was often correlated with a reservation price, mostly in terms of a sinecure: a pension, an appointment at a court or a university, or a sponsored job with an academy or scientific society.[41] The rules of the game in the Republic of Letters, as they were established in the second half of the seventeenth century, were credit by priority subject to verification. This 'credit' was a property right in that it attributed an innovation unequivocally to the person responsible.[42] The enhanced prestige was then often correlated with some appointment that provided the scientist with a reservation price, though the correlation was far from perfect. Others, such as Henry Cavendish, Joseph Banks, and Antoine Lavoisier were financially independent and did not need or expect to be compensated for their scientific work.

The other factor that facilitated the success of the Enlightenment as an intellectual movement in Europe was the institutional fluidity of intellectual activity. No single set of institutions dominated thought in Enlightenment Europe the way the Church had dominated in the medieval period and the way the Confucian mandarinate dominated Chinese thought. In Europe such institutional domination was absent, and within the Republic of Letters there was free entry and furious competition for patronage and clients. Peter Burke (2000: 37, 48) has suggested that universities tended to suffer from 'institutional inertia' and become conservative over time, so that only the founding of new ones kept them creative and lively. Professor Martin Luther was teaching theology at the University of Wittenberg, an institution that was only fifteen years old, and the University of Leyden, founded in 1575 as a Calvinist University, became a major innovator in its curriculum. But universities had to contend with the academies and courts of Europe to attract the best minds of Europe. The decentralized and multifocal distribution of wealth and power in Europe between Luther and Lavoisier led to a world of intellectual competition in which knowledge was both transmitted and augmented in ever more effective fashion.

There were other reasons for the success of the European Enlightenment. The *philosophes* of the eighteenth century were not a marginal group, struggling for recognition. Despite their opposition to the existing arrangements and their dreams of reform and improvement, they were more often than not part of the establishment, or, better put, part of *some* establishment. The triumph of the *philosophes* must be explained by their ability to act against the status quo from within the establishment. Many of the leading lights of the eighteenth-century *philosophes* and political economists were well-born and politically well-connected. Even when they ran foul of the regime, the relations rarely degenerated into hostility. This 'cosy fraternizing with the enemy', as Gay (1966: 24) calls it, did not come without a price, but it allowed the *philosophes* to be politically effective without necessarily threatening the status quo. In France, this relationship in the end imploded (though it was soon restored), but elsewhere it made it possible for their ideas to be adopted by the men who voted on policy decisions. All the same, throughout Europe the Enlightenment was a decentralized and free-enterprise endeavour, sometimes tolerated but rarely managed or sponsored by governments. Yet it was not unorganized: Enlightenment ideas found expression in the myriad of friendly societies, academies, masonic lodges and similar organizations of people who shared beliefs and traded knowledge. To be sure, there were a few figures of political power who were associated with and influenced by the Enlightenment, the best known of whom were the so-called 'enlightened despots' and some of their ministers. It stands to reason that an intellectual movement such as this can fail either because it is too close to the government or because it so marginalized that it can be ignored. Much of the European Enlightenment fell in between.

A brief comparison with China is instructive here. A dismissive argument that China never had an Enlightenment is incomplete. Some of the developments that we associate with Europe's Enlightenment closely resemble events in China, but the differences between the European and the Chinese Enlightenments are as revealing as the similarities. The Chinese attempt at Enlightenment in the eighteenth century was known as the school of *kaozheng* or 'evidentiary research'. In this school, abstract ideas and moral values gave way as subjects for discussion to concrete facts, documented institutions and historical events (Elman, 2001: 4). Chinese scholarship of this period was 'not inherently antipathetic to scientific study or resistant to new ideas' (De Bary, 1975: 205). It was based on rigorous research, demanded proof and evidence for statements, and shunned leaps of faith and speculation. It sounds promising, but in the end these scholars were primarily interested in philology, linguistics, and historical studies 'confident that these would lead to greater certainty about what the true words and intentions of China's ancient sages had been and, hence, to a better understanding of how to live in the present' (Spence, 1990: 103).[43] Equally significantly, unlike the European Enlightenment, the Chinese movement remained by and for the mandarinate, the ruling Confucian elite, which had little inclination for material progress.[44]

There were attempts at serious intellectual reform in China in the period under discussion. It could well be argued that the seeds of a Chinese Enlightenment were sown by Fang-I-Chih (1611–71), the author of a book meaningfully entitled *Small Encyclopedia of the Principles of Things*, which discussed potentially useful forms of propositional knowledge such as meteorology and geography. He was familiar with Western writings and quite influential in the *kaozheng* school of the eighteenth century. Peterson (1974: 401) has gone so far as to suggest that Fang was 'representative of the *possibility* in the seventeenth century that the realm of "things" to be investigated would center on physical objects, technology and natural phenomena'.[45] He argued that Fang's work paralleled the secularization of science in Europe. The real question, then, becomes what was different about China and the West that Fang did not become a figure comparable to Bacon, and that his new ideas remained only a 'possibility'.

The literature about the Chinese Enlightenment, conveniently summarized in Elman (2001), may have overstated its bias to literary and philological topics. There was considerable interest in astronomy and mathematics, and Chinese scholars carefully examined useful knowledge that seeped in from the West. Scholars such as Mei Wending (1633–1721) carefully compared Western mathematics and astronomy to Chinese knowledge, and pointed to advances that the West had made, though Chinese scholars often took the trouble of trying to show that this knowledge had already existed in ancient China. What was missing in China, however, were the institutional bridges that eighteenth-century Europe built between the *savants* and the *fabricants*. By creating communications not just within the scholarly community and between scholars and people in power, but eventually also between the realm of the scholar and those of the manufacturer, the farmer, and the navigator, the European Enlightenment redefined the agenda of research. Moreover, it placed best-practice knowledge and investigative techniques at the disposal of innovators, thus streamlining technological progress.

The tradition of *kaozheng* scholarship contained many elements that we associate with the European scientific revolution and the subsequent Enlightenment (Elman, 2001). *Kaozheng* scholars had an efficient network of information exchange and correspondence. The Jiangnan (Yangzi delta) area, in which many of the *kaozheng* scholars resided, contained many libraries, and the lending of books was a universal custom. In Beijing, an entire street was a major book emporium, and as in Europe, the publishing industry printed novels as well as classical texts. The scholarly community had a keen sense of assigning priority, and a notion of progress was implicit in their scholarship. Much like European scholars, Chinese Enlightenment scholars agreed that mathematics was one of the keys to concrete studies, as Jiao Xun (1763–1820) put it. Also as in Europe, information was organized in tabular form, and was often described in diagrams and maps. Gu Donggao's (1679–1759) book used these for information on the pre-Qin and Han periods (722–481 BC) and Yan Roju (1636–1704) counted and analysed citations from classical poetry. The scientists of the early Ch'ing period were convinced that their mathematical tools (trigonometry and geometry) had the power to explain nature as well as predict it. Yet, as Nathan Sivin (1975: 161) notes, 'in China the new tools were used to rediscover and recast the lost mathematical astronomy of the past and thus to perpetuate traditional values rather than to replace them'.

A telling example is the publication of Chinese encyclopedias. It is surely wrong to believe that Europeans were the only ones to realize the importance of reference books. The vast efforts of the Chinese Ch'ing emperors in publishing encyclopedias and compilations of knowledge under the Emperors K'ang Chi and Qian Long, above all the massive *Gujin tushu jicheng* compiled by Chen Menglei and published in 1726 (one of the largest books ever produced, with 10 000 chapters, 850 000 pages and 5000 figures), indicate an awareness of the importance of access to information. It stands to reason that the reference books produced in China served candidates for the state examinations and perhaps 'to help the mandarins in their work' (Burke, 2000: 175). The *Gujin tushu jicheng* was printed at the Wuyingdian, the Imperial Printing Office in Beijing. Altogether about 60 copies were made of it, a number that bears no comparison with the European encyclopedias, which were sold in large numbers.[46] It is revealing, for instance, that Chen was arrested and deported (twice), and that his name was removed from the project by the Emperor whose wrath he had incurred. The entire project was carried out under imperial auspices.[47] China did not have European-style universities, but it had numerous 'academies' (*shuyuan*) – in which candidates for the state bureaucracy could cram before the examinations (Elvin, 2004: 58).

Or consider the example of a seventeenth-century Chinese scholar Chu Shun-shui, one of the few Chinese intellectuals who can be compared with a European intellectual in his itinerancy. His knowledge was quite broad and extended to fields of practical knowledge such as architecture and crafts. Fleeing from China (he remained a supporter of the Ming dynasty, overthrown in 1644), first to Annam (Vietnam) and then to Japan, he acquired quite a following. Chu Shun-shui, in Julia Ching's words, was hardly a purely abstract philosopher, but 'the investigation of things referred less to the metaphysical understanding of the principle of material forces, and more to coping with concrete situations. At the same time, the extension of knowledge applied not only to knowledge of the Confucian classics, but also to all that is useful in life' (Ching, 1978: 217). This, again, sounds promising, but Chu's work remained unknown in China.

Chinese knowledge was different than European. It did not 'posit the existence of a uniform and predictable order in the physical universe' (Dikötter, 2003: 695) and did not rely on the mathematical tools that allowed the Europeans increasingly to apply their useful knowledge to engineering problems. Yet the view that these differences somehow handi-capped the Chinese and caused a 'failure' suffers from the hindsight bias that just because Europe created what became known as 'modern science', this was the *only* way that economic growth could have come about. As I have argued elsewhere (Mokyr, 2005d), evolutionary theory suggests that the actual outcomes we observe are but a small fraction of the outcomes that were feasible, and we simply have no way of imagining how Chinese useful knowledge would have evolved in the long run had it not been exposed to Western culture.

It is clear, however, that the Chinese Enlightenment, if that is the right term, did not produce what the European Enlightenment did. Its research agenda included little or no 'useful knowledge' and instead, in one succinct formulation, they were 'living out the values of their culture' (De Bary, 1975: 205). The 'chasm' between China's scientists and those who made things remained wide.[48] Mathematics and astronomy were applied, for instance, to calculating the size and shape of historical ceremonial bronze bells or recon-structing ancient carriages. Despite the fact that the *kaozheng* movement was born as a rebellious movement protesting the Manchu conquest of 1644, it could not remove itself from the establishment, and its agenda remained largely confined to what the court sponsored. If China's Imperial government was not interested in steering research in a direction that could benefit the economy, there seems to have been no other agency that had the interest or the capacity. The agenda of Chinese scholarship remained retro-spective. A programme devoted to proving ancient sages right and per-forming exegesis on their writings is a respectable intellectual activity, but it does not bring about the developments that Lucas could not stop thinking about. It seems wrong to dub the Chinese experience a failure. What is exceptional, indeed unique, is what happened in eighteenth-century Europe.

The European Enlightenment pushed a dual platform that was radical and revolutionary: reform institutions to promote efficiency and innovation, and bring the full force of human knowledge to bear on technology.[49] Without that synergy, long-term economic growth in the West might not have happened either. The Enlightenment was an indispensable element in the emergence of modern economic growth. Its belief in social progress through reason and knowledge was shocked repeatedly as the superiority of reason was thrown into doubt.[50] But the idea that useful knowledge is an engine of social progress has not lost any of its power, even as it was challenged, toned down, and refined in the two centuries since 1800. There was nothing pre-ordained or inevitable about that course of history. Indeed, it seems ex ante rather unlikely, and any competent economic historian can point to a dozen junctures where the process could have been derailed. The fruits of these changes were, of course, very late in the coming. Economic growth, in the sense that Lucas had in mind, does not take off *anywhere* before 1830. And yet, from a long-run perspective, the striking thing is not that it happened so long after the necessary precedent intellectual changes, but that it happened at all.

NOTES

*   The comments and suggestions of Kenneth Alder, Maristella Botticini, Wilfred Dolfsma, Margaret Jacob, Lynne Kiesling, Deirdre McCloskey, Edward Muir, Cormac Ó Gráda, Avner Greif and Richard Unger are acknowledged. I am indebted to Fabio Braggion, Chip Dickerson, Hillary King, and Michael Silver for loyal research assistance.
1.   For the most recent estimates of growth during the Industrial Revolution, see Mokyr (2004) and Harley (1998).
2.   This is true for the more moderate scholars in the so-called California school such as Wong (1997), Pomeranz (2000), and Goldstone (2002) as well as for the more extreme proponents such as Blaut (2000). Goldstone (2002: 330) feels that to even repeat such beliefs that have been 'abandoned by virtually all historians and sociologists' (with the minor exception of such obscure figures as David Landes and Jared Diamond) is 'embarrassing or seemingly absurd'.
3.   Horkheimer and Adorno ([1972] 1997), Gray (1995). This revulsion has deep philosophical roots in the works of Nietzsche and Heidegger, but the usefulness of the critique to historians interested in economic progress is doubtful. Even left-wing historians are embarrassed by notions that the Enlightenment inevitably led in some way to male domination, imperialism, totalitarianism, environmental degradation, and exploitation. Eric Hobsbawm notes with some disdain that this literature describes the Enlightenment as 'anything from superficial and intellectually naive to a conspiracy of dead white men in periwigs to provide the intellectual foundation for Western Imperialism' (see Hobsbawm, 1997: 253–65).
4.   The idea that the Enlightenment was somehow a French affair in which Britain played at best a supportive role is devastated by Porter (2000). For detailed data, see Mokyr (2005c). On cultural beliefs, see Greif (1994, 2005). Keynes's famous remark is to be found in Keynes (1936: 383–4): 'the power of vested interests is vastly exaggerated compared with the gradual encroachment of ideas . . . soon or late, it is ideas, not vested interests, which are dangerous for good or evil'.
5.   This point has been well made by Inkster (2004), whose analysis parallels what follows in certain respects. Inkster proposes, the term URK ('Useful and Reliable Knowledge'),

which is much like the term proposed by Kuznets, who preferred 'testable'. In my view *reliability* is an important characteristic of useful knowledge, but it seems less crucial than *tightness*, that is, the confidence and consensualness with which certain knowledge is held to be 'true'.

6. Linnaeus's belief that skilful naturalists could transform farming was widely shared and inspired the establishment of agricultural societies and farm improvement organizations throughout Europe. One source of confirmation of the belief in the possibility of economic progress may have been perceptions of agricultural progress. As Gascoigne (1994: 185) has noted, 'as the land bore more, better, and increasingly diversified fruits as a consequence of patient experiment with new techniques and crops, so, too, the need to apply comparable methods to other areas of the economy and society came to seem more insistent'.

7. Joseph Priestley, the great chemist, noted that 'If, by this means, one art or science should grow too large for an easy comprehension in a moderate space of time, a commodious subdivision will be made. Thus all knowledge will be subdivided and extended, and knowledge as Lord Bacon observes, being power, the human powers will be increased . . . men will make their situation in this world abundantly more easy and comfortable'. (Priestley, 176: 7). Adam Smith, in the 'Early Draft' to his *Wealth of Nations* (1976: 569–72) believed that the benefits of the 'speculations of the philosopher ... may evidently descend to the meanest of people' if they led to improvements in the mechanical arts.

8. By the mid-eighteenth century, for instance, the bulk of chemists had come to accept Herman Boerhaave's conviction that the transmutation of metals was impossible and that alchemy was a pseudo-science (Brock, 1992: 37).

9. The term is due to Cohen (2004: 118) who adds that in the seventeenth century useful applications of the new insights of science kept eluding their proponents.

10. Dickinson and Jenkins (1927: 16). Hills (1989: 53) explains that Black's theory of latent heat helped Watt compute the optimal amount of water to be injected without cooling the cylinder too much. More interesting, however, was his reliance on William Cullen's finding that in a vacuum water would boil at much lower, even tepid temperatures, releasing steam that would ruin the vacuum in a cylinder. In some sense that piece of propositional knowledge was essential to his realization that he needed a separate condenser.

11. William Shipley's credo was summed up in his 'plan' for the establishment of the Society of Arts (1754): 'Whereas the Riches, Honour, Strength and Prosperity of a Nation depend in a great Measure on Knowledge and Improvement of useful Arts, Manufactures, Etc . . . several [persons], being fully sensible that due Encouragements and Rewards are greatly conducive to excite a Spirit of Emulation and Industry have resolved to form [the Society of Arts] for such Productions, Inventions or Improvements as shall tend to the employing of the Poor and the Increase of Trade' (Allan, 1979: 192).

12. MacLaurin provided an ingenious solution (1735) to the problem of measuring the quantity of molasses in irregularly shaped barrels by the use of classical geometry. Not only did he solve the rather difficult mathematical problem with uncommon elegance, he also provided simple formulas, tables, and algorithms for the customs officers, that were used for many years (see Grabiner, 1998: 139–68).

13. One such example is Johann Joachim Becher, whose chemical theories constituted the foundation of eighteenth-century phlogiston chemistry, but who also worked for a variety of European governments as an engineering consultant and argued that his knowledge of medicine qualified him to write about politics because in both cases he was maximizing a social welfare function (Smith, 1994: 69). Scottish chemists such as William Cullen and Joseph Black were much in demand as consultants to farmers and ambitious textile manufacturers (Mokyr, 2002: 50–51).

14. Leonhard Euler, the most talented mathematician of the age, was concerned with ship design, lenses, the buckling of beams, and (with his less famous son Johann) contributed a great deal to hydraulics.

15. Naturalists of various types were equally regarded as contributing to the wealth of their nations. Originally botany and chemistry were subjects ancillary to medicine, and their

main proponents, such as Stahl, Cullen, and Boerhaave, were famous primarily as physicians. In the second half of the century this changed. Linnaeus's belief that skilful naturalists could transform farming was widely shared and inspired the establishment of agricultural societies and farm improvement organizations throughout Europe. After 1750, botanists, horticulturalists, and agronomers were working hand-in-hand through publications, meetings, and model gardens to introduce new crops, adjust rotations, improve tools and reform management.

16. The three were Alexandre Vandermonde, Claude Berthollet, and Gaspar Monge, who jointly published their 'Mémoire sur le fer', under the influence of the new chemistry of their master Antoine Lavoisier.

17. Thomas Sprat expressed it in the 1660s when he wrote that no New Atlantis (Bacon's ideal scientific community) was possible unless 'Mechanick Labourers shall have Philosophical heads; or the Philosophers shall have Mechanical hands' (see Sprat, 1702: 397). In its early days, the Royal Society invested heavily in the study of crafts and technology and commissioned a History of Trades, but this effort in the end failed (compare Hunter, 1989).

18. Nicholson was also a patent agent, representing other inventors. Around 1800 he ran a 'scientific establishment for pupils' on London's Soho Square. The school's advertisement announced that 'this institution affords a degree of practical knowledge of the sciences which is seldom acquired in the early part of life', and promised to deliver weekly lectures on natural philosophy and chemistry 'illustrated by frequent exhibition and explanations of the tools, processes and operations of the useful arts and common operations of society'.

19. In it, leading scientists, including John Dalton, Berzelius, Davy, Rumford, and George Cayley, communicated their findings and opinions. Yet it also contained essays on highly practical matters, such as an 'Easy Way of churning Butter' or a 'Description of a new Lamp upon M. Argand's Principle'.

20. Among his close friends were the agricultural improvers John Sinclair and Arthur Young, as well as two pillars of the Industrial Revolution, Matthew Boulton and Josiah Wedgwood. He was associated among others with the Society for the Arts, before taking over the Royal Society, which he ruled with an iron if benign hand (Drayton, 2000: ch. 4; Gascoigne, 1994: passim).

21. Pannabecker (1996, 1998) points out that the plates in the *Encyclopédie* were designed by the highly skilled Louis-Jacques Goussier who eventually became a machine designer at the Conservatoire des arts et métiers in Paris. They were meant to popularize the rational systematization of the mechanical arts to facilitate technological progress.

22. John R. Harris (2001: 219–21) has been even more sceptical of the importance of science relative to 'tacit' skills and has even argued that France's backwardness in steel-making was in part due to its reliance on scientists, who at first gave misleading and later rather useless advice to steel-makers.

23. Less well known but equally important is the work of Thomas Young (1773–1829), whose modulus of elasticity (1807) measured the resistance of materials under stress in terms of the pull in pounds that it would take to stretch a bar to double its original length. There were even some attempts to quantify precisely the amount of physical work one man could be expected to do in a day (Ferguson, 1971; Lindqvist, 1990).

24. The illustrations accompanying the *Encyclopédie* and the eighty volumes of the *Descriptions des Arts et Métiers* (1761–88) approached technical mastery. The eighteenth century witnessed a great deal of progress in 'technical representation', and by the middle of the eighteenth century technical draftsmanship was being taught systematically (Daumas and Garanger, 1969: 249). Alder (1998: 513) distinguishes between three levels of mechanical drawing in pre-revolutionary France: the thousands of workshops where experienced artisans taught free-hand drawing to their apprentices; state-sponsored schools in which drawing teachers taught basic geometry; and the advanced engineering schools in which mechanical drawing was taught by mathematicians.

25. Monge's technique essentially solved the problem of reducing three-dimensional entities to two dimensions while at the same time depicting the relationships between the parts

constituting the shape and configuration of the entity. In Alder's words, 'It marks a first step toward understanding how the way things are made has been transformed by the way they are represented' (1997: 140).

26. The clock and instrument maker John Whitehurst, a charter member of the Lunar Society, consulted for every major industrial undertaking in Derbyshire, where his skills in pneumatics, mechanics, and hydraulics were in great demand; Joseph Priestley worked as a paid consultant for his fellow 'lunatics' Wedgwood and Boulton (see Elliott, 2000: 83; Schofield, 1963: 22, 201). Another striking example is the emergence of so-called coal viewers who advised mine owners on the optimal location and structure of coal mines, the use of equipment, and similar specific issues.

27. Of the itinerant lecturers, the most famous was John T. Desaguliers. Desaguliers, a leading proponent of Newton with an international reputation (he lectured in the Netherlands), received a royal pension of £70 per annum as well as a variety of patents, fees, and prizes. His *Course of Mechanical and Experimental Philosophy* (1724) was based on the hugely popular lectures on science and technology with which he 'entertained his provincial listeners with combinations of scientific subjects and Providence and the Millennium'. Other British lecturers of note were William Whiston, one of Newton's most distinguished proponents and successor at Cambridge; James Jurin, master of the Newcastle Grammar School, who gave courses catering to the local gentlemen concerned with collieries and lead-mines; Peter Shaw, a chemist and physician; the instrument maker Benjamin Martin; Stephen Demainbray who lectured both in France and England and later became Superintendent of the King's Observatory at Kew; and the Revd. Richard Watson at Cambridge whose lectures on chemistry in the 1760s were so successful that he drew a patronage of £100 for his impoverished chair (see Stewart, 1992: *passim*). In France, the premier lecturer and scientific celebrity of this time was Abbé Jean-Antoine Nollet, whose fame rests on early public experiments with electricity (he once passed an electrical charge from a Leyden jar through a row of Carthusian monks more than a mile long). Nollet also trained and encouraged a number of his disciples as lecturers, as well as some of the most celebrated scientists of his age, such as Lavoisier and Monge. Similarly, Guillaume-François Rouelle's lectures on chemistry in the Jardin du roi drew an audience that included Rousseau, Diderot and even Lavoisier himself (Stewart, 2004). In Napoleonic France, the 'best scientific minds of the day' were lecturing to the public about steam engines, and it became common to regard some scientific training as a natural prelude for entrepreneurial activity (Jacob, 2004).

28. The lectures given by Humphry Davy were so popular that the carriages that brought his audience to hear him so clogged up Albermarle Street in London that it was turned into the first one-way street of the City.

29. Among those, Warrington Academy was one of the best, and the great chemist Joseph Priestley taught there for a while, though surprisingly he was made to teach history, grammar, and rhetoric (Schofield, 1963: 195).

30. Examples of the literature are Rodrik (2004), Rodrik et al. (2002) and Acemoglu et al. (2002). A convenient summary is provided in Helpman (2004).

31. This is precisely captured by Adam Smith (1976: 519): 'nations have been taught that their interests consisted in beggaring all their neighbours. Each nation has been made to look with an invidious eye upon the prosperity of all the nations with which it trades, and to consider their gain as its own loss.'

32. The canonical statement is by the great Belgian historian Henri Pirenne: 'the essential aim [of the craft guild] was to protect the artisan, not only from external competition, but also from the competition of his fellow-members'. The consequence was 'the destruction of all initiative. No one was permitted to harm others by methods which enabled him to produce more quickly and more cheaply than they. Technical progress took on the appearance of disloyalty' (1936: 185–6). For similar statements see, for example, Cipolla (1968), Deyon and Guignet (1980) and Horn (2006).

33. Among the 'enlightened thinkers' who believed in free markets but would make an exception for this case of a necessity were the French economist Pierre de Boisguilbert and Jeremy Bentham.

34. An early writer in the liberal tradition was the Siennese Sallustio Bandini writing in the 1730s. Tuscany turned out to be one of the first regions in Europe to dismantle its system of grain market management known as *abbondanza* (Persson, 2000: 142).
35. David Hume, while certainly no mercantilist, was of two minds about it and noted that a 'tax on German linens encourages home manufactures and thereby multiplies our people and our industry' (Hume [1742], 1985: 98). Alexandre Vandermonde, a noted mathematician and scientist, who turned to economics late in life and taught it at the newly founded École Normale, and who knew his *Wealth of Nations* inside out, never converted to free trade and preferred the protectionist doctrines of Smith's contemporary, James Steuart (Gillispie, 2004: 513).
36. Ricardo ([1817] 1971: ch. XIX). The chapter is entitled 'On sudden changes in the channels of trade'.
37. The *Zollverein* was preceded by the Prussian Maassen Tariff Law of 1818 which abolished all internal tariffs in Prussia and was influenced by a memorandum by G.J.C. Kunth, Beuth's mentor.
38. Carlos and Nicholas's (1990, 1996) example of the trading companies as examples of 'efficient monopolies' may be the one exception to this rule. Even in this case, the evidence has been contested (Ville and Jones, 1996).
39. The case of the famously pugnacious physician and chemist Paracelsus, who publicly burned the books of the canonical authorities in Basel in 1527, is illustrative. The Moravian religious leader and educational reformer Jan Amos Comenius, fleeing his native Czech lands from the Imperial forces, repeatedly found himself in politically uncomfortable circumstances and spent time in Poland, London, Paris, Sweden, and Amsterdam. In 1682, Pierre Bayle, a philosopher and polymath who annoyed Catholics and Calvinists in equal measure, left France and settled in Rotterdam. Similar mobility was practiced by many of the eighteenth-century *philosophes* (most famously Voltaire, Rousseau, and Christian Wolff), although by that time many intellectual establishments had realized the futility of repressing intellectual innovation and had basically given up on outright suppression of new ideas.
40. David's argument seems to assume that the main motive of natural philosophers was to secure such patronage positions rather than to impress their peers or contribute to knowledge. It also tends to overstate the ability of the scientific community to reach consensus on who were true winners in this tournament and the costs to princes associated with the sinecures awarded to mediocrities.
41. The economics of open science resemble in many ways the economics of open source software development (Lerner and Tirole, 2004), which has found that signalling to outsiders, peer recognition, and direct benefits all play a role.
42. In an earlier time, the absence of clear-cut rules discouraged open knowledge. Thus the architect Francesco di Giorgio Martini (1439–1501) complained that 'the worst is that ignoramuses adorn themselves with the labors of others and usurp the glory of an invention that is not theirs. For this reason the efforts of one who has true knowledge is oft retarded' (cited by Eamon, 1994: 88).
43. For instance, the great scholar Tai Chen who was 'a truly scientific spirit . . . whose principles hardly differed from those which in the West made possible the progress of the exact sciences. But this scientific spirit was applied almost exclusively to the investigation of the past' (Gernet, 1982: 513).
44. The literature about Confucian beliefs and practicality remains controversial. The Japanese sinologist Hattori Unichi flatly stated that Confucianism is neither utilitarian nor positivistic. He maintained that classical Confucianism and neo-Confucianism in general justify righteous action in terms of virtuous motivations rather than in terms of utility. These remarks point to an apparent ambivalence concerning practicality in Confucian philosophy; Confucian philosophy is practical in the sense of being concerned with morality, social interaction, and political activity, but it is not practical in the sense of being concerned with economy and technology.
45. Sivin (1975) is far more sceptical of Fang's abilities and has compared him with European scholasticism, stating that his work was 'antiquated'.

46. Darnton (1979) has estimated that in total, d'Alembert and Diderot's *Encyclopédie* sold about 25 000 copies. Given the many competitors in many languages that came out in the eighteenth century, the total number of encyclopedias alone, not counting the many compendia, dictionaries, lexicons, and similar books published in the eighteenth century, the total number of all reference books sold in the West is a large multiple of that figure.
47. Unlike the works of European encyclopedists, the *tushu jicheng* arose from the idea that the Emperor's task was to join the whole knowledge of the world to a unified cosmos (Bauer, 1966: 687).
48. This is well summed up by Nathan Sivin (1995: ch. VII): 'Science was done on the whole by members of the minority of educated people in China, and passed down in books. Technology was a matter of craft and manufacturing skills privately transmitted by artisans to their children and apprentices. Most such artisans could not read the scientists' books. They had to depend on their own practical and esthetic knowledge.'
49. Cohen (2004: 131) raises a similar point: how could one explain the simultaneous confluence of two seemingly independent streams of historical events, namely the growth of science and the willingness of Europeans to invest in large-scale projects embodying the new useful knowledge.
50. Indeed, even during the Enlightenment, the supremacy of reason over sentiment and sensitivity has been shown to be a flawed concept (Riskin, 2002).

REFERENCES

Acemoglu, Daron, Simon Johnson and James Robinson (2002), 'Reversal of Fortune: Geography and Institutions in the making of the Modern World's Income Distribution', *Quarterly Journal of Economics*, **117**: 1231–94.

Alder, Kenneth (1997), *Engineering the Revolution: Arms, Enlightenment, and the Making of Modern France*, Princeton, NJ: Princeton University Press.

Alder, Kenneth (1998), 'Making Things the Same: Representation, Tolerance and the End of the Ancien Régime in France', *Social Studies of Science*, **28**(4) (Aug.): 499–545.

Allan, D.G.C. (1979), *William Shipley: Founder of the Royal Society of Arts*, London: Scolar Press.

Bauer, Wolfgang (1966), 'The Encyclopedia in China', *Cahiers d'Histoire Mondiale*, **9**: 665–91.

Baumol, William J. (1993), *Entrepreneurship. Management, and the Structure of Payoffs*, Cambridge, MA: MIT Press.

Baumol, William (2002), *The Free-Market Innovation Machine: Analyzing the Growth Miracle of Capitalism*, Princeton, NJ: Princeton University Press.

Blaut, James M. (2000), *Eight Eurocentric Historians*, New York: Guilford Press.

Bourde, André J. (1967), *Agronomie et Agronomes en France au XVIIIe Siècle*, Vol. 1, Paris: S.E.V.P.E.N.

Bowers, Brian (1991), *Michael Faraday and the Modern World*, Wendens Ambo, Essex: EPA Press.

Brady, Alexander (1967), *William Huskisson and Liberal Reform: An Essay on the Changes in Economic Policy in the Twenties of the Nineteenth Century*, London: Oxford University Press.

Brock, William H. (1992), *The Norton History of Chemistry*, New York: W.W. Norton.

Brockliss, Laurence (2003), 'Science, the Universities, and other Public Spaces', in Roy Porter (ed.), *The Cambridge History of Science, Vol. 4: Eighteenth-century Science*, Cambridge: Cambridge University Press, pp. 44–86.

Burke, Peter (2000), *A Social History of Knowledge*, Cambridge: Polity Press.

Cardwell, Donald S.L. (1994), *The Fontana History of Technology*, London: Fontana Press.

Carlos, Ann and Stephen Nicholas (1990), 'Agency Problems in Early Chartered Companies: The Case of the Hudson's Bay Company' *Journal of Economic History*, **50**(4): 853–75.

Carlos, Ann and Stephen Nicholas (1996), 'Theory and History: Seventeenth-century Joint-stock Chartered Trading Companies', *Journal of Economic History*, **56**(4): 916–24.

Ching, Julia (1979), 'The Practical Learning of Chu Shun-shui, 1600–1682', in W. Theodore de Barry and Irene Bloom (eds), *Principle and Practicality: Essays in Neo-Confucianism and Practical Learning*, New York: Columbia University Press, pp. 189–229.

Cipolla, Carlo (1968), 'The Economic Decline of Italy', in Brian Pullan (ed.), *Crisis and Change in the Venetian Economy in the Sixteenth and Seventeenth Centuries*, London: Methuen.

Cohen, H. Floris (2004), 'Inside Newcomen's Fire Engine: The Scientific Revolution and the Rise of the Modern World', *History of Technology*, **25**: 111–32.

Darnton, Robert (1979), *The Business of Enlightenment*, Cambridge, MA: Harvard University Press.

Daumas, Maurice and André Garanger (1969), 'Industrial Mechanization', in Maurice Daumas (ed.), *A History of Technology and Invention*, vol. II, New York: Crown.

David, Paul A. (2004), 'Patronage, Reputation, and Common Agency Contracting in the Scientific Revolution', unpublished MS, Stanford University, August.

De Bary, W. Theodore (1975), 'Neo-Confucian Cultivation and the Seventeenth-century "Enlightenment"', in W. Theodore De Bary (ed.), *The Unfolding of Neo-Confucianism*, New York: Columbia University Press, pp. 141–206.

Deyon, Pierre and Philippe Guignet (1980), 'The Royal Manufactures and Economic and Technological Progress in France before the Industrial Revolution', *Journal of European Economic History*, **9**(3) (Winter): 611–32.

Dickinson, H.W., and Rhys Jenkins (1927), *James Watt and the Steam Engine*, London: Encore editions.

Dikötter, Frank (2003), 'China', in Roy Porter (ed.), *The Cambridge History of Science, Vol. 4: Eighteenth-century Science*, Cambridge: Cambridge University Press, pp. 688–98.

Drayton, Richard (2000), *Nature's Government: Science, Imperial Britain and the 'Improvement of the World'*, New Haven: Yale University Press.

Eamon, William (1994), *Science and the Secrets of Nature*, Princeton, NJ: Princeton University Press.

Ekelund, Robert B., Jr, and Robert D. Tollison (1981), *Mercantilism as a Rent-seeking Society*, College Station: Texas A&M University Press.

Ekelund, Robert B., Jr, and Robert D. Tollison (1997), *Politicized Economies: Monarchy, Monopoly, and Mercantilism*, College Station: Texas A&M University Press.

Elliott, Paul (2000), 'The Birth of Public Science in the English Provinces: Natural Philosophy in Derby, *c.* 1690–1760', *Annals of Science*, **57**: 61–101.

Elman, Benjamin (2001), *From Philosophy to Philology: Intellectual and Social Aspects of Change in Late Imperial China*, 2nd edn, Los Angeles: UCLA Asia-Pacific Institute.

Elvin, Mark (2004), 'Some Reflections on the Use of "Styles of Scientific Thinking" to Disaggregate and Sharpen Comparisons between China and Europe', *History of Technology*, **25**: 53–103.

Epstein, S.R. (1998), 'Craft Guilds, Apprenticeships, and Technological Change in Pre-industrial Europe', *Journal of Economic History*, **58**(3) (Sept.): 684–713.

Epstein, S.R. (2004), 'Knowledge-Sharing and Technological Transfer in Premodern Europe, *c.* 1200–*c.* 1800', unpublished manuscript, presented to the EHA Annual Conference, San Jose.

Ferguson, Eugene S. (1971), 'The Measurement of the "Man-Day"', *Scientific American*, **225**: 96–103.

Fox, Robert (2003), 'Science and Government', in Roy Porter (ed.), *The Cambridge History of Science, Vol. 4: Eighteenth-century Science*, Cambridge: Cambridge University Press, pp. 107–28.

Gascoigne, John (1994), *Joseph Banks and the English Enlightenment*, Cambridge: Cambridge University Press.

Gay, Peter (1966), *The Enlightenment: An Interpretation. The Rise of Modern Paganism*, New York: W.W. Norton.

Gernet, Jacques, (1982), *A History of Chinese Civilization*, Cambridge: Cambridge University Press.

Gillispie, Charles C. (1980), *Science and Polity in France at the end of the Old Regime*, Princeton, NJ: Princeton University Press.

Gillispie, Charles C. (2004), *Science and Polity in France: The Revolutionary and Napoleonic Years*, Princeton, NJ: Princeton University Press.

Goldstone, Jack A. (2002), 'Efflorescences and Economic Growth in World History: Rethinking the "Rise of the West" and the Industrial Revolution', *Journal of World History*, **13**(2): 323–89.

Golinski, Jan (1992), *Science as Public Culture: Chemistry and Enlightenment in Britain, 1760–1820*, Cambridge: Cambridge University Press.

Grabiner, Judith V. (1998), ' " Some disputes of Consequence": MacLaurin among the Molasses Barrels', *Social Studies of Science*, **28**(1): 139–68.

Gray, John (1995), *Enlightenment's Wake: Politics and Culture at the Close of the Modern Age*, London and New York: Routledge.

Greif, Avner (1994), 'Cultural Beliefs and the Organization of Society: A Historical and Theoretical Reflection on Collectivist and Individualist Societies', *Journal of Political Economy*, **102**(5): 912–41.

Greif, Avner (2005), *Institutions: Theory and History*, Cambridge: Cambridge University Press (forthcoming).

Harley, C. Knick (1998), 'Re-assessing the Industrial Revolution: A Macro View', in Joel Mokyr (ed.), *The British Industrial Revolution: An Economic Perspective*, Boulder: Westview Press, pp. 160–205.

Harris, John R. (2001), *Industrial Espionage and Technology Transfer*, Aldershot: Ashgate.

Helpman, Elhanan (2004), *The Mystery of Economic Growth*, Cambridge, MA: Harvard University Press.

Herman, Arthur (2001), *How the Scots Invented the Modern World*, New York: Crown.

Hills, Richard L. (1989), *Power from Steam: A History of the Stationary Steam Engine*, Cambridge: Cambridge University Press.

Hobsbawm, Eric (1997), 'Barbarism: A User's Guide', in Eric Hobsbawm, *On History*, New York: New Press, pp. 253–65.

Horkheimer, Max and Theodore W. Adorno (1976), *Dialectic of the Enlightenment*, New York: Continuum.

Horn, Jeff (2006), *The Path Not Taken: French Industrialization in the Age of Revolution, 1750–1830*, Cambridge, MA: MIT Press (forthcoming).

Hume, David ([1742] 1985), 'Of the Rise and Progress of the Arts and Sciences (1742)', in David Hume, *Essays: Moral, Political and Literary*, edited by Eugene F. Miller, Indianapolis: Liberty Fund.

Hunter, Michael (1989), *Establishing the New Science: The Experience of the Early Royal Society*, Woodbridge, Suffolk and Wolfeboro, NH: Boydell Press.

Inkster, Ian (2003), 'Technological and Industrial Change: A Comparative Essay', in Roy Porter (ed.), *The Cambridge History of Science, Vol. 4: Eighteenth-century Science*, Cambridge: Cambridge University Press, pp. 845–81.

Inkster, Ian (2004), 'Potentially Global: A Story of Useful and Reliable Knowledge and Material Progress in Europe, ca. 1474–1912', unpublished MS.

Jacob, Margaret C. (2004) 'Putting Science to Work', unpublished paper, presented to the History of Science meetings in Halifax, NS, July.

Jacob, Margaret C. and Larry Stewart (2004), *Practical Matter: Newton's Science in the Service of Industry and Empire, 1687–1851*, Cambridge, MA: Harvard University Press.

Jones, Eric L. (1981), *The European Miracle: Environments, Economies and Geopolitics in the History of Europe and Asia*, Cambridge: Cambridge University Press (2nd edn 1987).

Jones, Eric L. (1988), *Growth Recurring*, Oxford: Oxford University Press.

Kaplan, Steven L. (1976), *Bread, Politics and Political Economy in the Reign of Louis XV*, The Hague: Martinus Nijhoff.

Keynes, John Maynard (1936), *The General Theory of Employment, Interest, and Money*, New York: Harcourt, Brace.

Keyser, Barbara Whitney (1990), 'Between Science and Craft: The Case of Berthollet and Dyeing', *Annals of Science*, **47**(3) (May): 213–60.

Kindleberger, Charles P. (1975), 'The Rise of Free Trade in Western Europe, 1820–1875', *Journal of Economic History*, **35**(1) (March): 20–55.

Kranakis, Eda (1992), 'Hybrid Careers and the Interaction of Science and Technology', in Peter Kroes and Martijn Bakker (eds), *Technological Development and Science in the Industrial Age*, Dordrecht: Kluwer, pp. 177–204.

Landes, David S. (1998), *The Wealth and Poverty of Nations: Why Some Are So Rich and Some So Poor*, New York: W.W. Norton.

Lerner, Josh and Jean Tirole (2004), 'The Economics of Technology Sharing: Open Source and Beyond', NBER Working Paper 10956 (Dec.).

Levere, T.H., and G.L. E. Turner (2002), *Discussing Chemistry and Steam: The Minutes of a Coffee House Philosophical Society 1780–1787*, Oxford: Oxford University Press.

Lindqvist, Svante (1990), 'Labs in the Woods: The Quantification of Technology during the Late Enlightenment', in Tore Frängsmyr, J.L. Heilbron, and Robin E. Rider (eds), *The Quantifying Spirit in the 18th Century*, Berkeley: University of California Press, pp. 291–314.

Lipsey, Richard G., Kenneth Carlaw and Cliff Bekar (2006), *Economic Transformations: General Purpose Technologies and Sustained Economic Growth*, New York: Oxford University Press.

Lucas, Robert E. (1988), 'On the Mechanics of Economic Development', *Journal of Monetary Economics*, **22**: 3–42.

McClellan III, James (2003), 'Scientific Institutions and the Organization of Science', in Roy Porter (ed.), *The Cambridge History of Science, Vol. 4: Eighteenth-century Science*, Cambridge: Cambridge University Press, pp. 87–105.

Mokyr, Joel (2002), *The Gifts of Athena: Historical Origins of the Knowledge Economy*, Princeton, NJ: Princeton University Press.

Mokyr, Joel (2004), 'Accounting for the Industrial Revolution', in Paul Johnson and Roderick Floud (eds), *The Cambridge Economic History of Britain, 1700–2000*, Cambridge: Cambridge University Press, Vol. I, pp. 1–27.

Mokyr, Joel (2005a), 'Long-term Economic Growth and the History of Technology', in Philippe Aghion and Steven Durlauf (eds), *The Handbook of Economic Growth*, vol. III, Amsterdam: Elsevier, pp. 1113–80.

Mokyr, Joel (2005b), 'Mercantilism, the Enlightenment, and the Industrial Revolution', presented to the Conference in Honour of Eli F. Heckscher, Stockholm, May 2003. Forthcoming in Ronald Findlay, Rolf Henriksson, Håkan Lindgren, and Mats Lundahl (eds), *Eli F. Heckscher (1879–1952): A Celebratory Symposium*, Cambridge, MA: MIT Press.

Mokyr, Joel (2005c), 'The Intellectual Origins of Modern Economic Growth', *Journal of Economic History*, **65**(2) (June): 285–351.

Mokyr, Joel (2005d), 'King Kong and Cold Fusion: Counterfactual Analysis and the History of Technology', in Philip Tetlock, Ned Lebow, and Geoffrey Parker (eds), *The Unmaking of the West: Counterfactual Analysis in History and the Social Sciences*, Ann Arbor: Michigan University Press.

Needham, Joseph (1969), *The Grand Titration*, Toronto: University of Toronto Press.

Norberg, Kathryn (2003), 'Poverty', in Alan Charles Kors (ed.), *Encyclopedia of the Enlightenment*. Vol. 3, New York: Oxford University Press, pp. 347–53.

North, Douglass C. (1981), *Structure and Change in Economic History*, New York: W.W. Norton.

North, Douglass C. and Barry Weingast (1989), 'Constitutions and Commitment: The Evolution of Institutions Governing Public Choice in Seventeenth-century England', *Journal of Economic History*, **49**(4) (Dec.): 803–32.

Ogilvie, Sheilagh (2004), 'Guilds, Efficiency, and Social Capital: Evidence from German Proto-industry', *Economic History Review*, **57**(2): 286–333.

Pannebecker, John R. (1996), 'Diderot, Rousseau and the Mechanical Arts: Disciplines, Systems, and Social Context', *Journal of Industrial Teacher Education*, **33**(4): 6–22.

Pannebecker, John R. (1998), 'Representing Mechanical Arts in Diderot's Encyclopédie', *Technology and Culture*, **39**(1): 33–73.

Persson, Gunnar (2000), *Grain Markets in Europe, 1500–1900: Integration and Deregulation*, Cambridge: Cambridge University Press.

Peterson, Willard (1974), 'Fang-I-Chih: Western Learning and the "Investigation of Things"', in W. Theodore De Bary (ed.), *The Unfolding of Neo-Confucianism*, New York: Columbia University Press, pp. 369–411.

Peterson, Willard (1979), *Bitter Gourd: Fang I-Chih and the Impetus for Intellectual Change*, New Haven: Yale University Press.

Pirenne, Henri (1936), *Economic and Social History of Medieval Europe*, New York: Harcourt Brace & World.

Pomeranz, Kenneth (2000), *The Great Divergence: China, Europe, and the Making of the Modern World Economy*, Princeton, NJ: Princeton University Press.

Porter, Roy (2000), *The Creation of the Modern World: The Untold Story of the British Enlightenment*, New York: W.W. Norton.

Porter, Roy (2003), 'Introduction', in Roy Porter (ed.), *The Cambridge History of Science, Vol. 4: Eighteenth-century Science*, Cambridge: Cambridge University Press, pp. 1–20.

Priestley, Joseph (1768), *An Essay on the First Principles of Government and on the Nature of Political, Civil and Religious Liberty*, London: Printed for J. Doosley in Pall Mall.

Reynolds, Terry S. (1983), *Stronger than a Hundred Men: A History of the Vertical Water Wheel*, Baltimore: Johns Hopkins Press,

Ricardo, David ([1817] 1971), *Principles of Political Economy*, ed. R.M. Hartwell, Harmondsworth: Pelican Books.

Riskin, Jessica (2002), *Science in the Age of Sensibility: The Sentimental Empiricists of the French Enlightenment*, Chicago: University of Chicago Press.

Rodrik, Dani (2004), 'Getting Institutions Right: A User's Guide to the Recent Literature on Institutions and Growth', working paper, Harvard University, April.

Rodrick, Dani, Arvind Subramanian and Francesco Trebbi (2002), 'Institutions Rule: The Primacy of Institutions over Geography and Integration in Economic Development', NBER Working Paper no. 9305.

Root, Hilton (1994), *The Fountain of Privilege: Political Foundations of Markets in Old Regime France and England*, Berkeley and Los Angeles: University of California Press.

Rostow, Walt W. (1975), *How it all Began: Origins of the Modern Economy*, New York: McGraw Hill.

Rothschild, Emma (2001), *Economic Sentiments: Adam Smith, Condorcet, and the Enlightenment*, Cambridge, MA: Harvard University Press.

Schofield, Robert (1963), *The Lunar Society of Birmingham*, Oxford: Clarendon Press.

Shleifer, Andrei and Robert Vishny (1998), *The Grabbing Hand: Government Pathologies and their Cures*, Cambridge, MA: Harvard University Press.

Sivin, Nathan (1975), 'Wang Hsi-shan', in Charles Coulston Gillispie (ed.), *Dictionary of Scientific Biography*, New York: Charles Scribner's Sons, Vol. XIV, pp. 159–68.

Sivin, Nathan (1995), 'Why the Scientific Revolution did not take Place in China – or didn't it?', in *Science in Ancient China*, Aldershot: Variorum.

Smil, Vaclav (2005), *Creating the Twentieth Century: Technical Innovations of 1867–1914 and their Lasting Impact*, New York: Oxford University Press.

Smith, Adam (1978), *Lectures on Jurisprudence*, Edited by R.L. Meek et al., Oxford: Oxford University Press.

Smith, Adam (1976), *An Inquiry into the Nature and Causes of the Wealth of Nations*, ed. Cannan, Chicago: University of Chicago Press. Reprint. Oxford: Oxford University Press.

Smith, Pamela (1994), *The Business of Alchemy: Science and Culture in the Holy Roman Empire*, Princeton, NJ: Princeton University Press.

Spence, Jonathan (1990), *The Search for Modern China*, New York: W.W. Norton.

Sprat, Thomas (1702), *The History of the Royal-Society of London, for the Improving of Natural Knowledge*, London: Printed for Rob. Scot, Ri. Chiswell, Tho. Chapman, and Geo. Sawbridge.

Stewart, Larry (1992), *The Rise of Public Science*, Cambridge: Cambridge University Press.

Stewart, Larry (2004), 'The Laboratory and the Manufacture of the Enlightenment', unpublished manuscript, University of Saskatchewan.

Thompson, William Count Rumford ([1799] 1876), *The Complete Works of Count Rumford,* London: the American Academy of Arts and Sciences, Macmillan & Co.

Uglow, Jenny (2002), *The Lunar Men: Five Friends Whose Curiosity Changed the World*, New York: Farrar, Strauss and Giroux.

Ville, Simon and S.R.H. Jones (1996), 'Efficient Transactors or Rent-seeking Monopolists? The Rationale for Early Chartered Trading Companies', *Journal of Economic History*, **56**(4): 898–915.

Wong, R. Bin (1997), *China Transformed: Historical Change and the Limits of European Experience*, Ithaca: Cornell University Press.

Yeo, Richard (2003), 'Classifying the Sciences', in Roy Porter (ed.), *The Cambridge History of Science, Vol. 4: Eighteenth-century Science*, Cambridge: Cambridge University Press, pp. 241–66.

Young, Arthur (1772), *Political Essays concerning the Present State of the British Empire*, London: printed for W. Strahan and T. Cadell.

Zilsel, Edgar (1942), 'The Sociological Roots of Science', *American Journal of Sociology*, **47**(4): 544–60.

2. The knowledge-based economy and the triple helix model

Loet Leydesdorff

Few concepts introduced by evolutionary economists have been more successful than that of a 'knowledge-based economy' (Foray and Lundvall, 1996; Abramowitz and David, 1996; OECD, 1996). This assumption of a qualitative transition in economic conditions has become commonplace among policy-makers and mainstream economists. For example, the European Summit of March 2000 in Lisbon was specifically held 'to agree a new strategic goal for the Union in order to strengthen employment, economic reform and social cohesion as part of a knowledge-based economy' (European Commission, 2000). The findings of this meeting concluded that, among other things, 'the shift to a digital, knowledge-based economy, prompted by new goods and services, will be a powerful engine for growth, competitiveness and jobs. In addition, it will be capable of improving citizens' quality of life and the environment.'[1]

The metaphor of a 'knowledge-based economy' has raised a number of hitherto unanswered questions. For example, can such a large impact on the real economy be expected from something as elusive and poorly defined as the knowledge base of an economy (Skolnikoff, 1993)? Should one consider this concept merely as a rhetorical reflection of the optimism regarding the potential impact of ICT and the Internet during the latter half of the 1990s (Godin, 2006)? How would a knowledge-based economy be expected to differ from a market economy or a political economy?

In this chapter, I argue that one can expect a knowledge-based economy to exhibit dynamics different from those of a market-based or political economy. The systematic organization of knowledge production and control (Merton, 1973; Whitley, 1984) provides a third coordination mechanism to the social system in addition to the traditional mechanisms of economic exchange and political decision-making. From the perspective of complex systems and evolution theory, the interactions between these three coordination mechanisms can be expected to generate a knowledge base within the system.

1   WHAT IS THE KNOWLEDGE BASE OF AN ECONOMY?

How can a process such as the economy be based on something as ephemeral as 'knowledge'? In an introduction to a special issue on this topic, David and Foray (2002) voiced a caveat against using the metaphor of a knowledge-based economy. These authors cautioned that the terminology was coined recently and noted that 'as such, it marks a break in the continuity with earlier periods, more a "sea-change" than a sharp discontinuity' (p. 9). The authors suggest that the transformation can be analysed at a number of different levels. Furthermore, 'knowledge' and 'information' should be more carefully distinguished by analysing the development of a knowledge-based economy in terms of codification processes (Cowan and Foray, 1997; Cowan et al., 2000).

The focus of most economic contributions to the topic has hitherto remained on the *consequences* of knowledge-based developments, such as the impact of globalization on the relationships between competitors and between labour markets. The emergence of a knowledge-based economy is then invoked as a factor to explain historical developments and changes. However, the evolutionary dynamic of the knowledge base itself remain unexplained by these historical analyses. I do not wish to deny the social relevance of historical transitions and their impacts on the economy; on the contrary, my argument implies that knowledge-based dynamics can be expected to provide a coordination mechanism qualitatively different from the hitherto prevailing dynamics of politics and market-driven economics. The dynamic of knowledge production and control adds a degree of freedom to the complex system of social relations and coordination that needs to be explained. In other words, I focus on the knowledge base as an *explanandum* rather than as an *explanans* for its economic implications.

Under what conditions can a knowledge-based dynamics be expected to emerge in socio-economic systems? In order to operationalize, model, and eventually also measure the knowledge base of a system one must first flesh out the meaning of the concept. After the specification of the organization and codification of knowledge as an evolutionary mechanism, one is able to specify, among other things, why the emergence of a knowledge-based economy can be expected to induce 'globalization.' Why and how can a knowledge-based economy be considered a driving force of this social transformation? Furthermore, what can function as an indicator of the knowledge base operating within a system?

First, I will consider the theoretical side with a focus on the specification of knowledge-based innovation systems. Thereafter, I turn to the question of how the knowledge base can be operationalized and to whether this knowledge base can be measured and/or simulated. It will be argued that the concept of the knowledge base of an economy can be elaborated, and that this analysis results in an apparatus which provides a heuristics for empirical research and simulation studies.

2   THE EMERGENCE OF A KNOWLEDGE BASE

Knowledge enables us to codify the *meaning* of information. Knowledge can be considered as a meaning which makes a difference. Information can be more or less meaningful, given a perspective. However, meaning is provided from the perspective of hindsight. Providing meaning to an uncertainty (that is, Shannon-type information) can be considered as a first codification. Knowledge enables us to discard some meanings and retain others in a second layer of codifications. Knowledge itself can also be codified and codified knowledge can, for example, be commercialized. Thus, a knowledge-based system operates in recursive loops that one expects to be increasingly selective.

The knowledge base of a social system can thus be further developed over time (Cowan et al., 2000). Knowledge operates in the present in terms of informed expectations. Increasingly, codified anticipations drive a knowledge-based economy rather than its historical conditions (Lundvall and Borras, 1997). In other words, science-based representations of possible futures (for example, 'competitive advantages') feed back on the historical processes (Nonaka and Takeuchi, 1995). This orientation towards the future inverts the time axis locally. However, an inversion of the arrow of time may meta-stabilize a historically stabilized system. While stabilization and destabilization are historical processes, meta-stabilization potentially changes the dynamics of the system. A meta-stabilized system can under certain conditions be globalized (Coveney and Highfield, 1990; Mackenzie, 2001; Urry, 2003).

Before the emergence of a knowledge-based economy, the economic exchange of knowledge was first developed and stabilized as distinct from the exchange of commodities within the context of the market economy. For example, the patent system can be considered as a typical product of industrial competition in the late nineteenth century (Van den Belt and Rip, 1987). Patent legislation became crucial for regulating intellectual property when knowledge markets emerged increasingly in chemistry and later in electrical engineering (Noble, 1977). Patents package scientific knowledge so that new knowledge can function at the interface of science with the economy and be incorporated into knowledge-based innovations

(Granstrand, 1999; Jaffe and Trajtenberg, 2002). Patents thus provide a format for codifying knowledge contents for purposes other than the internal requirements of quality control in scientific communication.

The production and control of organized knowledge has existed as a subdynamic of the socio-economic system in advanced capitalist societies since approximately 1870 (Braverman, 1974; Noble, 1977). Schumpeter ([1939] 1964) is well-known for his argument that the dynamics of innovation upset the market mechanism (Nelson and Winter, 1982). While market forces seek equilibrium at each moment of time, novelty production generates an orthogonal subdynamic along the time axis. This has been modelled as the difference between factor substitution (the change of input factors along the production function) versus technological development (a shift of the production function towards the origin) (Sahal, 1981). Technological innovations enable enterprises to reduce factor costs in both labour and capital (Salter, 1960).

Innovative change *over time* (novelty production) and economic substitution at each *moment of time* can thus be considered as two analytically independent subdynamics, but these subdynamics may interact in the case of innovation. Improving a system innovatively presumes that one is able to handle the system purposefully. When this reflection is further refined by organizing knowledge, the innovative dynamic can be reinforced. This reinforcement will occur at some *places* more than at others. Thus, a third dimension pertinent to our subject can be specified: the geographical – and potentially national – distribution of whatever is invented, produced, traded, and retained. Nation-states, for example, can be expected to differ in terms of the relationship between the economy and their respective knowledge bases (Lundvall, 1992; Nelson, 1993). Different fields of science are organized nationally and/or internationally to varying degrees (Wagner and Leydesdorff, 2003; Walsh and Bayma, 1996).

Geographical units of analysis, economic exchange relations, and novelty production cannot be reduced to one another. However, they can be expected to interact to varying extents (Storper, 1997). Given these specifications one can create a model of the three dimensions and their interaction terms as shown in Figure 2.1.

The three dimensions provide us with different micro-operations of the social system because agents: (1) are differently positioned, (2) can maintain exchange relations and (3) learn from these relations with reference to their local positions. Figure 2.1 elaborates the conceptualization by displaying the interaction terms between each two of the three dimensions. In a modern society, these interactions are no longer synchronized ex ante. A knowledge-based economy is continuously disturbed by interactions at various interfaces and fails to be at rest. Interactions between the subdynamics generate

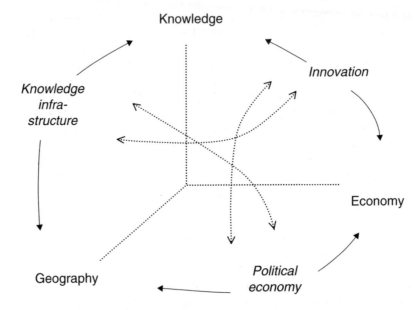

Figure 2.1   Three dimensions with their three first-order interaction terms

an evolutionary dynamics of transition *within* the system (Schumpeter, [1911] 1949).

In general, two interacting subdynamics can be expected to co-evolve along trajectories when the third dynamic is kept relatively constant. Over time, two subdynamics can lock into each other in a process of mutual shaping (Arthur, 1994; Callon et al., 2002; McLuhan, 1964). For example, during the formation of political economies in national systems during the nineteenth century knowledge production was first considered as a given (List, 1841; Marx, 1848, 1867).[2] Under the condition of constitutional stability in the various nation-states after 1870, *national systems of innovation* could gradually be developed among the axes of economic exchange and organized knowledge production and control (Noble, 1977; Rosenberg, 1976, 1982).

A hitherto stable context may begin to change historically. The erosion of relative stability in the nation-states after World War II has thus changed the conditions of innovation systems. When three subdynamics can interact, behaviour of the resulting systems can become complex. For example, a previously relatively stabilized coevolution between production and diffusion capacities within a national system can then increasingly be the subject of conflicting conditions of the local production and the world market. The multinational corporation thus emerged during the 1950s.

Alternatively, the other feedback term may globalize a historically stabilized trajectory of the technology into a technological regime (Dosi, 1982; Leydesdorff and Van den Besselaar, 1998).

When Lundvall (1988) proposed that the nation be considered as a first candidate for the *integration* of innovation systems, he formulated this claim carefully in terms of heuristics:

> The interdependency between production and innovation goes both ways . . . This interdependency between production and innovation makes it legitimate to take the national system of production as a starting point when defining a system of innovation. (Lundvall, 1988: 362)

The assumption of integrating innovation into production at the *national* level has the analytical advantage of providing us with an obvious system of reference. If the market is continuously upset by innovation, can the nation then perhaps be considered as another, albeit institutionally organized equilibrium (Aoki, 2001)? This specification of a stable system of reference enables the analyst to study, for example, the so-called 'differential productivity growth puzzle' which is generated by the different speeds of development among the industrial sectors (Nelson and Winter, 1975). This problem of the relative rates of innovation cannot be defined properly without the specification of a system of reference that integrates different sectors of an economy (Nelson, 1982, 1993). The solutions to this puzzle can accordingly be expected to differ among nation-states.

The historical progression varies among countries, and integration at the national level still plays a major role in systems of innovation (Skolnikoff, 1993). However, the emergence of transnational levels of government like the European Union, as well as the increased awareness of regional differences within and across nations, have changed the functions of national governments (Braczyk et al., 1998). 'Government' has evolved from a hierarchically fixed point of reference into a variable 'governance' that spans a variety of sub- and supranational levels. Larédo (2003) recently argued that this polycentric environment of stimulation has even become a condition for innovation policies in the European Union.

3 INTERACTIVE KNOWLEDGE PRODUCTION AND CONTROL

While a political economy can be indicated in terms of only two subdynamics (for example, as a 'dialectics' between production forces and production relations), a complex dynamics can be expected when three subdynamics are set free to operate upon one another (Li and Yorke, 1975; Leydesdorff, 1994). It will be argued here that the new configuration of three possible degrees of freedom – markets, governance, and knowledge production – can be modelled in terms of a triple helix of university–industry–government relations (Etzkowitz and Leydesdorff, 1997; Leydesdorff and Etzkowitz, 1998). Governance can be considered as the variable that instantiates and organizes systems in the geographical dimension of the model, while industry is the main carrier of economic production and exchange. Thirdly, academe can play a leading role in the organization of the knowledge production function (Godin and Gingras, 2000).

In this (neo-)evolutionary model of interacting subdynamics, the institutional dimensions cannot be expected to correspond one-to-one with the functions in the network carried by and between the agencies. Each university and industry, for example, has also a geographical location and is therefore the subject of regulation and legislation. In a knowledge-based system, functions no longer develop exclusively at the local level, that is, contained within the institutional settings. Instead, the interactions generate evolutionary dynamics of change in the relations at the network level. In other words, university–industry–government relations develop in terms of institutional arrangements that recombine three functions of the socio-economic system: (1) wealth generation and retention, (2) novelty production, and (3) control at the interfaces of these subdynamics. The functions provide a layer of development analytically different, but historically coupled to the institutional arrangements.

The first two functions (economy and science) can be considered as relatively open and 'universal' (Parsons, 1951; Luhmann, 1984). However, the third function of normative control bends the space of possible interactions reflexively back to the position of the operating units (for example, the firms and the nations) in the marketplace and at the research front, respectively. In this dimension, the question of what can be retained locally during the reproduction of the innovation processes becomes crucial. The advantages of entertaining a knowledge base can be incorporated only if the knowledge produced by the interacting fluxes can also be retained. In other words, the development of a knowledge base is dependent on the condition that knowledge production be socially organized.

The knowledge base of an economy can be considered as a second-order interaction effect in the historical trade-offs between functions and institutions. In other words, the interfaces between institutions and functions can be expected to resonate into co-evolutions in some configurations more than in others. However, these resonances remain incomplete because the co-evolving subdynamics are continuously disturbed by the third one. Therefore, the knowledge base cannot be stabilized and should not be reified

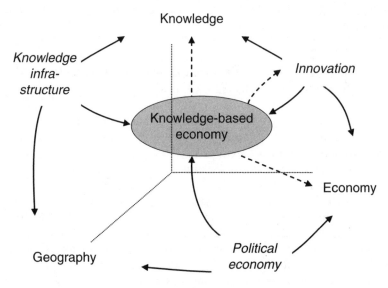

Figure 2.2　The first-order interactions generate a knowledge-based economy as a next-order system

reflexively. It remains merely an order of expectations pending as selection pressure upon the local configurations. The expectations, however, can be further codified through the use of knowledge. Knowledge can increasingly be codified in textual practices, for example, as 'scientific knowledge'.

Thus, one can distinguish between the stabilization of innovations along *technological trajectories* and the knowledge base as a next-order *regime* that remains emergent (Dosi, 1982; Sahal, 1985). As innovations are further developed along trajectories, a knowledge base becomes reflexively available as the evolutionary mechanism for restructuring of the historical trajectories. The next-order perspective of a regime rests as an additional selection environment on the trajectories. In terms of Figure 2.1, this second-order system can be added as shown in Figure 2.2.

In summary, the carriers of a knowledge-based system entertain a dually layered network: one layer of institutional relations in which they constrain each other's behaviour historically and one layer of functional relations in which they shape each other's expectations with reference to the future. The second-order interaction term (the knowledge base) remains a historical result of the first-order interactions in the knowledge infrastructure. An evolving knowledge base can be developed under the condition that the various interactions be left free to seek their own resonances, that is, in a self-organizing mode. This self-organization among the functions exhibits a dynamics potentially different from the organization of relations between the institutions.

4   THE GLOBALIZATION OF KNOWLEDGE PRODUCTION AND CONTROL

The availability and growth of a knowledge base reinforces the capacity of the system to develop solutions that improve on combinations developed hitherto. However, the knowledge base remains a reflexive construct that emerges endogenously within the system and is expected to remain under reconstruction. It self-organizes under the conditions of the organizations upon which it is created as a second-order layer. However, these second-order interaction terms can be expected to reflect changes as the first-order interaction terms change. Thus, a knowledge base may be replaced when the organizations change dramatically during periods of historical transition such as in Eastern Europe (and China!) after the demise of the Soviet Union. The horizon of expectations then changes.

Interacting expectations can provide a basis for changes in the behaviour of the carrying agents. These behavioural changes differ from the institutional imperatives and market incentives that have driven the system previously. While institutions and markets develop historically along the time axis, the knowledge-based structure of expectations drives the system in an anticipatory mode. Future-oriented planning cycles can be expected to become more important than current trends in the market. Thus, informed anticipations increasingly change the dynamics of the system from an agent-based perspective towards a more abstract knowledge-based one.

The social organization of knowledge production and control in R&D programmes has reinforced this knowledge-based subdynamic in the last century. Knowledge refines the communication by adding codification as a selection mechanism over time (while markets select at each moment of time). In other words, institutional dynamics develop along historical trajectories, but the knowledge base can be expected to function evolutionarily as the technological regime of the same system. The emerging regime remains pending as anticipated selection pressure generated and reproduced by the interactions among the lower-level subdynamics. The three subdynamics – which continue to develop recursively along their respective axes – are expected to interact in the complex dynamics of a knowledge-based economy.

Using ICT as its main medium, the knowledge-based economy can be expected to continue to expand and grow. Each knowledge-based subdynamic operates by reconstructing the past in the present on the basis of representations that contain informed expectations (for example, curves and functions on sheets of paper and computer screens). As the intensity and speed of communication between the carrying agencies increases, the codification of knowledge becomes a functional means to reduce the complexity in the communication. This emerging order of expectations remains accessible by reflexive agents. The expectations can be improved upon as they become more theoretically informed.

When the operation of a knowledge base is assumed, both participants and analysts are able to improve this understanding of the restructuring of the expectations at interfaces within the systems under study, which allows the codifications in the expectations to be further developed. For example, in a knowledge-based economy the price-mechanism of a market-based economy can increasingly be reconstructed in terms of price/performance ratios based on expectations about the life-cycles of technologies (Galbraith, 1967). Thus, more abstract and knowledge-intensive criteria are increasingly guiding economic and political decision-making.

5 THE OPERATION OF THE KNOWLEDGE BASE

The dynamics of a complex system of innovations based on the effects of second-order interactions are by definition non-linear (Allen, 1994). This non-linearity is a consequence of interaction terms among the subsystems and the recursive processes operating within each of them simultaneously. In the long run, the non-linear (interaction) terms can be expected to outweigh the linear (action) terms. For example, the *interaction* effects between 'demand pull' and 'technology push' can over time become more important for the systemic development of innovations than the sum of the linear action terms (Kline and Rosenberg, 1986; Mowery and Rosenberg, 1979).

As noted, trajectories can be stabilized when two of the three subdynamics co-evolve in a process of mutual shaping. For example, when a sector is innovated technologically, a 'lock-in' into a market segment may first shape a specific trajectory of innovations (Arthur, 1994). Learning curves can be steep, following a breakthrough in the marketplace (Arrow, 1962; Rosenberg, 1982). The third subdynamic, however, potentially meta-stabilizes a knowledge-based innovation system into its global regime. From this latter perspective, it is possible to compare different trajectories, but only by using a theoretical model (Scharnhorst, 1998). The model provides a basis for discussing alternatives beyond what has historically been available.

Analogously, when a science-based technology locks into a national state (for example, in the energy or health sector), a monopoly can be immunized against market forces for considerable periods of time. Over longer periods of time, however, these 'lock-ins' can be expected to erode because of the ongoing processes of 'creative destruction' (Schumpeter, 1943). Such creative destruction is based on recombinations of market forces with new insights (Kingston, 2003). Interaction effects among negative feedbacks, however, may lead to global crises that require the restructuring of the carrying layer of institutions (Freeman and Perez, 1988).

Historically, interactions betwen the subdynamics were first enhanced by geographical proximity (for example, within a national context or the context of a single corporation), but as the economic and technological dimensions of the systems globalized, dynamic scale effects became more important than static ones for the retention of wealth. Such dynamic scale effects through innovation were first realized by multinational corporations (Galbraith, 1967; Granstrand et al., 1997; Brusoni et al., 2000). They became a concern of governments in advanced industrialized countries after the (global) oil crises of the 1970s (OECD, 1980). Improving the knowledge base of these nations became a priority as science-based innovations were increasingly recognized as providing the main advantages to their economies (Rothwell and Zegveld, 1981; Freeman, 1982; Porter, 1990).

In other words, the relatively stabilized arrangements of a political economy endogenously generate the meta-stability of a knowledge-based system when the geographical units begin to interact and exchange more intensively in the economic and technological dimensions. Under the condition that the institutional make-up of the national systems must be restructured, the national and the international perspectives can induce an oscillation of a system between its stabilized and globalized states. The oscillating system uses its resources (for example, innovation) for the continuation of this 'endless transition' (Etzkowitz and Leydesdorff, 1998). From this perspective, the stimulation programmes of the European Union may have functioned as catalysts because these programmes have reinforced interactions between universities, industries, and governance at a transnational level (Frenken and Leydesdorff, 2004).

A previously stabilized system globalizes with reference to its next-order or regime level as an order of expectations. The knowledge base emerges by recursively codifying the expected information content of the underlying arrangements (Maturana and Varela, 1980; Fujigaki, 1998; Leydesdorff, 2001). Innovations can be considered as the historical carriers of this emerging system because they reconstruct and thus restabilize the relevant interfaces. Innovations instantiate the innovated systems in the present and potentially restructure existing interfaces in a competitive mode. In an innovative environment, the existing arrangements have to be continuously reassessed. For example, if one introduces high-speed trains, the standards and materials for constructing railways and rails may have to be reconsidered.

Once in place, a knowledge-based system thus feeds back on the terms of its construction by offering comparative improvements and advantages to the solutions found hitherto, that is, on the basis of previous crafts and skills. Knowledge intensity drives differentiation at the global level by providing us with alternative possibilities. However, the emerging system continues to operate locally in terms of institutions and solutions that organize and produce observable integration across interfaces. The production facilities provide the historical basis for further developing the knowledge-based operations. The complex knowledge-based system tends to resonate into a regime as a basin of attraction, but along a historical trajectory. This trajectory is evolutionarily shaped as a series of solutions to puzzles.

The expectations are heavily structured and invested with interests in finding solutions to puzzles. Some authors (for example, Gibbons et al., 1994; Nowotny et al., 2001) have claimed that the contemporary system exhibits de-differentiation between policy-making, economic transactions, and scientific insights due to the mutual 'contextualization' of these processes. These authors posit that a new mode of operation ('Mode 2') would have emerged at the level of the social system because of the dynamics of incorporating scientific knowledge. Indeed, the perpetual restructuring of the system which is guided by the knowledge base, can be expected to induce new institutional arrangements. Such rearrangements may include the temporary reversal of traditional roles between industry and the university, for example, in interdisciplinary research centres (Etzkowitz et al., 2000). Among codified expectations, however, exchanges are expected to remain highly structured (see Figure 2.3) and to continue to reproduce the differentiation for evolutionary reasons (Shinn, 2002).

Complex systems need both the *integration* of the various subdynamics into organizational formats (stabilization) and *differentiation* (globalization) in order to enhance further developments. This tension allows for

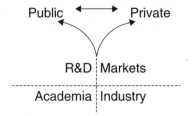

Figure 2.3   *Vertical and horizontal interfaces allow for functional and institutional reorganization*

meta-stabilization as a transitory state that can sustain both innovation and retention. In such systems, functions develop in interaction with one another and along their own axes, and thirdly in interaction with the exchanges between the institutions. At the interfaces between the economics of the market and the heuristics in R&D processes, translation mechanisms can be further developed that structure and codify these interactions over time. I gave above the example of developing the price mechanism into the price/performance criterion, but in innovative environments one can expect all criteria to become multivariate. For example, knowledge-based corporations organize a sophisticated interface between strategic (long-term) and operational (medium-term) planning cycles in order to appreciate and to update the different perspectives (Galbraith and Nathanson, 1978).

Since social coordination, communication, and control in a knowledge-based system no longer provide a single frame of reference, integration and differentiation can be expected to operate concurrently at the various interfaces, but without a priori synchronization at the systems level. In terms of the dynamics of the system, differentiation and integration can thus be considered as two sides of the same coin: integration may take different forms and differentiations can be relatively integrated (as subsystems). From an evolutionary perspective, the question becomes, where in the network can the relevant puzzles be solved and hence competitive edges be maintained? Thus, one can expect both geographically confined innovation systems and technological systems of innovation (Carlsson, 2002, 2006; Carlsson and Stankiewicz, 1991; Edqvist, 1997). The horizontal and vertical overlapping of systems and subsystems of innovation can be considered a hallmark of the knowledge-based economy.

In other words, the definition of a system of innovations becomes itself increasingly knowledge based in a knowledge-based economy since the subsystems are differently codified, yet interacting (at different speeds) in the reproduction of the system. Governance of a knowledge-based economy can only be based on a set of assumptions about the relevant systems. These assumptions are predictably in need of more informed revisions because one expects new formats to be invented at the hitherto stabilized interfaces.

6   NICHES

While the market can be considered in a first approximation as an open network seeking equilibrium, innovation requires closure of the network in terms of the relevant stakeholders (Callon, 1998). Innovations are generated and incubated by locally producing units such as scientific laboratories, artisan workshops, and communities of instrument makers, but in interaction with market forces. This provides innovation with both a market dimension and a technological dimension. The two dimensions are traded off at interfaces: what can be produced in terms of technical characteristics versus what can be diffused into relevant markets in terms of service characteristics (Lancaster, 1979; Saviotti, 1996; Frenken, 2006). Thus, a competitive edge can be shaped locally. Such a locally shielded network density can also be considered as a *niche* (Kemp et al., 1998).

Systems of innovation can be considered as complex systems because they are based on maintaining interfaces in a variety of dimensions. Problems at interfaces may lead to costs, but they can be solved more easily within niches than in their surroundings. Unlike organizations, niches have no fixed delineations. They can be considered as densities of interfaces in an environment that is otherwise more loosely connected. Within a niche, competitive advantages are achieved by reducing transaction costs (Biggiero, 1998; Williamson, 1985). Niches can thus be shaped, for example, within the context of a multinational and diversified corporation or, more generally, within the economy. In another context, Porter (1990) proposed analysing national economies in terms of *clusters* of innovation. Clusters may span vertical and horizontal integrations along business columns or across different types of markets. They can be expected to act as systems of innovation that proceed more rapidly than their relevant environments and thus are able to maintain a competitive edge.

Sometimes, the geographical delineation of systems of innovation in niches is straightforward, as in the case of the Italian industrial districts. These comprise often only a few valleys (Beccatini et al., 2003; Biggiero, 1998). For political reasons one may wish to define a system of innovation a priori as national or regional (Cooke, 2002). However, an innovation system evolves, and its shape is therefore not fixed (Bathelt, 2003). While one may entertain the *hypothesis* of an innovation system, the operationalization and the measurement remain crucial for the validation (Cooke and Leydesdorff, 2006). For example, Riba-Vilanova and Leydesdorff (2001) were *not* able to identify a Catalonian system of innovations in terms of knowledge-intensive indicators such as patents and publications despite references to this regional system of innovation prevalent in the literature on the basis of occupational indicators (Braczyk et al., 1998).

'National systems of innovation' have been posited for a variety of reasons, for example, because of the need to collect statistics on a national basis and in relation to national production systems (Lundvall, 1988; Nelson, 1993). In the case of Japan (Freeman, 1988), or in comparisons between Latin-American countries (Cimoli, 2000), such a delineation may provide better heuristics than those of the nations participating in the common frameworks of the European Union (Leydesdorff, 2000). Systems of innovation can be expected to vary in terms of their strengths and weaknesses in different dimensions. While one would expect a system of innovation in the Cambridge region (UK) to be science-based (Etzkowitz et al., 2000), the system of innovation in the Basque country is industrially based and reliant on technology centres that focus on applied research rather than on universities for their knowledge base (Moso and Olazaran, 2002). The evaluation of a 'system of innovation' can also vary according to the different perspectives of policy-making. While the OECD, for example, has focused on comparing national statistics, the EU has had a tendency to focus on changes in the interactions between the member states, for example, in transborder regions.[3]

Belgium provides an interesting example of regional differentiation. The country has been regionalized to such an extent that one no longer expects the innovation dynamics of Flanders to be highly integrated with the francophone parts of the country. In general, the question of which dimensions are relevant to the specificities of which innovation system requires empirical specification and research (Carlsson, 2006). However, in order to draw conclusions from such research efforts a theoretical framework is required. This framework should enable us to compare across innovation systems and in terms of relevant dimensions, but without an a priori identification of specific innovation systems. The systems under study provide the evidence, while the frameworks should carry the explanation of the differences.

Three such frameworks have been elaborated in innovation studies during the 1990s:

1. The approach of comparing (national) systems of innovation (Lundvall, 1988, 1992; Nelson, 1993; Edqvist, 1997).
2. The thesis of a new 'Mode 2' in the production of scientific knowledge (Gibbons et al., 1994; Nowotny et al., 2001).
3. The triple helix of university–industry–government relations (Etzkowitz and Leydesdorff, 1997, 2000; Leydesdorff and Etzkowitz, 1998).

I submit that the triple helix can further be elaborated into an *evolutionary* model that accounts for interactions between three dimensions (compare Lewontin, 2000; Ulanowicz, 1996). This generalized model will enable me to integrate three approaches: the 'Mode 2' thesis of the new production of scientific knowledge, the study of systems of innovation in evolutionary economics, *and* the neo-classical perspective on the dynamics of the market. In the triple helix model, the three micro-operations are first distinguished and then recombined.

7   DIFFERENT MICRO-FOUNDATIONS

In their seminal study entitled 'In Search of Useful Theory of Innovation', Nelson and Winter (1977) formulated their research programme as follows:

> Our objective is to develop a class of models based on the following premises. First, in contrast with the production function oriented studies discussed earlier, we posit that almost any nontrivial change in product or process, if there has been no prior experience, is an innovation. That is, we abandon the sharp distinction between moving along a production function and shift to a new one that characterizes the studies surveyed earlier. Second, we treat any innovation as involving considerable uncertainty both before it is ready for introduction to the economy, and even after it is introduced, and thus we view the innovation process as involving a continuing disequilibrium . . . We are attempting to build conformable sub-theories of the processes that lead to a new technology ready for trial use, and of what we call the selection environment that takes the flow of innovations as given. (Of course, there are important feedbacks.) (Nelson and Winter, 1977: 48f.)

These two premises led these authors to a programmatic shift in the analysis from a focus on the specification of expectations to observable firm *behaviour* and the development of industries along historical trajectories (Andersen, 1994). Thus, a 'heterodox paradigm' was increasingly generated (Storper, 1997). However, this shift in perspective has had epistemological consequences.

Both the neo-classical hypothesis of profit maximization by the operation of the market and Schumpeter's hypothesis of the upsetting dynamics of innovations were formulated as analytical perspectives. These theories specify expectations. However, the theory of the firm focuses on observable variation. The status of the model thus changed: analytical idealizations like factor substitution and technological development cannot be expected to develop historically in their ideal-typical forms. Nelson and Winter's first premise proposed focusing on the observables not as an *explanandum*, but as *variation* to be selected in selection environments (second premise). Innovation is then no longer to be explained, but trajectory formation among innovations functions as the *explanandum* of the first of the two 'conformable theories'. Trajectories enable enterprises to retain competences in terms of routines. Under evolutionary conditions of competition, one can expect the variation to be organized by firms along trajectories. Thus, the knowledge base is completely embedded in the institutional context of the firm. The relations between the evolutionary and the institutional perspective were thus firmly engraved in the research programme (Casson, 1997; Nelson, 1994).

The supra-institutional aspects of organized knowledge production and control are considered by Nelson and Winter (1977, 1982) as part of the selection environment. However, science and technology develop and interact at a global level with a dynamics different from institutional contexts (Leydesdorff, 2001). In the Nelson and Winter models, the economic uncertainty and the technological uncertainty cannot be distinguished other than in institutional terms (for example, market versus non-market environments). The undifferentiated selection environments generate 'uncertainty' both in the phase of market introduction and in the R&D phase. Thus, the two sources of uncertainty are not considered as a consequence of qualitatively different selection mechanisms which use different codes for the selections. The potentially different selection environments – geography, markets, knowledge – are not specified as selective subdynamics that may interact in a non-linear dynamics (including co-evolutions in organizational frameworks).

In other words, the models elaborated by Nelson and Winter were based on a biological model of selection operating blindly. Dosi (1982) added the distinction between 'technological trajectories' and 'technological regimes', but his theory remained within the paradigm of Nelson and Winter's theory due to its focus on innovative firm behaviour, that is, variation. Others have extended on these models by using aggregates of firms, for example, in terms of sectors (for example, Pavitt, 1984). However, the units of analysis remained institutionally defined.

In a thorough reflection on this 'post-Schumpterian' model, Andersen (1994) noted that firms (and their aggregates in industries) cannot be considered as the evolving units of an economy. He formulated his critique as follows:

> The limitations of Nelson & Winter's (and similar) models of evolutionary-economic processes are most clearly seen when they are confronted with the major alternative in evolutionary modeling which may be called 'evolutionary games'. . . . This difference is based on different answers to the question of 'What evolves?' Nelson and Winter's answer is apparently 'organisational routines in general' but a closer look reveals that only a certain kind of routines [*sic*] is taken into account. Their firms only interact in anonymous markets which do not suggest the playing of strategic games – even if the supply side may be quite concentrated. (Andersen, 1994: 144)

In summary, Nelson and Winter's models are formulated strictly in terms of the biological metaphor of variation and selection (Nelson, 1995).

Variation is organized along trajectories using a set of principles which is – for analytical reasons – kept completely separate from selection. The selection environments are not considered as differentiated (and thus at variance). The various selection mechanisms do not interact. Technological innovation is considered as endogenous to firm behaviour. The technological component in the selection environments is consequently not appreciated as a global effect of the interactions between firms.

It is argued here that the knowledge base can be considered as an attribute of the economy as a system. Although selection environments cannot be observed directly, they can be hypothesized as structural (sub)dynamics. This hypothesis is theoretically informed, but the model then becomes more abstract than an institutional one which begins with the observables. As Andersen (1994) noted, studies about evolutionary games begin with highly stylized starting points. These abstract assumptions can be compared with and traded off (for example, in simulations) against other hypotheses, such as the hypothesis of profit maximization prevailing in neo-classical economics. For example, one can ask to what extent an innovation trajectory can be explained in terms of the operation of market forces, in terms of its own internal dynamics of innovation, and/or in terms of interactions between the various subdynamics.

If selection mechanisms other than market choices can be specified – for example, in organized knowledge production and control – the interactions between these selection mechanisms can be made the subject of simulation studies. From this perspective, the observables and the trajectories are considered as the historically stabilized results of selective structures operating upon one another. In other words, the selection mechanisms span a phase space of possible events. The evolutionary progression is a result of continually solving puzzles at the interfaces between the subdynamics. Thus, the routines and the trajectories can be explained from a systems-theoretical perspective.

7.1   User–Producer Relations in Systems of Innovation

In an evolutionary model one can expect mechanisms to operate along the time axis other than the one prompted by the neo-classical assumption of profit maximization at each moment of time. While profit maximization remains pervasive at the systems level, this principle cannot explain the development of rigidities in the market, such as trajectories along the time axis (Rosenberg, 1976). In an evolutionary model, however, this (potentially stabilizing) subdynamic has to be specified in addition to market clearing. Thus, a second selection environment over time is defined in an evolutionary model.[4]

In general, the number of selection mechanisms determines the dimensionality of the model. Innovations take place at interfaces and the study of innovation requires therefore at least the specification of two systems of reference (for example, knowledge production and economic exchanges). It has been argued above that the emergence of a knowledge base requires the specification of three systems of reference. Before the three dynamics can interact, however, each selection mechanism has to be 'micro-founded' as an analytically independent operation of the complex system.

In his study about 'national systems of innovation' Lundvall (1988) argued that the learning process in interactions between users and producers provides a *micro-foundation* for the economy different from the neoclassical basis of profit maximization by individual agents. He formulated this as follows:

> The kind of 'microeconomics' to be presented here is quite different. While traditional microeconomics tends to focus upon decisions, made on the basis of a given amount of information, we shall focus upon a *process of learning*, permanently changing the amount and kind of information at the disposal of the actors. While standard economics tends to regard optimality in the allocation of a given set of use values as the economic problem, *par préférence*, we shall focus on the capability of an economy to produce and diffuse *use values with new characteristics*. And while standard economics takes an atomistic view of the economy, we shall focus upon the *systemic interdependence* between formally independent economic subjects. (Lundvall, 1988: 349f.)

After arguing that the interaction between users and producers belonging to the same national systems may work more efficiently for reasons of language and culture, Lundvall (1988: 360 ff.) proceeded by proposing the nation as the main system of reference for innovations. Optimal interactions in user–producer relations enable developers to reduce uncertainties in the market more rapidly and over longer stretches of time than in the case of less coordinated economies (Hall and Soskice, 2001; compare Teubal, 1979). I discussed this above when defining the function of niches.

Lundvall's theory about user–producer interactions as a microfoundation of economic wealth production at the network level can be considered as a contribution beyond his original focus on national systems. The relational system of reference for the micro-foundation is different from individual agents with preferences. The concept of 'systems of innovation' was generalized to cross-sectoral innovation patterns and their institutional connections (Carlsson and Stankiewicz, 1991; Edqvist, 1997; Whitley, 2001). User–producer relations contribute to the creation and maintenance of a system as one of its subdynamics. In an early stage of the development of a technology, for example, a close relation between technical specifications and market characteristics can provide a specific design with a competitive advantage (Rabeharisoa and Callon, 2002).

In other words, proximity can be expected to serve the incubation of new technologies. However, the regions of origin do not necessarily coincide with the contexts that profit from these technologies at a later stage of development. Various Italian industrial districts provide examples of this flux. As local companies develop a competitive edge, they have tended to move out of the region, generating a threat of deindustrialization which has continuously to be countered at the regional level (Beccatini et al., 2003). This mechanism is further demonstrated by the four regions designated by the EU as 'motors of innovation' in the early 1990s. These regions – Catalonia, Lombardia, Baden-Württemberg, and Rhône-Alpes – were no longer the main loci of innovation in the late 1990s (Krauss and Wolff, 2002; Viale and Campodall'Orto, 2002). Such observations indicate the occurrence of a bifurcation resulting when the rate of diffusion becomes more important than the local production. Diffusion may reach the level of the global market, and thereafter the globalized dimension can feed back on local production processes, for example, in terms of deindustrialization. Given the globalization of a dominant design, firms may even compete in their capacity to destroy knowledge bases from a previous period (Frenken, 2006).

In summary, a system of innovation defined as a localized nation or a region can be analysed in terms of the stocks and flows contained in this system. Control and the consequent possibility of appropriation of the competitive edge emerge from a recombination of institutional opportunities and functional requirements. In some cases and at certain stages of the innovation process, local stabilization in a geographic area may prove beneficial, for example, because of the increased puzzle-solving capacity in a niche. However, at a subsequent stage this advantage may turn into a disadvantage because the innovations may become increasingly locked into these local conditions. As various subdynamics compete and interact, the expectation is a more complex dynamics. Therefore, the institutional perspective on a system of innovation has to be complemented with a functional analysis.

7.2 'Mode 2' in the Production of Scientific Knowledge

The 'Mode 2' thesis of the new production of scientific knowledge (Gibbons et al., 1994) implies that the contemporary system has more recently gained a degree of freedom under the pressure of globalization and the new communication technologies. What seemed to be institutionally rigid under a previous regime (for example, nation-states) can be made flexible under this new regime of communication. In a follow-up study,

Nowotny et al. (2001) specified that the new flexibility is not to be considered as only 'weak contextualization'. The authors argue that a system of innovation is a construct that is continuously undergoing reconstruction and can be reconstructed even *in the core of its operations*. This 'strong contextualization' not only affects the selections themselves, but also the structure in the selections over time. The possibilities for novelty and change are limited more in terms of our capacity to reconstruct expectations than in terms of historical constraints.

How does one allocate the capacities for puzzle-solving and innovation across the system when the system boundaries become so fluid? The authors of the Mode-2 thesis answered as follows:

> There is no longer only one scientifically 'correct' way, if there ever was only one, especially when – as is the case, for instance, with mapping the human genome – constraints of cost-efficiency and of time limits must be taken into account. There certainly is not only one scientifically 'correct' way to discover an effective vaccine against AIDS or only one 'correct' design configuration to solve problems in a particular industry. Instead, choices emerge in the course of a project because of many different factors, scientific, economic, political and even cultural. These choices then suggest further choices in a dynamic and interactive process, opening the way for strategies of variation upon whose further development ultimately the selection through success will decide. (Nowotny et al., 2001: 115f.)

The perspective, consequently, is changed from interdisciplinary to *transdisciplinary*. The global perspective provides us with more choices than were realized hitherto. Reflections (which the authors consider as a property of the communication) enable us to make this difference in the discourse. Such reflexive communications add another dimension to the reflection by individual agents.

While Lundvall (1988) had focused on interaction and argued that communications can stabilize the local innovation environment for agents, these authors argue that communications enable us to entertain a global perspective on the relevant environments. In other words, communications can be expected to develop an internal dynamics between local interactions and global perspectives. The global perspective adds a dynamic that is different from the historical one which follows the time axis. While the latter focuses on the opportunities and constraints of a given unit (for example, a region) in its historical context, the discourse enables us to redefine the system of reference by contextualizing and analysing the subjects under study from the perspective of hindsight. Thus, the focus shifts from the historical reconstruction of a system by 'following the actors' (Latour, 1987) to the functional analysis of an innovation system operating in the present. The robustness of this construct depends not on its historical generation, but on the present level of support that can be mobilized from other subsystems of society (for example, the economy or the political systems involved).

What does this model add to the model of 'national innovation systems' in terms of providing a different micro-foundation? Lundvall's microeconomics were grounded in terms of communication and interaction between users and producers rather than in terms of the individual preferences of agents. The authors of 'Mode 2' define another communication dynamic relevant to the systems of innovation. This other perspective is possible because a network contains a dynamic both at the level of the nodes and at the level of the links. While agency can be considered as a source of communication – and can be expected to be reflexive, for example, in terms of learning and entertaining preferences – an agent necessarily has a position at a node in the network (Burt, 1982). The links of a communication system operate differently from the nodes in the network. The systems of reference, however, are different. Nodes represent agents and the links represent the relations between them.

Categories like reflexivity and knowledge can be expected to have different meanings from one layer of the network to another. For example, agents entertain preferences, but the structure of communication provides some agents with more access than others. In addition to actions which generate the variations, the dynamics of communications, that is, at the level of the links, are able to generate changes at the systems level, that is, in terms of changes in the structural selection mechanisms. These changes are endogenous to the system because they can be the result of non-linear interactions between previously stabilized aggregates of actions. Recursion and interaction add non-linear terms to the aggregations of micro-actions.

Luhmann (1984) was the first to propose that communication be considered as a system of reference distinct from agency. He emphasized the analytical advantages of this hypothesis (for example, Luhmann, 1996). The two systems of agency and communication are 'structurally coupled' in the events, like the columns and rows of a matrix. An interaction can be attributed as an action to the actor, while it can be expected to function as a communication within the respective communication system (Maturana and Varela, 1980; Leydesdorff, 2001). In addition to communicating in terms of first-order exchange relations, social systems communicate reflexively by providing meaning to communications from the perspective of hindsight.

Global perspectives can be focused when the communications are increasingly codified. For example, scientific communications may enable us to deconstruct and reconstruct phenomena in ever more detail. As noted above, the price mechanism could be further refined in terms of price/performance ratios. The differentiation of the communication into various functions enables the social system to process more complexity than in a hierarchically controlled mode. However, under this condition one can expect to lose a central point of coordination as the interacting (sub)systems of communication become increasingly differentiated in terms of their potential functions for the (uncoordinated) self-organization of the system. This communication regime reshapes the existing communication structures as in a cultural evolution. In other words, selection mechanisms other than 'natural' ones reconstruct the system from various perspectives.

For example, in scientific communications 'energy' has a meaning different from its meaning in political discourse. While economists and politicians are able to worry about 'shortages of energy', 'energy' is defined as a conserved quantity in physics. Words may have different meanings in other contexts. Thus, the evolutionary dynamics of social communication adds another layer of complexity to the first-order dynamics of the exchange. Institutionalization and organization stabilize the communication structures historically, but by providing meaning to the communication one is able to generate a global perspective (Husserl, [1929] 1973; Urry, 2003).

In summary, the communicative layer provides society with a selection environment for historical institutions. Unlike variation, selection remains deterministic albeit that in the case of communication systems selections operate probabilistically. Thus, the selection mechanisms cannot be observed directly. However, the specification of the expectation guides the observation. Furthermore, the communication structures of the social system are complex because the codes of the communication have been differentiated historically. Communications develop along the various axes, but they can additionally be translated into each other by using the different codes at the interfaces reflexively. Thus, systems of translation are generated. A translation adds an interface to the translated system.

For example, interaction terms among codes of communication emerged as a matter of concern within knowledge-based corporations when interfaces between R&D and marketing had increasingly to be managed (Galbraith, 1967). In university–industry–government relations three types of communications are interfaced. Frictions at the interfaces between the institutional layers and the dynamics of mutual expectations produce noise that can sometimes be locked-in and thus provide a competitive advantage. The systems thus generated can regain a degree of freedom which was previously locked into a co-evolution, in a later stage using the third dimension. The utilization of the degrees of freedom between institutions and functions among the three subsystems interacting in a triple helix increasingly provides the knowledge-based advantages in the economy.

7.3   A Triple Helix of University–Industry–Government Relations

The systems of innovation approach defined innovation systems in terms of (aggregates of) institutional units of analysis. 'Mode 2' analysis defined innovations exclusively in terms of reconstructions on the basis of emerging perspectives in communication. The triple helix approach combines these two perspectives as different subdynamics of the systems under study. However, this model enables us to include the dynamics of the market as a third perspective with the micro-foundation of neo-classical economics in natural preferences. Thus, one can assume that innovation systems are driven by various subdynamics and to varying extents. Consequently, the discussion shifts from an ontological one about what an innovation system 'is', or the epistemological question of how it should be defined, to the methodological question of how one can study innovation systems in terms of their different dimensions and subdynamics.

In the triple helix model, the main institutions of the knowledge-based economy have first been defined as university, industry, and government (Etzkowitz and Leydesdorff, 1995). These institutional carriers of an innovation system can be expected to entertain a dually layered network: one layer of institutional relations in which they constrain each other's behaviour, and another layer of functional relations in which they shape each other's expectations. Three functions have to be recombined and reproduced at the systems level: (1) wealth generation in the economy, (2) novelty generation by organized science and technology, and (3) control of these two functions locally for the retention and reproduction of the system. The layers can be expected to feed back onto each other, thus changing the institutional roles, the selection environments, and potentially the evolutionary functions of the various stakeholders in each subsequent round.

Within this complex dynamic, the two mechanisms specified above – user–producer interactions and reflexive communications – can be considered as complementary to the micro-foundation of neo-classical economics. First, each agent or aggregate of agencies is positioned differently in terms of preferences and other attributes. Second, the agents interact, for example in economic exchange relations. This generates the network perspective. Third, the arrangements of positions (nodes) and relations (links) can be expected to contain information because not all network positions are held equally and links are selectively generated and maintained. The expected information content of the distributions can be *recognized* by relevant agents at local nodes. This recognition generates knowledge within these agents and their organizations. Knowledge, however, can also be processed as discursive knowledge in the network of

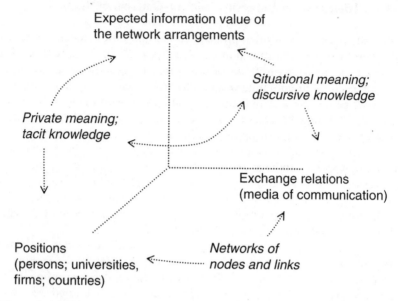

Figure 2.4   Micro-foundation of the triple helix model of innovation

exchange relations. Knowledge that is communicated can be further codified, for example, as discursive knowledge in the sciences. Figure 2.4 summarizes this configuration.

With this visualization I intend to make my argument epistemologically consistent by relating the various reflections (Cowan et al., 2000; Lundvall and Borras, 1997) to the underlying dimensions of the triple helix model. The three analytically independent dimensions of an innovation system were first distinguished in Figure 2.1 (above) as (1) the geography which organizes the positions of agents and their aggregates; (2) the economy which organizes the exchange relations; and (3) the knowledge content which emerges first with reference to either of these dimensions. Given these specifications, we were able to add the relevant interaction terms. The second-order interaction between these interactions then provided us with the possibility of the development of a knowledge base endogenous to the system under study. Figure 2.4 specifies this as an interaction between discursive and tacit knowledge. This second-order interaction may generate configurational knowledge as an order of expectations. The three different micro-foundations (preferences of agents, learning in interaction, anticipation in the learning through codification) can thus be distinguished reflexively with reference to the analytically distinguished dimensions.

8 THE TRIPLE HELIX: A PROGRAMME OF EMPIRICAL STUDIES AND SIMULATIONS

I have argued that the triple helix can be elaborated into a neo-evolutionary model which enables us to recombine sociological notions of meaning processing, economic theorizing about exchange relations, and insights from science and technology studies regarding the organization and control of knowledge production. The further codification of meaning in scientific knowledge production can add value to the exchange (Foray, 2004; Frenken, 2006). This model can serve as heuristics, but should not be reified. Its abstract and analytical character enables us to explain current transitions towards a knowledge-based economy as a new regime of operations.

Unlike biological models that focus on observable realities as variation with reference to 'natural' selection mechanisms, the triple helix model focuses primarily on the specification of the selection mechanisms. Three helices are sufficiently complex to understand the social reproduction of the dynamics of innovation (Leydesdorff, 1994; Leydesdorff and Etzkowitz, 1998; Lewontin, 2000). What is observable can be specified as relative equilibria at interfaces between different selection mechanisms operating upon each other. When repeated over time, a *co*-variation can be developed into a *co*-evolution, and a next-order, that is, more complex, system can be generated in a process of 'mutual shaping' (McLuhan, 1964).

The differentiation in terms of selection mechanisms can be both horizontal and vertical. Vertically the fluxes of communications are constrained by the institutional arrangements that are shaped in terms of stabilizations of previous communications. Horizontally, these communications are of a different nature because they can use different codes. For example, market transactions are different from scientific communications. Market transactions can also be cross-tabled with organizational hierarchies (Williamson, 1985), but from the perspective of a triple helix model, this would require the specification of two different dynamics: (1) markets can be organized at different levels (for example, at local, national, and global levels), and (2) control mechanisms can be made the subject of political or managerial governance by taking a different angle. While the control mechanisms at interfaces can be considered as functional for the differentiation between communications, the hierarchy in the organization provides us with a multi-level problem within the institutional dimension.

In summary, the functional perspective is different from the institutional one. Functional communications evolve; institutional relations function as retention mechanisms which respond to functional incentives. The specification of functions in the socio-economic analysis requires reflexivity. All reflections can again be made the subject of communication.

Thus, one can study a triple helix at different levels and from different perspectives. For example, one can study university–industry–government relations from a (neo-)institutional perspective (for example, Etzkowitz et al., 2000; Gunasekara, 2006) or one can focus on the relations between university science and the economy in terms of communications (for example, Langford et al., 1997; Leydesdorff, 2003). Different interpretations of the triple helix model can be at odds with each other and nevertheless inform the model. Each metaphor stabilizes a geometrical representation of an otherwise more complex dynamics.

Innovation can be considered as the reflexive recombination at an interface, such as between a technological option and a market perspective. Specification of the two different contexts requires theorizing. For the purpose of innovation, the perspectives have to be translated into each other, for example, in terms of a plan. Such translations potentially reinforce the research process by raising new questions, for example, by comparing across different contexts, yet with reference to emerging phenomena. Competing hypotheses derived from different versions of the triple helix can be explored through formal modelling and appreciated through institutional analysis. The case studies inform the modelling efforts about contingencies and boundary conditions, while the simulation model enables us to relate the various perspectives. In summary, the triple helix model is sufficiently complex to encompass the different perspectives of participant observers (for example, case histories) and, from an analytical perspective, to guide us heuristically in searching for options newly emerging from the interactions.

What is the contribution of this model in terms of providing heuristics to empirical research? First, the neo-institutional model of arrangements between different stakeholders can be used in case-study analysis. Given the new mode of knowledge production, case studies can be enriched by raising the relevance of the three major dimensions of the model. This does not mean to disclaim the legitimacy of studying, for example, academic–industry relations or government–university policies, but one can expect more interesting results by observing the interactions of the three subdynamics. Second, the model can be informed by the increasing understanding of complex dynamics and simulation studies from evolutionary economics (for example, Malerba et al., 1999; Windrum, 1999). Third, the second-order perspective adds to the meta-biological models of evolutionary economics the sociological notion of meaning being exchanged between the institutional agents (Luhmann, 1984; Leydesdorff, 2001).

Finally, on the normative side of developing options for innovation policies, the triple helix model provides us with an incentive to search for mismatches between the institutional dimensions in the arrangements and the social functions carried by these arrangements. The frictions between the two layers (knowledge-based expectations and institutional interests), and among the three domains (economy, science, and policy) provide a wealth of opportunities for puzzle solving and innovation. The evolutionary regimes are expected to remain in transition because they are shaped along historical trajectories (Etzkowitz and Leydesdorff, 1998). The knowledge-based regime continuously upsets the political economy and the market equilibria as different subdynamics. Conflicts of interest can be deconstructed and reconstructed, first analytically and then perhaps also in practice in the search for solutions to problems of economic productivity, wealth retainment, and knowledge growth.

The rich semantics of partially conflicting models reinforces a focus on solving puzzles among differently codified communications reflexively. While the lock-ins and the bifurcations are systemic, that is, largely beyond control, further developments require variety and self-organization of the interactions between the subsystems. New resonances between selections can shape trajectories in co-evolutions and the latter may recursively drive the system into new regimes. This neo-evolutionary framework assumes that the processes of both integration and differentiation remain under reconstruction. While Neurath's (1932/33: 206) metaphor that 'the ship is repaired on the open sea' focused at that time exclusively on science, a knowledge-based society has internalized the new dynamic of knowledge production and control into the economy at both the micro- and the macro-level.

NOTES

1. See the Conclusions of the EU Presidency at http://www.europarl.eu.int/summits/lis1_en.htm#b.
2. Marx (1857) extensively discussed the technological condition of industrial capitalism. For example, he formulated as follows:

   > Nature does not build machines, locomotives, railways, electric telegraphs, selfacting mules, etc. These are the products of human industry; natural resources which are transformed into organs of the human control over nature or one's practices in nature . . . The development of the fixed assets shows to what extent knowledge available at the level of society is transformed into immediate productive force, and therefore, to what extent the conditions of social life itself have been brought under the control of the general intellect and have been transformed accordingly. Crucial is the degree to which the socially productive forces are produced not only as knowledge, but as immediate organs of social practice, that is, of the real process of living. (Marx, 1857: 594; my translation)

   Thus, Marx's focus remained on the historical state of the development of science and technology, and the integration of this condition into the political economy.

3. The Maastricht Treaty (1991) assigned an advisory role to the European Committee of Regions with regard to economic and social cohesion, trans-European infrastructure networks, health, education, and culture (Council of the European Communities, 1992). This role was further strengthened by the Treaty of Amsterdam in 1997, which envisaged direct consultations between this Committee of Regions and the European Parliament and extended the advisory role to employment policy, social policy, the environment, vocational training, and transport.
4. The comparison between different states (for example, using different years) can be used for the comparative static analysis, but the dynamics along the time axis are then not yet specified.

REFERENCES

Abramowitz, M. and P.A. David (1996), 'Measuring Performance of Knowledge-based Economy', in *Employment and Growth in the Knowledge-Based Economy*, Paris: OECD, pp. 35–60.

Allen, P.M. (1994), 'Evolutionary Complex Systems: Models of Technology Change', in L. Leydesdorff and P. Van den Besselaar (eds), *Evolutionary Economics and Chaos Theory: New Directions for Technology Studies*, London/ New York: Pinter, pp. 1–18.

Andersen, E.S. (1994), *Evolutionary Economics: Post-Schumpeterian Contributions*, London: Pinter.

Aoki, M. (2001), *Towards a Comparative Institutional Analysis*, Cambridge, MA: MIT Press.

Arrow, K.J. (1962), 'The Economic Implications of Learning by Doing', *Review of Economic Studies*, **29**: 155–73.

Arthur, W.B. (1994), *Increasing Returns and Path Dependence in the Economy*, Ann Arbor: University of Michigan Press.

Bathelt, H. (2003), 'Growth Regimes in Spatial Perspective 1: Innovation, Institutions and Social Systems', *Progress in Human Geography*, **27**(6): 789–804.

Beccatini, G., M. Bellandi, G. Dei Ottati, and F. Sforzi (2003), *From Industrial Districts to Local Development: An Itinerary of Research*, Cheltenham, UK and Northampton, MA, USA: Edward Elgar.

Biggiero, L. (1998), 'Italian Industrial Districts: A Triple Helix Pattern of Problem Solving', *Industry and Higher Eductation*, **12**(4): 227–34.

Braczyk, H.-J., P. Cooke and M. Heidenreich (eds) (1998), *Regional Innovation Systems*, London/ Bristol, PA: University College London Press.

Braverman, H. (1974), *Labor and Monopoly Capital. The Degradation of Work in the Twentieth Century*, New York/London: Monthly Review Press.

Brusoni, S., A. Prencipe and K. Pavitt (2000), 'Knowledge Specialization and the Boundaries of the Firm: Why Do Firms Know More Than They Make?' *Administrative Science Quarterly*, **46**: 597–621.

Burt, R.S. (1982), *Toward a Structural Theory of Action*, New York: Academic Press.

Callon, M. (1998), *The Laws of the Market*, Oxford and Malden, MA: Blackwell.

Callon, M., C. Méadel and V. Rabeharisoa (2002), 'The Economy of Qualities', *Economy and Society*, **31**(2): 194–217.

Carlsson, B. (ed.) (2002), *New Technological Systems in the Bio Industries – An International Study*. Boston/Dordrecht/London: Kluwer Academic Publishers.

Carlsson, B. (2006), 'Internationalization of Innovation Systems: A Survey of the Literature', *Research Policy*, **35**(1): 56–67.

Carlsson, B. and R. Stankiewicz (1991), 'On the Nature, Function, and Composition of Technological Systems', *Journal of Evolutionary Economics*, **1**(2): 93–118.

Casson, M. (1997), *Information and Organization: A New Perspective on the Theory of the Firm*, Oxford: Clarendon Press.

Cimoli, M. (ed.) (2000), *Developing Innovation Systems: Mexico in a Global Context*, London: Continuum.

Cooke, P. (2002), *Knowledge Economies*, London: Routledge.

Cooke, P. and L. Leydesdorff (2006), 'Regional Development in the Knowledge-based Economy: The Construction of Advantages', *Journal of Technology Transfer*, **31**(1): 5–15.

Council of the European Communities (1992), *Treaty on European Union*, Luxembourg: Office for Official Publications of the European Communities.

Coveney, P. and R. Highfield (1990), *The Arrow of Time*, London: Allen.

Cowan, R. and D. Foray (1997), 'The Economics of Codification and the Diffusion of Knowledge', *Industrial and Corporate Change*, **6**: 595–622.

Cowan, R., P. David and D. Foray (2000), 'The Explicit Economics of Knowledge Codification and Tacitness', *Industrial and Corporate Change*, **9**(2): 211–53.

David, P.A. and D. Foray (2002), 'An Introduction to the Economy of the Knowledge Society', *International Social Science Journal*, **54**(171): 9–23.

Dosi, G. (1982), 'Technological Paradigms and Technological Trajectories: A Suggested Interpretation of the Determinants and Directions of Technical Change', *Research Policy*, **11**: 147–62.

Edqvist, C. (ed.) (1997), *Systems of Innovation: Technologies, Institutions and Organizations*, London: Pinter.

Etzkowitz, H. and L. Leydesdorff (1995), 'The Triple Helix – University–Industry–Government Relations: A Laboratory for Knowledge-based Economic Development', *EASST Review*, **14**: 14–19.

Etzkowitz, H. and L. Leydesdorff (1997), *Universities and the Global Knowledge Economy: A Triple Helix of University–Industry–Government Relations*, London: Pinter.

Etzkowitz, H. and L. Leydesdorff (1998), 'The Endless Transition: A "Triple Helix" of University–Industry–Government Relations', *Minerva*, **36**: 203–8.

Etzkowitz, H. and L. Leydesdorff (2000), 'The Dynamics of Innovation: From National Systems and "Mode 2" to a Triple Helix of University–Industry–Government Relations', *Research Policy*, **29**(2): 109–23.

Etzkowitz, H., A. Webster, C. Gebhardt and B.R.C. Terra (2000), 'The Future of the University and the University of the Future: Evolution of Ivory Tower to Entrepreneurial Paradigm', *Research Policy*, **29**(2): 313–30.

European Commission (2000), 'Towards a European Research Area', Brussels, 18 January, at http://europa.eu.int/comm/research/era/pdf/com2000-6-en.pdf.

Foray, D. (2004), *The Economics of Knowledge*, Cambridge, MA and London: MIT Press.

Foray, D. and B.-A. Lundvall (1996), 'The Knowledge-based Economy: From the Economics of Knowledge to the Learning Economy', in *OECD Documents: Employment and Growth in the Knowledge-based Economy*, Paris: OECD, pp. 11–32.

Freeman, C. (1982), *The Economics of Industrial Innovation*, Harmondsworth: Penguin.

Freeman, C. (1988), 'Japan, a New System of Innovation', in G. Dosi, C. Freeman, R. R. Nelson, G. Silverberg and L. Soete (eds), *Technical Change and Economic Theory*, London: Pinter, pp. 31–54.

Freeman, C. and C. Perez (1988), 'Structural Crises of Adjustment, Business Cycles and Investment Behaviour', in G. Dosi, C. Freeman, R.R. Nelson, G. Silverberg and L. Soete (eds), *Technical Change and Economic Theory*, London: Pinter, pp. 38–66.

Frenken, K. (2006), *Innovation, Evolution and Complexity Theory*, Cheltenham, UK and Northampton, MA, USA: Edward Elgar.

Frenken, K. and L. Leydesdorff (2004), 'Scientometrics and the Evaluation of European Integration', in J. Ulijn and T. Brown (eds), *Innovation, Entrepreneurship and Culture: The Interaction between Technology, Progress and Economic Growth*, Cheltenham, UK and Northampton, MA, USA: Edward Elgar, pp. 87–102.

Fujigaki, Y. (1998), 'Filling the Gap between Discussions on Science and Scientists' Everyday Activities: Applying the Autopoiesis System Theory to Scientific Knowledge', *Social Science Information*, **37**(1): 5–22.

Galbraith, J.K. (1967), *The New Industrial State*, Harmondsworth: Penguin.

Galbraith, J.R. and D.A. Nathanson (1978), *Strategy Implementation: The Role of Structure and Process*, St Paul, MN: West Publishing Company.

Gibbons, M., C. Limoges, H. Nowotny, S. Schwartzman, P. Scott and M. Trow (1994), *The New Production of Knowledge: The Dynamics of Science and Research in Contemporary Societies*, London: Sage.

Godin, B. (2006), 'The Knowledge-based Economy: Conceptual Framework or Buzzword', *Journal of Technology Transfer*, **31**(1): 17–30.

Godin, B. and Y. Gingras (2000), 'The Place of Universities in the System of Knowledge Production', *Research Policy*, **29**(2): 273–8.

Granstrand, O. (1999), *The Economics and Management of Intellectual Property: Towards Intellectual Capitalism*, Cheltenham, UK and Northampton, MA, USA: Edward Elgar.

Granstrand, O., P. Patel and K. Pavitt (1997), 'Multitechnology Corporations: Why They Have "Distributed" Rather Than "Distinctive" Core Capabilities', *California Management Review*, **39**: 8–25.

Gunasekara, C. (2005), 'Reframing the Role of Universities in the Development of Regional Innovation Systems', *Journal of Technology Transfer*, **31**(1): 101–13.

Hall, P.A. and D.W. Soskice (eds) (2001), *Varieties of Capitalism: The Institutional Foundations of Comparative Advantage*, Oxford: Oxford University Press.

Husserl, E. ([1929] 1973), *Cartesianische Meditationen Und Pariser Vorträge* [*Cartesian Meditations and the Paris Lectures*], The Hague: Martinus Nijhoff.

Jaffe, A.B. and M. Trajtenberg (2002), *Patents, Citations, and Innovations: A Window on the Knowledge Economy*, Cambridge, MA and London: MIT Press.

Kemp, R., J. Schot and R. Hoogma (1998), 'Regime Shifts to Sustainability through Processes of Niche Formation. The Approach of Strategic Niche Management', *Technology Analysis and Strategic Management*, **10**(2) 175–95.

Kingston, W. (2003), *Innovation: The Creative Impulse in Human Progress*, Washington, DC: Leonard R. Sugerman Press.

Kline, S. and N. Rosenberg (1986), 'An Overview of Innovation', in R. Landau and N. Rosenberg (eds), *The Positive Sum Strategy: Harnessing Technology for Economic Growth*, Washington, DC: National Academy Press, pp. 275–306.

Krauss, G. and H.-G. Wolff (2002), 'Technological Strengths in Mature Sectors – an Impediment of an Asset of Regional Economic Restructuring? The Case of

Multimedia and Biotechnology in Baden-Württemberg', *Journal of Technology Transfer*, **27**(1): 39–50.

Lancaster, K.J. (1979), *Variety, Equity and Efficiency*, New York: Columbia University Press.

Langford, C.H., R.D. Burch and M.W. Langford (1997), 'The "Well-stirred Reactor": Evolution of Industry–Government–University Relations in Canada', *Science and Public Policy*, **24**(1): 21–7.

Larédo, P. (2003), 'Six Major Challenges Facing Public Intervention in Higher Education, Science, Technology and Innovation', *Science and Public Policy*, **30**(1): 4–12.

Latour, B. (1987), *Science in Action*, Milton Keynes: Open University Press.

Lewontin, R. (2000), *The Triple Helix: Gene, Organism, and Environment*, Cambridge, MA and London: Harvard University Press.

Leydesdorff, L. (1994), 'Epilogue', in L. Leydesdorff and P. Van den Besselaar (eds), *Evolutionary Economics and Chaos Theory: New Directions for Technology Studies*, London and New York: Pinter, pp. 180–92.

Leydesdorff, L. (2000), 'Are EU Networks Anticipatory Systems? An Empirical and Analytical Approach', in D.M. Dubois (ed.), *Computing Anticipatory Systems – Casys'99*, Woodbury, NY: American Physics Institute.

Leydesdorff, L. (2001), *A Sociological Theory of Communication: The Self-Organization of the Knowledge-Based Society*, Parkland, FL: Universal Publishers: at http://www.upublish.com/books/leydesdorff.htm.

Leydesdorff, L. (2003), 'The Mutual Information of University–Industry–Government Relations: An Indicator of the Triplex Helix Dynamics', *Scientometrics*, **58**(2): 445–67.

Leydesdorff, L. and H. Etzkowitz (1998), 'The Triple Helix as a Model for Innovation Studies', *Science and Public Policy*, **25**(3): 195–203.

Leydesdorff, L. and P. Van den Besselaar (1998), 'Technological Development and Factor Substitution in a Non-Linear Model', *Journal of Social and Evolutionary Systems*, **21**: 173–92.

Li, T.-Y. and J.A. Yorke (1975), 'Period Three Implies Chaos', *American Mathematical Monthly*, **82**: 985–92.

List, F. (1841), *The National Systems of Political Economy*, London: Longman (1904 edn).

Luhmann, N. (1984), *Soziale Systeme. Grundriß einer allgemeinen Theorie*, Frankfurt a. M.: Suhrkamp.

Luhmann, N. (1996), 'On the Scientific Context of the Concept of Communication', *Social Science Information*, **35**(2): 257–67.

Lundvall, B.-Å. (1988), 'Innovation as an Interactive Process: From User–Producer Interaction to the National System of Innovation', in G. Dosi, C. Freeman, R. Nelson, G. Silverberg and L. Soete (eds), *Technical Change and Economic Theory*, London: Pinter, pp. 349–69.

Lundvall, B.-Å. (ed.) (1992), *National Systems of Innovation*, London: Pinter.

Lundvall, B.-Å. and S. Borras (1997), *The Globalising Learning Economy: Implication for Innovation Policy*, Luxembourg: European Commission.

Mackenzie, A. (2001), 'The Technicity of Time', *Time & Society*, **10**(2/3): 235–57.

Malerba, F., R. Nelson, L. Orsenigo and S. Winter (1999), ' "History-Friendly" Models of Industry Evolution: The Computer Industry', *Industrial and Corporate Change*, **8**(1): 3–35.

Marx, K. (1848), *The Communist Manifesto* (translated by Samuel Moore in 1888) Harmondsworth: Penguin (1967 edn).

Marx, K. (1857), *Grundriße der Kritik der politischen Oekonomie*, Moscow: Marx-Engels-Lenin Institute (1939 edn).

Marx, K. (1867), *Das Kapital I*, Hamburg: Meisner.

Maturana, H.R. and F.J. Varela (1980), *Autopoiesis and Cognition: The Realization of the Living*, Dordrecht: Reidel.

McLuhan, M. (1964), *Understanding Media: The Extension of Man*, New York: McGraw-Hill.

Merton, R.K. (1973), *The Sociology of Science: Theoretical and Empirical Investigations*, Chicago and London: University of Chicago Press.

Moso, M. and M. Olazaran (2002), 'Regional Technology Policy and the Emergence of an R&D System in the Basque Country', *Journal of Technology Transfer*, **27**(1): 61–75.

Mowery, D.C. and N. Rosenberg (1979), 'The Influence of Market Demand upon Innovation: A Critical Reveiw of Some Empirical Studies', *Research Policy*, **8**: 102–53.

Nelson, R.R. (ed.) (1982), *Government and Technical Progress: A Cross-Industry Analysis*, New York: Pergamon.

Nelson, R.R. (ed.) (1993), *National Innovation Systems: A Comparative Analysis*, New York: Oxford University Press.

Nelson, R.R. (1994), 'Economic Growth via the Coevolution of Technology and Institutions', in L. Leydesdorff and P. Van den Besselaar (eds), *Evolutionary Economic and Chaos Theory: New Directions in Technology Studies*, London and New York: Pinter, pp. 21–32.

Nelson, R.R. (1995), 'Recent Evolutionary Theorizing about Economic Change', *Journal of Economic Literature*, **33**(1): 48–90.

Nelson, R.R. and S.G. Winter (1975), 'Growth Theory from an Evolutionary Perspective: The Differential Productivity Growth Puzzle', *American Economic Review*, **65**: 338–44.

Nelson, R.R. and S.G. Winter (1977), 'In Search of Useful Theory of Innovation', *Research Policy*, **6**: 35–76.

Nelson, R.R. and S.G. Winter. (1982), *An Evolutionary Theory of Economic Change*, Cambridge, MA: Belknap Press of Harvard University Press.

Neurath, O. (1932/33), 'Protokollsätze', *Erkenntnis*, **3**: 204–14.

Noble, D. (1977), *America by Design*, New York: Knopf.

Nonaka, I. and H. Takeuchi (1995), *The Knowledge Creating Company*, Oxford and New York: Oxford University Press.

Nowotny, H., P. Scott and M. Gibbons (2001), *Re-Thinking Science: Knowledge and the Public in an Age of Uncertainty*, Cambridge: Polity.

OECD (1980), *Technical Change and Economic Policy*, Paris: OECD.

OECD (1996), *OECD Economic Outlook, No. 60*, Paris: OECD.

Parsons, T. (1951), *The Social System*, New York: The Free Press.

Pavitt, K. (1984), 'Sectoral Patterns of Technical Change: Towards a Theory and a Taxonomy', *Research Policy*, **13**: 343–73.

Porter, M.E. (1990), *The Competitive Advantage of Nations*, London: Macmillan.

Rabeharisoa, V. and M. Callon (2002), 'The Involvement of Patients' Associations in Research', *International Social Science Journal*, **54**(171): 57–65.

Riba-Vilanova, M. and L. Leydesdorff (2001), 'Why Catalonia Cannot be Considered as a Regional Innovation System', *Scientometrics*, **50**(2): 215–40.

Rosenberg, N. (1976), 'The Direction of Technological Change: Inducement Mechanisms and Focusing Devices', in *Perspectives on Technology*, Cambridge: Cambridge University Press, pp. 108–25.

Rosenberg, N. (1982), *Inside the Black Box: Technology and Economics*, Cambridge: Cambridge University Press.

Rothwell, R. and W. Zegveld (1981), *Industrial Innovation and Public Policy*, London: Pinter.

Sahal, D. (1981), *Patterns of Technological Innovation*, Reading, MA: Addison Wesley.

Sahal, D. (1985), 'Technological Guideposts and Innovation Avenues', *Research Policy*, **14**: 61–82.

Salter, W.E.G. (1960), *Productivity and Technical Change*, New York: Cambridge University Press.

Saviotti, P.P. (1996), *Technological Evolution, Variety and the Economy*, Cheltenham, UK and Brookfield, UT, USA: Edward Elgar.

Scharnhorst, A. (1998), 'Citation-Networks, Science Landscapes and Evolutionary Strategies', *Scientometrics*, **43**(1): 95–106.

Schumpeter, J. ([1911] 1949), *The Theory of Economic Development*, Cambridge, MA: Harvard University Press.

Schumpeter, J. ([1939] 1964), *Business Cycles: A Theoretical, Historical and Statistical Analysis of Capitalist Process*, New York: McGraw-Hill.

Schumpeter, J. (1943), *Socialism, Capitalism and Democracy*, London: Allen & Unwin.

Shinn, T. (2002), 'The Triple Helix and New Production of Knowledge: Prepackaged Thinking on Science and Technology', *Social Studies of Science*, **32**(4): 599–614.

Skolnikoff, E.B. (1993), *The Elusive Transformation: Science, Technology and the Evolution of International Politics*, Princeton, NJ: Princeton University Press.

Storper, M. (1997), *The Regional World – Territorial Development in a Global Economy*, New York: Guilford Press.

Teubal, M. (1979), 'On User Needs and Need Determination. Aspects of a Theory of Technological Innovation', in M.J. Baker (ed.), *Industrial Innovation. Technology, Policy and Diffusion*, London: Macmillan Press, pp. 266–89.

Ulanowicz, R.E. (1996), 'The Propensities of Evolving Systems', in E.L. Khalil and K.E. Boulding (eds), *Evolution, Order and Complexity*, London and New York: Routledge, pp. 217–33.

Urry, J. (2003), *Global Complexity*, Cambridge: Polity.

Van den Belt, H. and A. Rip (1987), 'The Nelson–Winter–Dosi Model and Synthetic Dye Chemistry', in W.E. Bijker, T.P. Hughes and T.J. Pinch (eds), *The Social Construction of Technological Systems. New Directions in the Sociology and History of Technology*, Cambridge, MA: MIT Press, pp. 135–58.

Viale, R. and S. Campodall'Orto (2002), 'An Evolutionary Triple Helix to Strengthen Academy–Industry Relations: Suggestions from European Regions', *Science and Public Policy*, **29**(3): 154–68.

Wagner, C.S. and L. Leydesdorff (2003), 'Seismology as a Dynamic, Distributed Area of Scientific Research', *Scientometrics*, **58**(1): 91–114.

Walsh, J.P. and T. Bayma (1996), 'Computer Networks and Scientific Work', *Social Studies of Science*, **26**(3): 661–703.

Whitley, R.D. (1984), *The Intellectual and Social Organization of the Sciences*, Oxford: Oxford University Press.

Whitley, R.D. (2001), 'National Innovation Systems', in N.J. Smelser and P.B. Baltes (eds), *International Encyclopedia of the Social and Behavioral Sciences*, Oxford: Elsevier, pp. 10303–9.
Williamson, O. (1985), *The Economic Institutions of Capitalism*, New York: Free Press.
Windrum, P. (1999), 'Simulation Models of Technological Innovation: A Review', *American Behavioral Scientist*, **42**(10): 1531–50.

3. Reputation, leadership and communities of practice: the case of open source software development

Paul Muller[*]

1 INTRODUCTION

Numerous recent contributions (Brown and Duguid, 1991; Amin and Cohendet, 2000) have pointed out the importance of so-called communities of practice in a knowledge economy. The prominence of those communities has been perceived in several fields of enquiry, such as the knowledge-based theory of the firm (Cohendet and Llerena, 2003; Brown and Duguid, 2001), open source software development (Kogut and Metiu, 2001) or industrial clusters (Dahl and Pedersen, 2004). The argument frequently put forward is that communities of practice lie at the core of collective learning and collective invention processes (see, for example, Cowan and Jonard, 2003) since they rely on a constant exchange of knowledge and information related to the considered practice. Those communities which are characterized by the absence of any contractual scheme aiming at regulating their members' individual behaviours prove to be particularly efficient in treating the issue of knowledge within the firm. Indeed, many authors (for example, Hodgson, 1998; Witt, 1998) have pointed out the shortcomings of contractual approaches to coordination such as transaction costs economics (Williamson, 1975) when dealing with knowledge.

Still, very little is known about the internal organization of communities of practice. As Von Hippel and Von Krogh (2003: 218) put it:

> We need to understand . . . the nature and emergence of social categories in such projects . . . Many observers of the open source software phenomenon point to the paramount role many leaders have had in the development of an open source software project.

In this way, the rationale, dynamics and consequences of the emergence of such a centralized structure (in the power enjoyed by members) remain rather unclear. Moreover, as pointed out by Kogut and Metiu (2001) in the case of open source software development, communities seem to display different types of organizations, characterized by different levels of centralization. At one end of the spectrum, the Linux community is characterized by a high degree of centralization: Linus Torvalds and a few of his trusted 'lieutenants' concentrate most of the power (especially in terms of rights of decision concerning the project) of the community. At the other end of the spectrum, the Apache[1] community is characterized by a high level of decentralization: each important decision concerning the development of the project is subject to a debate among members of the community.

Following those observations, the theoretical questions we address are: how do centralized structures in communities of practice emerge? How do they influence the activity of those communities? The argument we develop is the following. The emergence of community leaders is the outcome of a self-organizing process involving reputation. Moreover, leadership plays the role of a coordination device for the activity of community members.

In the remainder of this chapter, we adapt the theoretical framework we propose to the particular issue of open source software. However, we stress the fact that it can apply to numerous types of communities, ranging from scientific communities to communities in the frame of the knowledge-based theory of the firm. This contribution is organized as follows. Section 2 is devoted to a description of the notion of community of practice around three basic features: a domain of definition, interactions among members and the construction of a shared repertoire of resources. In Section 3, we give an outline of a theory of leadership applied to communities of practice. Then, we make use of the notion of reputation by linking it to the notion of leadership. It is notably shown that reputation constitutes a basic condition to the emergence and the exercise of leadership. In Section 4, we propose a simulation model accounting for the emergence and the evolution of the structure of communities of practice. In Section 5, we describe the statistics as well as the starting settings of the simulation model described in Section 4. In Section 6, the main results of the model are presented. It is shown that the emergence and evolution of the community's relational structure is the direct outcome of a self-organizing process stemming from the accumulation of individual decisions made by community members.

2   COMMUNITIES OF PRACTICE: THEORETICAL BACKGROUND

In a broad way, communities of practice represent groups of people engaged in common practices and interacting constantly in order to develop their competences (Brown and Duguid, 1991; Lave and Wenger, 1991;

Wenger, 1998). These interactions, which may occur on a direct, face-to-face basis or through indirect contacts (in particular in the case of virtual open source software – OSS – communities) consist of the disclosure and the evaluation of 'best practices' as well as any piece of information or piece of knowledge related to the relevant practice. Through those social habits of knowledge disclosure, community members are able to engage in collective learning processes. Wenger (2001) pointed out three main characteristics shared by communities of practice:

- *The domain*   The fact that a community of practice is focused on a shared practice implies that members share a common level of knowledge of the domain. A community does not therefore merely consist in a network of acquaintances or a group of friends. In the case of OSS, members of the community have to enjoy some degree of mastery in computer science in order to contribute to the project (as Lakhani and von Hippel, 2003, pointed out in their case study of the Apache project, members of the Apache community have, at the very least, to be sufficiently skilled in computer sciences to pinpoint a bug or a problem in the software, thus contributing to its improvement).
- *Interactions*   Members, bound together by a common interest, freely devoted to joint activities, try to help each other, exchange advice and share information. The existence of interactions between members is central since it differentiates communities of practice from other types of communities (in the sociological sense – people sharing some common traits) such as people having the same job or the same title or people belonging to the same social class.
- *The development of a shared repertoire of resources*   Members of a community of practice develop a shared repertoire of resources which is made up of experiences or tools. In OSS communities, this repertoire of resources is generally provided in two ways: the source code of the project and a discussion forum. The source code constitutes the outcome of the most important and valuable contributions to the project. Thus, the source code constitutes a synthesis of the communitarian progress in the assigned task and fulfils the same task as publications in the scientific community. However, it only constitutes the tip of the iceberg. The everyday life of the community is best accounted for by the discussion forum which constitutes the most complete repository of resources since it stores all communications made by members to the community. Those communications may consist in problem reports and solutions related to those problems. But, they may also be the scene of disputes and disagreements related to a given point of the project.

Thus, a community of practice is defined by a domain of focus, interactions between members and the development of a shared repertoire of common resources. Since they are characterized by the absence of any contractual scheme (differentiating them from teams in the agency literature), agents are able freely to set the nature of their commitment to the community. Individual commitment is defined along two dimensions: the field of expertise and the depth of the communitarian experience. Dealing with the first dimension of individual commitment, a basic hypothesis underlying the existence of communities of practice corresponds to the fact that members are endowed with differentiated experiences (which may be dealing with the community's practice or not). Such a heterogeneity leads them to specialize in a given field of inquiry (Amin and Cohendet, 2003) which is determined by the personal background of the individual.

Such specialization effects have been notably emphasized in a study of the Freenet project[2] (von Krogh et al., 2003). It was shown that each member of the project tends to specialize in the development of very specific functionalities of the software (for instance, some may specialize in the user interface, some other specialize in the cryptography modules). Moreover, individuals choose to specialize in the domains in which the contributing costs are low (the solution is already 'on the shelf' because the individual already had to tackle similar problems) or in domains in which contributions are most personally rewarding (because they refer to the individual's personal field of interest) (von Hippel and von Krogh, 2003).

This specialization in specific functionalities implies that each member develops particular knowledge related to a field of enquiry while ignoring other parts of the project. The adoption of those particular learning and knowledge creation trajectories contribute to shaping members' personal perspectives about the communitarian current and prospective activity. Those personal perspectives might differ from each other. For instance, two programmers working on different modules of the same project would put the emphasis on the development of their own activity to the detriment of other modules they perceive as less central. A consequence of this task and knowledge specialization lies in the fact that each member is endowed with different objectives and motivations (Leibenstein, 1987).

Along with their type of expertise, members are defined by the depth of their communitarian experience. This corresponds to the time spent by the individual in the community and conditions his/her level of understanding of the social norms and customs of the community as well as his/her level of knowledge of the practice. In a study of the Apache helpdesk, Lakhani and von Hippel (2003) observe that a significant share of the contributions are sent by a hard-core of Apache developers and users: 50 per cent of the contributions were actually sent by only 10 per cent of the contributors.

By contrast, most of the members adopt a relatively passive attitude and only send a few contributions.

Such heterogeneity in individual knowledge and behaviour implies some shortcomings in terms of task coordination and of work coherence. Furthermore, they might be aggravated by the potential appearance of conflict among members of the community. However, these limitations can hardly be addressed by the classical approaches to organizations. Several reasons can be put forward. First, one of the basic characteristics of communities of practice lies in the fact that they do not rely on any contractual scheme. This implies that the contributions of their members are the product of their free will: they are able to decide whether or not to contribute to the community and the nature of their contribution. In this manner, agents enjoy the freedom to set the amount as well as the nature of their contributions (due to their autonomy) without necessarily expecting any equivalent feedbacks from the community.

Second, communities rely on the existence of trust between members (see Cohendet and Diani, 2003). This is due to the fact that the environment of communities is commonly evolving. Members have to adapt their behaviour to those evolutions. Thus, trust constitutes an efficient coordinating device by allowing a certain degree of flexibility in the behaviours. As underlined by Adler (2001: 218):

> While trust is a complex, multifaceted phenomenon, the complementarities between the components of each of its four key dimensions enable trust to function as a highly effective coordinating mechanism. Groups whose cohesion is based primarily on mutual trust are capable of extraordinary feats. Trust is therefore usefully seen as a third coordination mechanism . . .

In contrast, Leibenstein (1987) pointed out the fact that hierarchies coordinated specialized tasks notably by a close intertwining between incentives and sanction mechanisms. However, to be effective and credible, those mechanisms require the implementation of monitoring systems aiming at assessing the level of effort of each member. Such monitoring systems can, in turn, be interpreted as an evidence of a lack of confidence of the hierarchy in the members of the organization. As a consequence, an atmosphere of distrust tends to flourish within the organization.

Apart from the adoption of common norms of behaviour (see Muller, 2004a, for further developments on this point), the problems of task coordination and of work coherence are partially solved by the adoption of a modular structure for the source code of the software. A modular structure allows the product to be split into separate subparts (modules) with low interactions between them (Baldwin and Clark, 1997; Langlois, 2002). In such a structure, changes in one module do not affect the behaviour and the performances of other modules, decreasing the need for information flows between individuals working on different modules. However, the adoption of a modular structure for the project output might not be sufficient. The questions of the entity designing it and of the selection process of the code to be integrated into the program remain. As the project starts, those questions are of limited scope since the tasks of architecture definition and of code selection are usually held by its instigator. As the project grows in size, those issues become crucial as they are linked to the coherence of the repertoire of resources and, therefore, to the coherence of the whole community. The solution to those concerns lies in the emergence of community leaders. Their primary tasks are to impose coherence on the community knowledge base by influencing community members in the choice of their learning tasks and by selecting contributions to be included into the community repertoire of resources. The next sections are devoted to a description of the functions and the emergence of those leaders.

3 LEADERSHIP: FUNCTIONS AND ATTRIBUTES

It has been previously argued that one of the basic traits of open source communities and, more generally, of communities of practice, lies in the specialization of knowledge and of tasks. Thus, community members tend to interact only with a few other individuals and have only a very partial knowledge of the functioning of the whole community. This raises coordination problems which may eventually lead to inefficiencies in its functioning. Those coordination problems might be solved by the emergence of community leaders. The way in which leadership exerts influence on the community has apparently raised little interest, although its existence has been widely observed, especially in the literature on open source software (Bezroukov, 1999; Kogut and Metiu, 2001).

In a very basic way, leadership is exercised through an influence on information and knowledge flows, thus directing members' decisions (Aghion and Tirole, 1997; Hermalin, 1998; Foss, 2001). Such an influence on information and knowledge flows is the outcome of two joint effects: the ability to constrain communication flows and a privileged access to information and knowledge. The first attribute of community leaders corresponds to their ability to constrain communication flows. This ability is provided by the leaders' roles as mediators (in the sense of Schelling, 1960). Mediators, because of their central status within the communication network of the community, have the ability to regulate and to direct the communication flows. By doing this, they have the faculty to direct the work of the community (or, at least, the sub-community a leader is heading). Indeed, as pointed out by Schelling, a 'mediator does more than simply constrain communications – putting limits on the order of offers, counter-offers, and so forth – since he can invent contextual material of his own and make potent suggestions. That is, he can influence the other players' expectations on his own initiative, in a manner that both parties cannot help mutually recognizing. When there is no apparent agreement, he can create one by his own power to make a dramatic suggestion' (1960: 144).

Second, community leaders enjoy a privileged access to information and knowledge. This enhanced access is the outcome of the multiplication of relationships and interactions involving the leaders. Individuals, while facing uncertainty about the outcome of their actions, tend to mimic the behaviour of leaders because they believe that leaders enjoy more accurate information and knowledge. This gives rise to informational mimesis effects. This concept of informational mimesis was developed by Orléan (2001) and constitutes an extension of the concepts of informational cascade (Bikchandani et al., 1992; Orléan, 1995) and of recruitment behaviours (Kirman, 1993). More precisely, Orléan introduced the concept of informational mimesis[3] to explain the behaviour of individuals who, facing a high degree of uncertainty, choose to copy the behaviour of individuals supposed to possess more accurate information. A leader is supposed to have access to richer and more accurate information and might make more relevant decisions. Knowing this, it is rational to copy the leader's behaviour. The same mechanism applies in the frame of communities of practice where members are facing high degrees of uncertainty concerning the selection of the most relevant pieces of information with regard to their activity. This uncertainty in the process of decision-making leads them to mimic the behaviour of individuals who, they believe, possess more accurate information. Those individuals correspond to community leaders who are characterized by their ability to concentrate the information and knowledge flows in the community.

The ability to perform mediation and informational mimesis is the outcome of the higher visibility a leader enjoys (at least) within the part of the community he belongs to. The visibility of an individual is closely tied to reputation within the community.[4] Visibility, for instance, of a contribution (pieces of code or any advice related to the purpose of the community) corresponds to the probability of this contribution being perceived by other members and, eventually, modifying their decisions. Differences in visibility might be, *in fine*, the outcome of differentials in the reputations of the individuals in the community. Indeed, individuals are endowed with what Herbert Simon called 'scarcity of attention', the ability of humans to process only a small portion of the information that comes to their senses at any time. This scarcity of attention leads them to direct their cognitive capabilities towards some specific information and to engage in a selection process. In the frame of a community, and under the assumption that any piece of information perfectly diffuses, members would be unable to process all of them. They have no option but to select signals following criteria such as their perceived relevance and the reputation of the member at the origin of the piece of information. Reputation, by enhancing one's ability to influence individuals' decisions, plays an important role in the process of leadership building.

Community leaders fulfil their role by the influence they exert on information flows. However, their role and their power are limited, thus differentiating leaders from gurus in the context of a sect. A key feature of communities of practice lies in the autonomy of the members. They are able to freely set the level as well as the nature[5] of their activity devoted to the community without any coercive constraint. In OSS communities, individuals are free to contribute or not to the project, to disclose code (contributing directly to the project) or simply to disclose advice or bug reports. To be sound, leadership has to be legitimized by the other members of the community (Weber, 1990). In our case, the legitimation of a community's leadership relies on two key phenomena: the compliance with the social norms prevailing within the community[6] and trust. This issue of community leaders' legitimacy is discussed in more depth in Cohendet et al. (2003), Muller (2004a) and Muller (2004b). It is central for the community's cognitive coherence since legitimized leadership helps prevent members from forking. Forking sees a division of community members between competing communities. This implies a reduction of cognitive resources available for both projects, threatening their survival. Forking arises out of the questioning of leaders' choices by other community members, those decisions being considered by the latter as not beneficial for the community (Bezroukov, 1999; Lerner and Tirole, 2000).

4 A SIMPLE MODEL OF LEADERSHIP BUILDING

Leadership solves coordination problems through the combined action of mediation and informational mimesis. The building of leadership constitutes the outcome of the accumulation of interpersonal interactions. The formal model we present in this section constitutes an implementation of the previously outlined theoretical framework.

The final structure of the social network forming the community is determined by individual decisions made by agents characterized by heterogeneous behaviours, as opposed to models of network structure such as random graphs (Erdős and Rényi, 1959) or 'small worlds' (Watts and Strogatz, 1998; Watts, 1999). Moreover, our model departs from traditional models of network formation (Jackson and Wolinsky, 1996; Jackson and Watts, 2002) because it assumes cooperative behaviours from individuals. Finally, the individual characteristics governing relationship-binding decisions are endogenous. Thus, the dynamics of the model refer rather to the literature on scale-free networks (Barabási and Albert, 1999).

4.1   The Individual Characteristics

At time 0, let us consider n programmers located on an undirected,[7] sparsely connected random graph $G_0 = (V, \Gamma_0)$, where $V = \{1, \ldots, n\}$ is the set of hackers (vertices) and $\Gamma_0 = \{\Gamma_0^i, \forall i \epsilon V\}$ is the list of connections (where $\Gamma_0^i = \{j \epsilon V | \{ij\} \epsilon G_0\}$, representing the link between programmers i and j, constitutes the neighbourhood of agent i at time 0 or, similarly, the set of individual i's acquaintances at time 0).

We only consider 'strong ties' in the present model. This focus is motivated by several factors. First, programmers engaged in strong, enduring relationships, are involved in the construction of trust and of mutual empathy (Nooteboom, 2003). A high degree of trust, by increasing the leaders' capacity to influence their partners' behaviours, forms a basic prerequisite for the efficiency of leadership (see Muller, 2004a, 2004b for further developments on this point). Furthermore, although we acknowledge the capacity of any programmer to disclose a piece of information to any other member of the community, those latter relationships can only be considered as weak ties by being ephemeral. They do not engage both partners to invest personal time and resources for the construction of trust. Those weak ties are characterized by the lower capacity of partners to influence each other because they are missing the trust and empathy dimensions in the relationship. In this way, they appear to have a lower impact in the coordinating task of community leaders than strong ties. Thus the construction of leadership appears to be best accounted for by the observation of the dynamics of strong ties within the community's social network.

A second argument related to the mere consideration of strong ties in the model is technical and is related to the readability of the results. By contrast with strong ties, weak ties do not require the existence of close, enduring relationships. Rather, a tie can be considered as weak when two partners exchange advice or information in a very irregular and sporadic way. This does therefore not entail the construction of trust and of mutual empathy. Pushing this reasoning further, one could also consider that a weak tie exists for two individuals having only interacted a few times (this being common in communities of practice[8]). It follows that accounting for weak ties in the model would translate into the construction of a very dense network, each member being connected to almost all other individuals. This, of course, raises issues concerning the readability of the results of the simulation since it will become very difficult to monitor any evolutions in the distribution of ties within the community.

Each programmer $i \in V$ is characterized by an absolute degree of commitment to the community, φ_i, which is assumed to be fixed over time. This level of commitment is positively related to the level of activity of the individual within the community and might be understood as the level of agent i's interest in the common enterprise.

Beside any consideration related to the level of commitment, each agent benefits from relationships established within the community. The benefits stemming from those relationships may be numerous and take the form of a greater access to tacit knowledge or to some information which might be of use to the development of personal knowledge and competences. However, those gains are submitted to decreasing returns since the multiplication of strong ties implies decreases in the efficiency of collective learning (see Hansen, 1999; Granovetter, 1973). This is due to the conjunction of two factors. The first factor corresponds to the fact that individuals are assumed to be boundedly rational: as the number of acquaintances increases, the volume of knowledge and information coming from each acquaintance that the individual is able to process decreases. Moreover, while multiplying the number of partners, an individual might find increasing redundancies in the knowledge held by each of them. It follows that the marginal gain coming from the binding of new strong ties steadily decreases while the marginal cost of preserving them remains constant.

Finally, the construction and maintaining of strong ties implies that both partners have to engage resources dedicated to the maintaining and the development of the relationship. Those resources may, for instance, correspond to the time and efforts spent in knowledge codification (Cowan and Foray, 1997; Cowan et al., 2000). Thus, the building of strong ties implies some cost for both partners.

For the sake of simplicity, the gains and costs arising from relationships are expressed as a function of the number of acquaintances a member of the community enjoys. From the preceding discussion on individual characteristics, the behaviour of agent i, during the rewiring process, is given by function $\Phi(k_{i,t}, \varphi_i)$, which is formalized in equation (3.1).

$$\Phi(k_{i,t}, \varphi_i) = \begin{cases} k_{i,t}^\gamma - ck_{i,t} + \varphi_i & \text{if } k_{i,t}^\gamma + \varphi_i > ck_{i,t} \\ 0 & \text{otherwise} \end{cases} \qquad (3.1)$$

where $k_{i,t}$ corresponds to the degree (or, similarly, the number of i's acquaintances at time t), c represents the individual cost of a relationship and φ_i, the degree of commitment of individual i to the community. The return of any new relationship is decreasing at rate γ. It is assumed that individuals are of two types: either they are highly committed to the community (that is, they choose to contribute extensively to the community's work) or they choose to slightly commit (by choosing to profit from other agents' contributions), leading, respectively, to $\varphi_i = \varphi_{max}$ and $\varphi_i = \varphi_{min}$ with $\varphi_{max} > \varphi_{min}$. Such a distinction based on the level of commitment to the community has been documented in several contributions on open source software (for example, Von Krogh et al., 2003; Hertel et al., 2003). We define $\Delta\varphi = \varphi_{max} - \varphi_{min}$ as the difference in commitment between agents of the system. Highly committed agents and slightly committed agents respectively represent a share π and $1 - \pi$ of the total number of agents in the system.

4.2 The Dynamics of the System

The aim of the model is to show the structuring process of a community of practice and, more specifically, of an open source community, as the outcome of the dynamics of reputation among its members. The dynamics of our system lies thus at the individual level. Periodically, members of the system take the decision to cease a relationship. The individual initiating this relationship-breaking connects with another member of the community according to the reputation of the latter.

At time 0, a sparse random graph including n agents is built, those agents being individual programmers involved in an open source project. At each timestep, an individual decides to break an existing relationship with one of his acquaintances. This decision is motivated by the fact that the relationship is running short of trust.[9] He tries then to bind a new relationship with another member of the community. At this stage, reputation plays a crucial role by reducing the uncertainty associated with the actual competences and behaviour of other members of the community.[10] Reputation is a key variable in the process of relationship binding. The agent having severed the existing relationship first tries to link up with the individual with the highest reputation. If he doesn't succeed (that is, the latter doesn't agree to interact), he then tries to link up with the individual with the second-best reputation. The process continues until he finds an individual to link up with.

However, in contrast to the relationship breaking-up process, which might be led in an unilateral way, the rewiring process requires the mutual consent of both individuals, the individual originating the rewiring process and the potential recipient. In this perspective, at the end of the process, if, for the former, his personal number of acquaintances does not change, the latter's personal network increases of one node. Thus, the actual rewiring decision can be described as the outcome of a two-step process. First, individuals try to link with other agents according to their reputation. Second, the decision of latter agents whether to accept or not to bind a new relationship with the former is conditioned by their behaviour function (given by equation (3.1)).

It comes out that individual i rewires with individual j with the following probability:

$$\Pi(j \in \Gamma_t^i \mid j \notin \Gamma_{t-1}^i) = \frac{k_{j,t-1}\Phi(k_{j,t-1}, \varphi_j)}{\sum\limits_{s \in V - \{\Gamma_{t-1}^i\}} (k_{s,t-1}\Phi(k_{s,t-1}, \varphi_s))} \tag{3.2}$$

5 NUMERICAL ANALYSIS

Since network models are particularly hard to deal with in an analytical way, we apply the methodology provided by numerical simulation. Ultimately, our interest lies in the evolution of the structure of communities of practice and the conditions of the emergence of community leaders. It has been previously argued that leaders fulfil their coordinating task through informational mimesis and mediation.

5.1 Statistics

The structuring effects of the social network characterizing the community can be captured by making use of two main indicators. The statistics of interest correspond to measures of degree centrality and betweenness centrality. The distribution of degree (corresponding to the number of acquaintances) among individuals constitutes a standard measure of an actor's centrality in the social network (Wasserman and Faust, 1994):

$$\forall i \in V, k_{i,t} = \#\Gamma_t^i \tag{3.3}$$

The distribution of degree allows us to assess the ability of each individual to collect information and, by doing this, to be subject to informational mimesis (which corresponds to the first attribute of community leaders). It is here assumed that the higher the number of acquaintances, the more an individual collects information and knowledge through interpersonal interactions. Knowing this, members of the community tend to copy the behaviour of individuals enjoying high degree values. It follows that, through their behaviour, agents enjoying high degree values are able to influence others' actions. This causal relationship between degree centrality and influence in a social network has been extensively discussed in the social network literature. In this way, Bonacich (1972) identified the number of acquaintances an actor enjoys as one of the basic factors underlying influence within a social network.

The second statistic, betweenness centrality, corresponds to a measure of the proportion of all geodesics[11] linking any pairs of vertices (which are distinct from each other and from *i*) which pass through vertex *i*. Betweenness is approximately a measure of the number of times an individual occurs on a shortest path between two distinct members of the community (Freeman, 1979). Let g_{jk} be the number of shortest paths (geodesics) linking nodes *j* and *k*. Among those, let $g_{jk}(n_{i,t})$ be the number of geodesics linking *j* and *k* and containing *i* at time *t* (with $i \neq j$, $i \neq k$). The betweenness of node *i* is given by:

$$C_B(n_{i,t}) = \sum_{j,k \in V - \{i\}: j < k} \left(\frac{g_{jk}(n_{i,t})}{g_{jk}} \right) \tag{3.4}$$

An actor's betweenness refers to the ability to bridge two distant parts of a graph. This property was notably highlighted in Granovetter's (1973) famous contribution. Granovetter viewed those bridges as constituting an accelerating factor in the diffusion of ideas or innovations. However, this author devoted little consideration to the possibility that individuals involved in such bridges could also derive power from their specific situation. In fact, people acting as bridges can choose to favour the diffusion of some categories of information over some others by selecting the pieces of information to be disclosed and retaining some others. It follows that such behaviours entail modifications in partners' behaviour, thus influencing their own behaviour.

The use of degree and betweenness centrality indices allows us to monitor the emergence of leaders since both measures account for the function and attributes of community leaders emphasized in Section 3. On the one hand, leaders are members characterized by significantly higher levels of activity within the community than their peers and, on the other hand, they enjoy the capacity to influence communication flows within the community. As argued by Freeman (1979), while degree centrality forms a measure of activity, betweenness centrality forms a measure of the capacity to control communication flows. Extending the argument of Freeman (1979), degree centrality constitutes a measure of the past and of the present activity of leaders. First, a main factor affecting the high degree values characterizing community leaders lies in their high levels of reputation. This reputation is, in turn, the outcome of their high levels of activity within the community: members having significantly contributed to the community's cognitive activity are likely to affirm numerous new acquaintances. Second, once established, community leaders are likely to receive numerous communications from their acquaintances. It follows that they are at the centre of higher levels of communication activity than other members of the community.

However, activity only represents one aspect of the exercise of leadership and the other aspect lies in the capacity of leaders to control communication flows. In this manner, betweenness centrality constitutes a complementary measure to degree centrality in accounting for the two aspects of leadership. Indeed, betweenness constitutes an accurate measure of an individual's ability to perform the function of mediator, which corresponds to the second attribute of leadership.

For both degree and betweenness centrality measures, the main concern in this model is about the evolution of the relational structure of a community. This is assessed by studying the evolution of average measures for both degree and betweenness. Both measures are closely linked to an individual's capacity to influence individual behaviours. In this way, since a basic feature of the model lies in the distinction between highly engaged individuals and slightly engaged individuals, average measures of degree and betweenness for highly and slightly committed individuals are separately computed.

5.2 Settings

The basic structure of the simulation is as follows. We start with a random graph of $N = 250$ individuals linked to, on average, 10 individuals. Those links are bidirectional. The original network is a relatively sparse graph as it contains $250 \times 10/2 = 1250$ distinct edges[12] (for a complete graph, the total number of edges would be $250 \times 249/2 = 31\,125$, so only 4 per cent of the possible connections are active). Simulations are run for 15 000 periods by which fluctuations in the statistics become marginal.

A major concern of this model is the assessment of the impact of discrepancies (in the degree of commitment) on the relational dynamics of the community. Those gaps take two forms. Discrepancies of the first type, symbolized by the parameter Δ_φ, correspond to a gap in the degree of commitment. The second type of discrepancy, symbolized by π, corresponds to the share of highly committed individuals in the community. The parameters we vary are therefore two. The first parameter to be varied is the share π of highly engaged individuals. The choice of π as a varying parameter is motivated by the observation that the organization of communities of

Table 3.1   Parameter settings

Parameter	Definition	Value
	Individual characteristics	
γ	Individual's behaviour elasticity	0.1
c	Marginal cost of a relationship	0.01
φ_{min}	Degree of commitment for slightly committed individuals	0.1
$\varphi_{Max}(\Delta\varphi)$	Degree of commitment for highly committed individuals (gap between highly committed and slightly committed individuals)	0.5 (0.4) − 0.8 (0.7) − 1.5 (1.4)
π	Share of highly committed individuals	0.1 − 0.3 − 0.5

practice (and, in particular, open source communities) tends to stretch between two polar cases. At one extreme, they adopt an organization of the Linux type. Such a community, which evolves around Linus Torvalds, relies on his very strong leadership. In practice, the development process is very centralized, few individuals enjoying high degrees of recognition within the community. This case might correspond to the situation of low π values. At the other extreme, the process of development might be federal: an important share of the community members enjoys a significant influence over the development process. This case, which corresponds to the situation of high π values, is exemplified by the Apache community.

The second parameter to be varied corresponds to the differential in the levels of commitment of each individual, $\Delta\varphi = \varphi_{max} - \varphi_{min}$. This allows us to assess the impact of this gap on the structure of the community. The values of the parameters are given in Table 3.1.

6   RESULTS

In Section 6.1, we describe the structuring dynamics giving rise to the emergence of leadership by evaluating in particular the dynamics of degree and betweenness for highly and slightly committed individuals. In Section 6.2, we discuss the results by drawing a parallel between the results of the simulation model and open source communities.

6.1   The Dynamics of the System and the Emergence of Leadership

Figure 3.1 shows the evolution of the average degree for highly engaged and slightly engaged individuals. As in the figures that follow, the results are

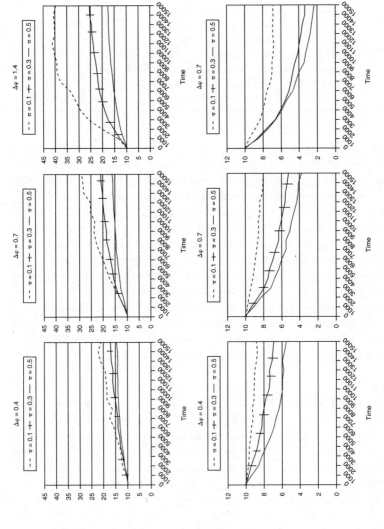

Figure 3.1 Evolution of average degree for highly committed (upper panels) and slightly committed (lower panels) individuals

shown in several panels. In the left-hand panels, the value of Δ_φ is 0.4, indicating a low gap between highly engaged individuals and slightly engaged ones. In the middle panels, the value of Δ_φ is 0.7. The right-hand panels show a wide gap, the value of Δ_φ being 1.4. In all panels various value of π are shown (corresponding to the share of highly committed individuals in the system). The parameter π takes several values: 0.1, 0.3 and 0.5. Upper (respectively lower) panels depict the evolution of the average degree for high (respectively slight) contributors to the community.

The average degree for high contributors increases over time (Figure 3.1). On the other hand, the average degree for low contributors steadily decreases. This constitutes strong evidence of an increase in the variability of degree among members of the community, most of the links being directed towards highly committed individuals. This can be interpreted as a strong polarization of the social network of the community where high contributors attract a significant share of the links.

For highly committed individuals (upper panels), the impact of both parameters under control on the relational dynamics seems to be rather balanced. We nevertheless observe that the impact of the share of highly committed individuals (π) tends to be slightly more important than the impact of discrepancies in the levels of commitment (Δ_φ) (especially for low values of π). This might be explained in the following way: individual reputation is positively correlated with the degree of commitment. As fewer individuals enjoy a high reputation, other members of the community, when faced with the decision of binding a new relationship enjoy knowledge about only a few individuals. It follows that fewer individuals enjoy new relationships, giving rise to higher discrepancies in the average degree between highly and slightly committed individuals. This is evidenced by the gaps between the curves in each panel.

Both parameters seem to have a marginal effect on the speed of convergence toward the final values of degree, except in the case in which the share of highly committed individuals is 10 per cent. Indeed, in this latter case, it seems that the higher the gap in the commitment levels, the higher the speed of convergence. For slightly committed individuals (lower panels), the impact of both parameters (the gap in the levels of commitment and the share of highly committed individuals) is more ambivalent. In this case, the effect induced by the share of highly committed individuals (π) outperforms the impact of the gap in the levels of commitment.

As evidenced in Figure 3.2, the evolution of the average betweenness centrality for high (respectively slight) contributors follows the same pattern of evolution as the average degree (Figure 3.1). Indeed, betweenness is defined as the ability to constrain communication flows between members of the community. Its measure corresponds approximately to the number of times

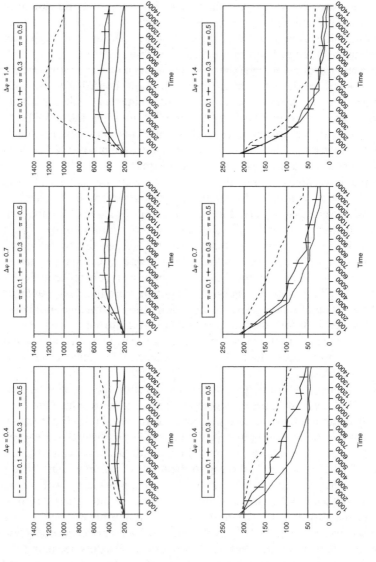

Figure 3.2 Evolution of average betweenness for highly committed (upper panels) and slightly committed (lower panels) individuals

an individual occurs on a shortest path (geodesic) between two distinct individuals. Thereby, higher values of degree increase the individual's probability of belonging to a geodesic between those individuals, increasing in turn the individual's betweenness.

For highly committed individuals, most of the impact of the discrepancies in the degrees of commitment, Δ_φ, arise for low values of π. When the share of highly committed individuals is low ($\pi = 10\%$), one can observe that the higher the gap between highly and slightly committed individuals, the higher the highly committed individuals' betweenness centrality. For higher values of π, the value of Δ_φ does not have a significant effect on the dynamics of betweenness centrality. For slightly committed individuals, the values of both parameters, Δ_φ and π, do not have a significant impact on the final values of average betweenness. However, they determine the speed of convergence to those final values: the higher the value of Δ_φ and the lower the value of π, the quicker the convergence towards the final average values of betweenness centrality.

6.2 Simulation Results and OSS Communities

The aim of this section is to compare the results of our simulation study to real cases of communities of practice. Open source software communities are of particular interest since they stretch between two polar types of organization (Kogut and Metiu, 2001). At one extreme, they adopt an organization of the Linux type. In this case, the community organization is very centralized, including multiple layers; new layers being added as the project and the community grow in size. This case corresponds to the situation of a low π value. As evidenced in the simulation results, central members of the community enjoy a very strong leadership status. First, since they enjoy high betweenness centrality values, they are able to act as efficient mediators (Figure 3.2). Second, they are able to concentrate a significant share of the links in the community. This may imply that they are subject to strong informational mimesis effects (Figure 3.1). As evidenced by Bezroukov (1999), the Linux community is structured as an authoritarian mode of governance. Only a small share of the members are allowed to include modifications into the source code of the project. This insures a higher coherence in the outcome of the project.

At the other extreme lies the Apache model. Apache has adopted a coalitional type of organization which corresponds to a high π value (Kogut and Metiu, 2001). This model of community is characterized by weak leadership. First, the ability of highly committed individuals to function as mediators is limited by the fact that they enjoy low betweenness centrality values (Figure 3.2). Second, since they enjoy only low degree values, the extent to which they are subject to informational mimesis effects might be limited.

7   CONCLUSION

Communities of practice are acknowledged as a central concept in the knowledge-based theory of the firm as well as in open source software development. This is due to the fact that they constitute the *locus* of collective learning and of knowledge exchange processes. Still, the question of the basic mechanisms underlying the working of communities of practice has been poorly explored (excepted in the literature on open source software). We tackle, more precisely, the question of the mechanisms ensuring the coordination of agents in communities of practice. Traditional explanations (for example, Wenger, 1998, 2001) have emphasized the existence of a shared domain of focus or, similarly, on a common practice, the existence of interactions between members and on the development of a shared repertoire of resources. However, such communities rely on the specialization of their members, implying some degree of heterogeneity in the knowledge held by the agents. In this chapter we propose that leadership provides a mechanism coordinating heterogeneous agents in communities of practice through mediation and informational mimesis effects. Mediation corresponds to the leaders' ability to constrain communication flows. Informational mimesis corresponds to the fact that the leaders' behaviour is copied by the other members of the community because the latter believe that the former possess richer and more accurate information inducing their particular behaviour.

Leadership translates into the social network describing the community through significant higher values for degree (underlying the individual's ability to be subject to informational mimesis) and for betweenness (underlying his/her ability to operate as a mediator). Our simulation focusing on the relational dynamics in communities of practice allow us to draw some conclusions. First, leaders emerge out of the accumulation of individual decisions of members of the community, constituting thus a self-organizing process. Second, small differences in individual behaviours may induce significant differences in the social position of agents, the most committed ones becoming leaders (enjoying, on average, higher degree and betweenness centralities). Third, the nature of this leadership is closely tied to the share of highly committed individuals in the community. On the one hand, a high share of highly committed individuals implies a distributed leadership, inducing a coalitional style of community governance. On the other hand, a low share of highly committed individuals, by restricting the access to leadership to a few people, implies a more authoritarian style of governance.

However, leadership doesn't constitute the only device coordinating communities of practice. In fact, the issue of social norms is central (Muller, 2004a). First, they provide a mechanism ensuring the legitimacy of community leaders. Indeed, the quality of leadership can only be assessed relative to the social norms prevailing in the community: since reputation and trust build relative to these norms, legitimate leaders are those exhibiting a high degree of compliance (Bowles and Gintis, 1998). Second, norms provide a coordination device. This is due to the fact that they allow the definition of a set of behaviours considered as acceptable in the frame of the community (Bowles and Gintis, 1998), thus contributing to a convergence of the members' behaviours. For instance, social norms can have an effect on individuals' behaviours by encouraging some customs and prohibiting others (such as cheating, stealing and so on). Therefore, a deeper understanding of the internal coordination mechanisms occurring within communities of practice has to include the co-evolution of norms, leadership and trust.

NOTES

* This research has been partly undertaken during a stay at the Maastricht Economic Research Institute on Innovation and Technology (MERIT). Financial support provided by the Marie Curie Multipartner Training Program is gratefully acknowledged. This work has greatly benefited from comments by participants at MERIT Seminars and the 2003 European Association of Evolutionary Political Economics Conference held in Maastricht. Comments by Markus Becker, Patrick Cohendet, Robin Cowan and Wilfred Dolfsma are gratefully acknowledged. The usual disclaimer applies. This paper was awarded the Herbert Simon Young Scholar Prize for 2003 by the European Association of Evolutionary Political Economics.

1. Lakhani and von Hippel (2003: 924) describe Apache as 'a web server software used on web server computers connected to the Internet . . . A typical server waits for clients' requests, locates the requested resource, applies the requested method to the resource, and sends the response back to the client.'
2. The Freenet software corresponds to a peer-to-peer software allowing for the dissemination of information over the Internet. This software fulfils the same tasks as other peer-to-peer software such as Napster.
3. Orléan describes informational mimesis as 'this particular mimesis which consists in copying other individuals because one believes they have a better knowledge about the situation. To put it differently, we mimic other people because we believe that they are better informed' (author's translation).
4. Reputation is here understood as a set of information concerning recurring past behaviours, which may be submitted to a reassessment according to information updates. Besides, reputation may feature public properties in the sense that it is revealed to the entire community and must be the object of a consensus. When reputation is taken in a positive way, it implies a decrease in the uncertainty associated with the absence of any previous relationships in such a way that reputation is mostly useful in relationships

characterized by a strong uncertainty and where expectations about a behaviour would otherwise have been practically impossible (Kreps, 1990).
5. Differentiations in the nature of the activities fulfilled by members constitute an outcome of the specialization of tasks and of knowledge which constitutes the root of communities of practice.
6. The relationship between social norms and leadership is discussed in Muller (2004a).
7. Since the maintaining of any relationship requires the mutual consent of both partners, the graph describing the social network of the community is undirected.
8. As exemplified in web-based forums (for example, the case of the Apache helpdesk analysed by Lakhani and von Hippel, 2003), people can commonly disclose pieces of information or of knowledge to other members without necessarily wishing to engage in a lasting relationship. The existence of such behaviours can be explained by their altruistic character and by the fact that disclosing the piece of information required is often at low cost since the piece of information is already possessed and is not considered as strategic.
9. In order to keep the dynamics of the simulation as simple as possible, it is assumed that the individual initiating the relationship break up is randomly drawn.
10. Reputation is here approximated by the degree of the individual (corresponding to the number of acquaintances). The use of this proxy is motivated by our former discussion on reputation: since it constitutes a device reducing the uncertainty associated with the competences and the behaviour of an individual, there is a positive correlation between reputation and the number of acquaintances an individual enjoys. Moreover, it avoids the introduction of extra variables into the model, keeping it as simple as possible.
11. Geodesic binding agents i and j correspond to the smallest path linking i and j.
12. Since the links are assumed to be bidirectional, to obtain the number of nodes of the system, one has to divide the sum of degrees of the system by two for the following reason. Let's assume one edge $\{ij\}$ linking two nodes i and j; since the link is bidirectional, the degree of i and of j are increasing by 1 unit each.

REFERENCES

Adler, P.S. (2001), 'Market, Hierarchy and Trust: The Knowledge Economy and the Future of Capitalism', *Organization Science*, **12**(2): 215–34.

Aghion, P. and J. Tirole (1997), 'Formal and Real Authority in Organizations', *Journal of Political Economy*, **105**: 1–29.

Amin, A. and P. Cohendet (2000), 'Organisational Learning and Governance through Embedded Practices', *Journal of Management and Governance*, **4**: 93–116.

Amin, A. and P. Cohendet (2003), *Architecture of Knowledge: Firms, Capabilities and Communities*, New York: Oxford University Press.

Baldwin, C.Y. and K.B. Clark (1997), 'Managing in an Age of Modularity', *Harvard Business Review*, **75**(5): 84–93.

Barabási, A.L. and R. Albert (1999), 'Emergence of Scaling in Random Networks', *Science*, **286**: 509–12.

Bezroukov, N. (1999), 'Open Source Software Development as a Special Type of Academic Research (Critique of Vulgar Raymondism)', *First Monday*, **4**: http://www.firstmonday.org/issues/issue4_10/bezroukov/index.html.

Bikchandani, S., D. Hirshleifer and I. Welch (1992), 'A Theory of Fads, Fashion, Custom, and Cultural Changes as Informational Cascades', *Journal of Political Economy*, **100**: 992–1026.

Bonacich, P.F. (1972), 'Factoring and Weighting Approaches to Clique Identification', *Journal of Mathematical Sociology*, **2**: 113–20.

Bowles, S. and H. Gintis (1998), 'The Moral Economy of Communities: Structured Populations and the Evolution of Prosocial Norms', *Evolution & Human Behavior*, **19**: 3–25.

Brown, J.S. and P. Duguid (1991), 'Organizational Learning and Communities of Practice: Toward a Unified View of Working, Learning and Innovation', *Organization Science*, **2**: 40–57.

Brown, J.S. and P. Duguid (2001), 'Knowledge and Organization: A Social-practice Perspective', *Organization Science*, **12**: 198–213.

Cohendet, P. and M. Diani (2003), 'L'organisation comme une communauté de communautés: croyances collectives et culture d'entreprise', *Revue d'Economie Politique*, **113**(5): 697–721.

Cohendet, P., M. Diani, J. Li and P. Muller (2003), 'The Formation of Trust in Knowledge Intensive Communities', Symposium 'La Structure Cognitive de la Confiance', Paris, April 25–27.

Cohendet, P. and P. Llerena (2003), 'Routines and Incentives: The Role of Communities in the Firm', *Industrial and Corporate Change*, **2**: 271–97.

Cowan, R. and D. Foray (1997), 'The Economics of Codification and the Diffusion of Knowledge', *Industrial and Corporate Change*, **6**: 595–622.

Cowan, R. and N. Jonard (2003), 'The Dynamics of Collective Invention', *Journal of Economic Behavior & Organization*, **52**: 513–32.

Cowan, R., P.A. David and D. Foray (2000), 'The Explicit Economics of Knowledge Codification and Tacitness', *Industrial and Corporate Change*, **9**(2): 211–53.

Dahl, M.S. and C.Ø.R. Pedersen (2005), 'Knowledge Flows through Informal Contacts in Industrial Clusters: Myth or Reality?', *Research Policy*, **33**(10): 1673–83.

Erdős, P. and A. Rényi (1959), 'On Random Graphs', *Publicationes Mathematicae*, **6**: 290–97.

Foss, N.J. (2001), 'Leadership, Beliefs and Coordination: An Explorative Discussion', *Industrial and Corporate Change*, **10**: 357–88.

Freeman, L.C. (1979), 'Centrality in Social Networks: Conceptual Clarification', *Social Networks*, **1**: 215–39.

Granovetter, M.S. (1973), 'The Strength of Weak Ties', *American Journal of Sociology*, **78**(6): 1360–80.

Hansen, M.T. (1999), 'The Search-transfer Problem: The Role of Weak Ties in Sharing Knowledge across Organization Subunits', *Administrative Science Quarterly*, **44**(1): 82–111.

Hermalin, B.E. (1998), 'Toward an Economic Theory of Leadership: Leading by Example', *American Economic Review*, **88**: 1188–1206.

Hertel, G., S. Niedner and S. Herrmann (2003), 'Motivation of Software Developers in Open Source Projects: An Internet-based Survey of Contributors to the Linux Kernel', *Research Policy*, **32**: 1159–77.

Hodgson, G.M. (1998), 'Competence and Contract in the Theory of the Firm', *Journal of Economic Behavior & Organization*, **35**: 179–201.

Jackson, M.O. and A. Watts (2002), 'The Evolution of Social and Economic Networks', *Journal of Economic Theory*, **106**: 265–95.

Jackson, M.O. and A. Wolinsky (1996), 'A Strategic Model of Social and Economic Networks', *Journal of Economic Theory*, **71**: 44–74.

Kirman, A. (1993), 'Ants, Rationality, and Recruitment', *Quarterly Journal of Economics*, **111**: 137–56.

Kogut, B. and A. Metiu (2001), 'Open-source Software Development and Distributed Innovation', *Oxford Review of Economic Policy*, **17**: 2.

Kreps, D.M. (1990), 'Corporate Culture and Economic Theory', in J.E. Alt and K.A. Shepsle (eds), *Perspectives on Positive Political Economy*, Cambridge: Cambridge University Press, pp. 90–143.

Lakhani, K.R. and E. von Hippel (2003), 'How Open Source Software Works: "free" User-to-User Assistance', *Research Policy*, **32**: 923–43.

Langlois, R.N. (2002), 'Modularity in Technology and Organization', *Journal of Economic Behavior & Organization*, **49**: 19–37.

Lave, J. and E. Wenger (1991), *Situated Learning: Legitimate Peripheral Participation*, Cambridge: Cambridge University Press.

Leibenstein, H. (1987), *Inside the Firm: The Inefficiencies of Hierarchy*, Cambridge, MA: Harvard University Press.

Lerner, J. and J. Tirole (2000), 'The Simple Economics of Open Source', NBER Working Paper no. 7600.

Muller, P. (2004a), 'Autorité et gouvernance des communautés intensives en connaissances: une application au développement du logiciel libre', *Revue d'Economie Industrielle*, **106**: 49–68.

Muller, P. (2004b), 'Reputation, Trust, and the Dynamics of Leadership within Communities of Practice', paper presented at the 3rd ETE Workshop, January 29–30, Sophia-Antipolis, France.

Nooteboom, B. (2003), 'Learning to Trust', Symposium 'La structure cognitive de la confiance', Ecole des Hautes Etudes en Sciences Sociales, Paris, 25–27 September.

Orléan, A. (1995), 'Bayesian Interactions and Collective Dynamics of Opinion: Herd Behavior and Mimetic Contagion', *Journal of Economic Behavior & Organization*, **28**: 257–74.

Orléan, A. (2001), 'Comprendre les foules spéculatives: mimétismes informationnel, autoréférentiel et normatif', in J. Gravereau and J. Trauman (eds), *Crises Financiers*, Paris: Economica.

Raymond, E.S. (2000), 'The Cathedral and the Bazaar': http://www.tuxedo.org/~esr.

Schelling, Thomas (1960), *The Strategy of Conflict*, Cambridge, MA: Harvard University Press.

Von Hippel, E. and G. Von Krogh (2003), 'Open Source Software and the "Private-Collective" Innovation Model: Issues for Organization Science', *Organization Science*, **14**: 209–23.

Von Krogh, G., S. Spaeth and K.R. Lakhani (2003), 'Community, Joining and Specialization in Open Source Software Innovation: A Case Study', *Research Policy*, **32**: 1217–41.

Wasserman, S. and K. Faust (1994), *Social Network Analysis: Methods and Applications*, Cambridge: Cambridge University Press.

Watts, D.J. (1999), *Small Worlds: The Dynamics of Networks between Order and Randomness*, Princeton, NJ: Princeton University Press.

Watts, D.J. and S.H. Strogatz (1998), 'Collective Dynamics of "Small World" Networks', *Nature*, **393**: 440–42.

Weber, M. (1990), *Wirtschaft und Gesellschaft: Grundriß der verstehenden Soziologie*, 5th edition, Tübingen: Mohr Siebeck.

Wenger, E. (1998), *Communities of Practice: Learning, Meaning and Identity*, Cambridge: Cambridge University Press.

Wenger, E. (2001), 'Communities of Practice', in N.J. Smelser and P.B. Baltes (eds), *International Encyclopaedia of the Social & Behavioral Sciences*, Amsterdam: Elsevier Science, 2339–42.

Williamson, O.E. (1975), *Markets and Hierarchies: Analysis and Antitrust Implications*, New York: The Free Press.

Witt, U. (1998), 'Imagination and Leadership – the Neglected Dimension of an Evolutionary Theory of the Firm', *Journal of Economic Behavior & Organization*, **35**: 161–77.

4. New firms evolving in the knowledge economy: problems and solutions around turning points

Erik Stam and Elizabeth Garnsey

1 INTRODUCTION

Economic firms are institutions, sustained by corporate law and fiscal arrangements. They are basic units of the market economy and drivers of change. In the knowledge economy, new firms have proliferated as a result of the lowering of barriers to entry by information technologies and the associated emergence of new economic activities. But it is still difficult to understand these newcomers to the economy or the basis of the growth on which their innovative contribution depends. The bulk of economic studies of new firms offer cross-sectional analyses and/or focus only on growth indicators. Few theoretically grounded studies examine their internal dynamics. Studies of internal processes tend to be stage models of growth, which have been criticized as empirically unsound and theoretically ungrounded (Storey, 1997; Bhidé, 2000). What is required is a conceptual scheme that is theoretically informed and has conceptual affinities with other current work (for example, resource-based, evolutionary and complexity) and which supports empirical comparisons between new firms. In this chapter we show how the work of Penrose (1995) on the growth of established firms can be the basis for a dynamic conceptual approach to the study of new firms.

This chapter uses a process-oriented, longitudinal approach in comparing the start up and growth experience of 25 case study firms. The focus is on problem solving activities in the early life of the entrepreneurial firm. We analyse the problems and their solutions around turning points that mark a shift from a growth episode into a stagnation or setback. Where a number of problems can be solved at once, several growth processes may take place, for example, a venture's technological resources may be created in the course of commissioned research or technical consultancy for customers, which yields revenues. New firms often turn to others for help in solving the problem, for example, through subcontracting. The solution of early problems leads to the development of competence that enables the firm to respond to changing opportunities and threats. An important lesson from evolutionary economics is the contribution of problem-solving to the development of routines and competences (compare Nelson and Winter, 1982; Coriat and Dosi, 1998). These routines and competences are essential to understanding the firm's development. Few new firms achieve growth on sustained and substantial basis. These successful firms accumulate resources which enable them to reorient themselves in response to changes in opportunity structure without succumbing to resource shortages. These become leaders among the new generation of firms.

   In-depth examination of case studies identifies common development processes during the life course of new firms. This study examines growth paths of a number of new Netherlands' firms, and focuses on the turning points which mark their growth experience. This enables us to draw general conclusions about growth phases and syndromes in young firms. Their experience reveals the way in which new firms grow by co-evolving with others, forming connections and partnerships with the complementary organizations that characterize the networked division of labour in the knowledge economy (compare Autio and Garnsey, 1997). The key question in this chapter is: how and why do new firms develop? In order to answer this we will analyse the growth paths of new firms and the turning points in these paths.

2   CONCEPTUAL FRAMEWORK

Although the knowledge economy has brought many opportunities for new firms to emerge and evolve, new firms continue to face endemic problems. These problems and their solutions are important drivers of heterogeneity among firms. There have been many studies on these drivers shaping firm heterogeneity. On the one hand, there is a long tradition of empirical and conceptual studies on problems in relation to growth stages of new firms (Churchill and Lewis, 1983; Greiner, 1972; Kazanjian, 1988; Miller and Friesen, 1984; Terpstra and Olson, 1993). However, these studies have been widely criticized as empirically unsound and/or theoretically ungrounded (Bhidé, 2000; Levie and Hay, 1998; Storey, 1997). On the other hand, there are advanced theoretical approaches such as the resource-based perspective (Barney, 1991; Foss, 1997), the (dynamic) capabilities approach (Teece et al., 1997; Dosi et al., 2000) and evolutionary economics[1] (Nelson and Winter, 1982). These theoretical approaches have been criticized for their neglect of firm growth and change, and the lack of a clear conceptual model of the endogenous creation of new resources and competences

(Foss, 1997: 351–2). These approaches have been largely aimed at explaining short-term performance of firms (resource-based perspective and dynamic capabilities approach) or long-term change in industries, technologies and the economy as a whole (evolutionary economics). The dynamic capabilities approach aims at explaining innovation (new products, production processes, alliances). This approach could also be useful for studying specific changes in the life course of the firm, since it deals with the competences developed by a firm and in that way also provides insight into why certain changes in the organization have been realized successfully or not (Eisenhardt and Martin, 2000). However, for explaining the long-term development of new firms a developmental approach is needed, which explains how and why new firms evolve.

Development and Growth of New Firms

A developmental approach focuses on processes of change in new firms (Garnsey, 1998; Rathe and Witt, 2001; Stam, 2003) and builds heavily on the work of Penrose (1995). Such an approach aims at explaining endogenous processes of change, and explicitly takes entrepreneurship into account.[2] Development is an iterative, non-linear process in which the new firm must continually adapt to unfolding opportunities. The development of new firms is driven by both internal and external dynamics. In this approach opportunities and resources are necessary conditions for the creation of a firm (compare Sorenson, 2003). Perception of an opportunity to create value triggers the process of new firm formation. The recognition of such an opportunity is determined by the imagination of the entrepreneur. This opportunity can be developed with the resources to which entrepreneurs have direct access, with the resources they can acquire outside the firm or those they can create internally (resource mobilization). Direct or indirect access to resources is necessary to develop this opportunity into a commercial output. These resources are subsequently deployed in order to develop and produce the product or service. Thus the new firm creates a productive base in the form of, for example, technological competences or expertise in R&D. Often external co-producers are needed for specific modules to be added to the final product or service offering. In order to bring this final product or service offering to the market, commercial capabilities[3] are needed, such as legal, marketing and sales expertise. These form the firm's commercial base, which also includes its reputation, or dealer network. To create value for customers on an ongoing basis, a firm needs a productive and commercial base of some kind. In more abstract terms this means that the firm is able to generate resources through its productive and commercial activities.

In order to survive in a market economy, entrepreneurs have to solve basic problems. They need some way of accessing and mobilizing initial resources; they have to develop and produce the good or service and connect to suppliers and customers. The need for production and sale of goods and services to be sustained at a profit remains the central problem after problems of start up and early growth have been solved. Once the firm is up and running, returns from the resource generation process can be accumulated; the firm itself becomes an asset once it has an asset base. The asset base can be measured by the market value of the firm on the stock market or on the market for mergers and acquisitions. This value can only precisely be established when the firm exits (via a buy-out, a takeover, or bankruptcy) or realizes an initial public offering (IPO). Investments in the firm that enlarge its asset base can be used to support further growth, whether through further exploration or through exploitation of existing opportunities.

Once a firm is functioning as an economic unit achieving returns, the question arises as to how and why its further development takes place. It might survive without growing, but ambitious entrepreneurs have or develop an intention to grow the business. However, there are several limitations to the growth (that is, rate of expansion) of firms. Metcalfe (1998: 45) identifies five specific kinds of limitation to growth: 'in relation to the ability to purchase inputs and sell output as determined by the growth of relevant market environments; in relation to the availability of internal and external finance to expand capacity; in relation to the managerial implications of growth for the ability to control costs (Penrose, 1995); in relation to the growth of rival firms and thus the specific market of the firm; and in relation to the ability to imagine and articulate growth opportunities'. According to Metcalfe (1998: 45) all of these elements come together to determine the economic fitness of the firm. Kazanjian (1988) distinguishes six categories of dominant problems to growth in technology-based new ventures: those related to organizational systems, sales/marketing, people, production, strategic positioning, and external relations.

Further growth often requires inputs of resources before returns have been realized to pay for these. Reorganization of the firm may be a prerequisite for further growth. These necessary reorganizations constitute the 'turning points' in the development of the firm. When critical problems are solved successfully, the firm is able to continue to grow. However, solutions are hard to come by. This developmental approach shares with the stage models of growth (for example, Greiner, 1972; Kazanjian, 1988; Hanks et al., 1993) the focus on dominant problems in the life of new firms. However, the latter type of studies focus on taxonomies of problems in distinctive stages and assume that firms progress sequentially across one specific sequence of stages. The developmental approach focuses on feedback effects as these problems are faced and solved and lead to the further development of the firm. Certain developmental *processes* are common in new firms as they mobilize and build resources to form a resource base capable of generating market returns. Firms that face and solve similar developmental problems in sequence may go through similar phases of activity (Garnsey, 1998). Researchers have identified such regularities in firms producing similar products on the basis of similar business models (for example, Bell and McNamara (1991) on US computer hardware ventures). But different problems arise in firms that engage in different kinds of activities and are addressed in different ways, using different types of business models. The building of different kinds of resource base involves different sequences of activity. We have seen that problems may be addressed in parallel, or may recur. Moreover firms may or may not inherit a resource base from another organization through de-merger or spin-out. Thus there are no invariant phases of activity as new firms emerge; instead there are common requirements for development into an economically viable unit, achieved in a variety of ways.

The new firm's experience is shaped by changes inside the firm and changes in the firm's environment (compare Tushman and Romanelli, 1990; Romanelli and Tushman, 1994). Changes inside the firm may be of a quantitative nature, for example, increases in resources and activities, but also of a more qualitative nature, involving a changing organizational structure and/or strategy, and the development of competence through learning. In a competence-based view, the existence, structure and boundaries of the firm can be explained by the associated existence of individual or team competences which are in some way fostered and maintained by that firm (Hodgson, 1999: 247–8). Competence is built cumulatively within the firm through team-based learning (Penrose, 1995). Competence is the product of problem-solving activities and enables the firm to respond to changing opportunities and threats.[4] This is achieved as the new firm develops problem-solving skills and embeds these in procedures and routines.[5] These competences can be found in the productive and commercial base in Figure 4.1.

As Penrose emphasized, the 'opportunity environment' depends on the entrepreneur's perceptions. But Penrose recognized that these perceptions are confronted by reality. Evolutionary theory represents the firm's environment as the source of selection forces that actually determine whether significant others choose to do business with the new entrant. This evolutionary issue is not directly addressed in modern resource-based theory (Foss, 1997). Selection processes are experienced through the firm's interactions with resource providers (including investors, the knowledge environment, and labour sources), co-producers, customers, and competitors

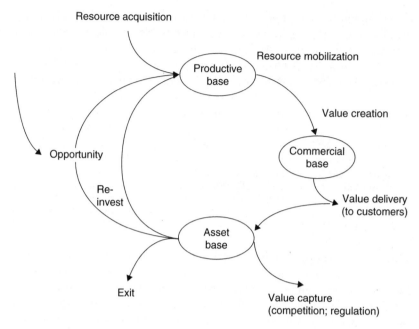

Figure 4.1   Internal and external dynamics of new firm development

and regulators. Important features of the new firm's environment are the operations of the capital market that affect conditions of exit, merger and acquisition. The firm's environment may involve changes in the firm's input markets and its output markets. Important aspects of input markets are the supply of resources by resource providers, and the possibility of co-producing with other organizations or hiring or contracting personnel. The growth and decline of product markets, and the changing level of competition are important aspects of the output markets. A key question in this respect is how firms and the markets and networks in which they operate co-evolve (Rathe and Witt, 2001; Richardson, 1972).

Figure 4.1 represents the internal and external dynamics involved in firm development. The ovals refer to resources and competences that accumulate over time as experience builds up and returns are reinvested in the firm's resource base (compare Dierickx and Cool, 1989, on 'asset stocks'). The firm's resource base is represented in terms of a productive base, a commercial base, and an asset base for clarity, though in practice they are not separable.

In principle a new firm could embark on many different growth trajectories. Each firm has its individual and unique characteristics. Consequently, initial conditions and resource endowments incline the system in a certain direction, but the actual path taken is unpredictable because it is subject to contingent occurrences and singular initiatives. Nevertheless, the processes that contribute to their development have common features (Garnsey, 1998; McGrath, 2002). Opportunities must be detected and input resources accessed and mobilized in order to generate further resources on an ongoing basis for a firm to survive in a market economy. Thus for all firms, there is an initial opportunity search process:

> The productive activities of such a firm are governed by what we shall call its 'productive opportunity', which comprises all of the productive possibilities that its 'entrepreneurs' see and can take advantage of. A theory of the growth of firms is essentially an examination of the changing productive opportunity of firms; in order to find a limit to growth, or a restriction on the rate of growth, the productive opportunity of a firm must be shown to be limited in any period. (Penrose, 1995: 31–2)

This productive opportunity set refers to the opportunities that an entrepreneur recognizes in the firm's environment and can take advantage of on the basis of its tangible and intangible resources. Other processes are commonly found in a new firm's early development as it seeks to solve problems facing all new firms. Concepts from the resource-based view (compare Foss, 1997) and evolutionary economics (Nelson, 1991) can throw light on some of these processes.

In contrast to growth, development is not based on quantitative indicators. There are quantitative growth indicators that could to some extent represent the internal dynamics represented in Figure 4.1: for example, the productive base in number of employees, the commercial base as level of turnover, and the asset base as the current market value of the firm. The development of firms can be represented in terms of the maturity of their resource base. Start-up is characterized by the emergence and formation of an initial productive base. A new firm that is surviving is able to achieve returns on its activities, which means it has some kind of commercial base (legal and marketing services). Firms that have entered into early growth have not only shown ability to survive in a specific product-market, but have also generated surplus profits in this or additional other markets, which have been invested in their productive base. These investments often lead to an increase of the number of employees in the firm. Before they have reserves to see them through fluctuations in their trading performance firms are vulnerable and their growth is at best intermediate. Many firms never emerge from this phase, facing a continual struggle to overcome short-term fluctuations. Finally, some firms are able to accumulate resources in a growing productive and asset base. Competitive advantage of firms is a necessary condition for the accumulation of resources. The advantage is reinforced through reinvestment of extra profits ('internal accumulation', compare Steindl, 1952). The implication is that as firms grow, investments to expand the productive base for existing products is no longer constrained by access to finance. As firms grow, new opportunities may also be identified – positively affected by the increased knowledge base of the firm – and investment in new product development may even become 'institutionalized' (compare dynamic capabilities: Teece et al., 1997; Eisenhardt and Martin, 2000). This resource accumulation process provides reserves (compare Cyert and March, 1963, on 'organizational slack'), which provide a buffer for external shocks and also the means to explore new opportunities, without endangering the current resource generation process.

3   RESEARCH DESIGN AND METHOD

We have chosen a longitudinal and retrospective, case-based research method to compare and explain the development of evolving firms, drawing on both qualitative and quantitative evidence. We start with quantitative evidence which points to uneven and discontinuous growth in new firms in our sample (see Garnsey et al., 2006, for a discussion of the methods used). Though this evidence does not directly map developmental processes, it does show that turning points, interruptions and setbacks are common in new firms, while the qualitative evidence relates these metrics to underlying growth processes. Our research is in two parts. First a database is assembled to explore the growth paths of a group of evolving firms. This part provides background information on the development of evolving firms, in so far as quantitative growth indicators can measure this over time. Second, we conduct a series of comparative in-depth case studies to investigate more thoroughly the problems and solutions around turning points in the firms' development. The case studies involve the life histories of these evolving firms as told by the founder-entrepreneurs (company life history analysis: compare Van Geenhuizen et al., 1992), but also a survey on indicators about the size, nature, inter-organizational relations and spatial organization of the firm. Key events affecting the development of the firms were uncovered with the critical incident technique (compare Chell and Pittaway, 1998; Cope and Watts, 2000). In addition to these data obtained in the interview, other data from company archives, the press and other media were collected. The empirical evidence will be used to answer three research questions:

1. What growth paths of young fast-growing firms can be distinguished?
2. Why are there turning points in their growth paths?
3. How can the different growth paths be explained?

The Sample

The sample consisted of 16 knowledge-based service firms, four biomedical, three shipbuilding, and two graphics-media firms (see Table 4.1). We used the data of these firms to address the first two research questions, while we

Table 4.1   Characteristics of the firms in the research sample

Name	Sector	Current specialization	No. of employees
A	Knowledge services	Communication and organization advice	148
B	Knowledge services	Organization advice	250
C	Knowledge services	Organization advice	40
D	Knowledge services	Organization advice	26
E	Knowledge services	Market research	90
F	Knowledge services	Information and communication technology	140
G	Knowledge services	Information and communication technology	110
H	Knowledge services	Labour market services	200
I	Knowledge services	Government and education services	110
J	Knowledge services	Government services	300
K	Knowledge services	Information and communication technology	42
L	Knowledge services	Information and communication technology	85
M	Knowledge services	Information and communication technology/New media	170
N	Knowledge services	Industrial automation	90
O	Knowledge services	Datamining	20
P	Knowledge services	Information technology	30
Q	Biomedical	Tissue engineering	95
R	Biomedical	Therapeutics research and development	140
S	Biomedical	Development and marketing of diagnosis and therapy products	26
T	Biomedical	Development and marketing of products for diagnosis	15
U	Shipbuilding	Development and production of composite constructions	23
V	Shipbuilding	Custom boat-building	52
W	Shipbuilding	Houseboat-building	42
X	Graphics-media	Printing and graphic design	31
Y	Graphics-media	Printing, graphic design, and multimedia	34

used a subsample with contrasting cases to answer the last research question (compare Eisenhardt, 1989; Pettigrew, 1995).

The evolving firms have been operationally defined as firms that have survived the first four years of existence (which are generally characterized by the highest failure rates), but are not older than 10 years (which means that they probably have not become mature and managerial firms, and that the founder-entrepreneur could probably be traced). They had to have created at least 20 FTEs (full-time equivalents), which is a crude indicator of company success and evolution. Finally, these are independent firms, that is, owner-managed (with a majority stake in the firm). We have a 'control group' matching successful, rapidly growing firms: evolving firms that did not continually grow (experiencing stagnation or even setbacks). This prevents a 'success-bias' to some extent; a problem of former studies like Kazanjian (1988) and Terpstra and Olson (1993). Only the minority of the sampled firms grew in a continuous way.

Operational Definition of Firm Growth

There are many indicators of firm growth: indicators in terms of input (employees, investment funds), throughput (productivity), output (sales, revenues, profits), and valuation (assets, book value, market capitalization). The various measures capture different dimensions of growth and are not necessarily aligned, though they may be (Vaessen, 1993; Storey, 1997; Delmar et al., 2003). Here we draw on the available data on employment of the sample of evolving firms. Growth paths are traced using quantitative employment indicators, in contrast with the development paths, which are based on qualitative indicators of development processes. The data points making up the growth paths are compressed and termed 'B' for a reduction in employment greater than 5 per cent, 'G' for an increase in employment greater than 5 per cent, and 'P' for a change in employment in either direction of less than 5 per cent (between two subsequent years, with a change of at least two employees). The resulting measures were coded to represent the turning points in evidence and presented as archetypal growth paths (compare Garnsey and Heffernan, 2003). In this study the operational definition of the start is the formal registration at the local Chamber of Commerce: the point zero in the growth paths. From a developmental perspective, however, development processes begin earlier than this. After the start-up phase, the growth paths start to diverge. After the initial start-up firms may experience growth, setback, or plateau (or sequences of these patterns).

4   GROWTH PATHS EXPLORED

In this section we will address the first research question – What growth paths of young fast-growing firms can be distinguished? We examined the data on an exploratory basis to see whether it was possible to summarize trends without losing relevant information on comparative growth paths. Among the sample were firms with a continuous growth path that began early on. For the group of firms with a delayed onset of growth, several years may elapse before they exhibit growth. A somewhat different order of growth is characteristic of the plateau path. These firms begin to grow quite soon, but for a few years after this, growth stagnates. The fourth growth path is the least regular. Firms in this phase suffer from one or more set-backs during their life course, but they differ with respect to the other characteristics of their growth path (delayed growth: firm I; continued growth: firms C, D, and H; plateau: firm O). The sequence and duration of the growth phases during the life course of the evolving firms are shown in Table 4.2.

There is clear evidence of uneven growth. During a favourable economic cycle, only nine firms grew continuously over the period studied, with another three firms growing continuously after a delay, or a preparatory period. The firms with continuous growth had already gone beyond the 50-employees size within five years after their start (firms J, N, Q, R). Another eight firms experienced periods of interrupted growth, staying temporarily on a plateau. Only five firms had serious setbacks, with two of them also experiencing plateaus.[6] Judged by the low incidence of setbacks, this is a successful sample of start-ups (compare Hugo and Garnsey, 2002; Garnsey and Heffernan, 2003). Most firms have grown in an organic way, but four have also grown through takeovers (firms E, H, and Y) or a merger (firm R). The biomedical firms Q and R were recently successful in realizing an initial public offering (IPO). The growth curves of the cases in the different types of growth paths are shown in Figure 4.2.

5   PROBLEMS AND PROBLEM-SOLVING

In this section we will analyse the problems of evolving firms that have led to stagnation or setbacks during their life course and on how these problems are solved. We will focus on the firms experiencing delayed early growth, long periods of stagnation and/or growth setbacks.

In a market economy, a necessary condition for a firm to thrive is a resource generation process that allows outputs to be sold at more than their production and delivery costs. Almost all case-study firms have realized

Table 4.2   Sequence and duration of growth phases in the growth paths

Firm		1	2	3	4	5	6	7	8	9	10	11
						Age (in years)						
Continuous	**A**	G	G	G	G	G	G	G	G	G	G	
growth	**B**	G	G	G	G	G	G	G	G	G		
(G→G)	**J**	G	G	G	G	G	G					
	K	G	G	G	G	G	G	G				
	L	G	G	G	G	G	G	G	G			
	N	G	G	G	G	G	G					
	Q	G	G	G	G							
	R	G	G	G	G							
	S	G	G	G	G	G	G	G	G	G	G	G
Delayed	**E**	P	G	G	G	G	G	G	G	G	G	
growth	**G**	P	P	G	G	G	G	G	G	G		
(P→G)	**P**	P	P	G	G	G	G	G	G			
Plateau	**F**	G	G	G	P	P	G	G	G			
(G→P)	**M**	G	P	P	G	G	G	G	G	G		
	T	G	P	G	G	G	G	G				
	U	G	G	G	G	P	P	G	G			
	V	G	G	G	G	P	P	G	G	G	G	
	W	G	G	G	G	G	P	G	G			
	X	G	G	P	G	G	G					
	Y	G	G	P	P	P	P	G	G	P		
Setback	**C**	G	G	G	G	G	G	G	G	B	B	
(G→B)/	**D**	G	G	G	G	G	G	B	G			
Mixed	**H**	G	G	G	G	B	G	G	G	G	G	
	I	P	P	B	G	G	G	G	G	G	G	G
	O	G	G	B	G	G	P	G	G	G	B	

Note: Codes of the growth phases: S = **S**tart-up (first formal year of existence); P = **P**lateau (employment change less than 5% per year); G = **G**rowth (employment growth at least 5% per year); B = Set**B**ack (employment decline at least 5% per year).

such a resource generation process, and can thus be regarded as viable for the time being. The firms that had not yet reached viability were the biomedical firms Q and R. Those that had only done so recently are the knowledge service firm O, and shipbuilding firm W (only a very short profitable period after start-up). During the period of financial dependence these firms could only survive because they continued to receive inputs from resource providers (formal investors) who believed in their long-term profitability.

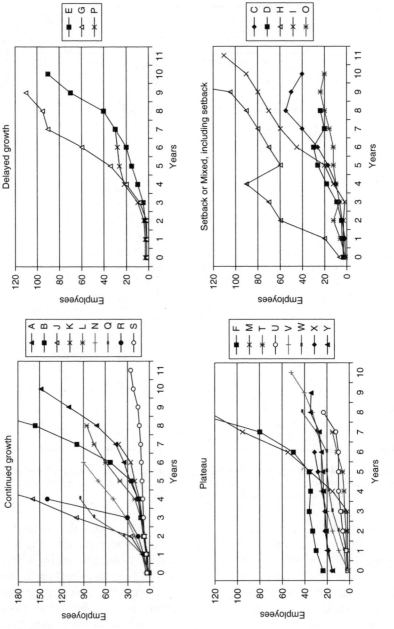

Figure 4.2   Growth paths of the sample of evolving firms

Clearly, choice of activity has important implications for the need for resources of all kind, not the least for financial capital. Knowledge service firms have to mobilize only a few tangible resources such as computer and office facilities, while shipbuilding and graphics-media firms need many more tangible resources, and thereby financial resources. Higher resource needs are more difficult to sustain, and are a challenge to continuous growth. This is a factor in the plateau growth exhibited by the shipbuilding and graphics-media cases in our study. The creation of an enduring input–output process requires certain essential input and output relationships. As it takes form, the firm becomes an open system interacting with others in the production environment.

Essential input relationships are internal to the character of the activity in question (compare Sayer, 1992). Biomedical firms stand out in this respect; they need considerable investment for specific facilities (such as laboratories), and highly-skilled scientific and technical labour. Many of these biomedical firms grow in employment terms (productive base) before they reach the initial survival phase (commercial base) enabling a minimum scale of operation. These firms also face the growth problems associated with the early growth phase after initial survival. The venture capitalists of the biomedical firms Q and R compelled these firms to change their organization and control structure at an earlier stage than that in which problems could arise. The growth of these firms was thus reinforced by the accumulated experience of their financial relationships, even before they entered the initial survival phase.

The evolving firms with delayed growth have failed to grow after their start-up. In some cases this can be the result of a demanding resource mobilization process before resources for growth are obtained, but this does not apply to the current case studies. The entrepreneurs of the evolving firms with a delayed growth path were willing to grow, but lacked the opportunity to expand, or were constrained by other factors in the first instance.[7] One example of such a constraint is a non-competition clause in an agreement with the former employer (firm G). A delayed start can be substituted by serial entrepreneurship; that is to say, by setting up another business until the constraints on growth have elapsed.

In only a few cases was delayed growth related to a lack of opportunities. Often delayed growth cannot be accounted for by one reason alone, but rather by a combination of reasons. The reasons for delayed growth as stated by the entrepreneurs are summarized in Table 4.3.

There are limits to a firm's *rate* of growth (Penrose, 1995: 194), but why do some new ventures actually stagnate or decline? These firms face problems they have been unable to resolve. The reasons for the plateaus are summarized in Table 4.4. In one case the entrepreneurial team did not work

Table 4.3   Reasons for delayed growth

Source of problem	Reasons stated
Internal	Entrepreneurs wanted to do everything themselves (no delegation) (E)
External	Two-year embargo on approaching customers and employees of former employer (G); internet not yet accepted as general communication medium (G); constrained market opportunities (because of regulations) (I)

Table 4.4   Reasons for the plateau

Source of problem	Reasons stated
Internal	Organization structure (F); part-time entrepreneur, next to two academic studies (M); lack of marketing competence (T); too busy with production and too few marketing efforts (V); conflict between partners in the entrepreneurial team (W); capital shortage (W); organization structure (W); problems with coordinating businesses in two regions (X)
External	Problems with recruitment of new personnel (F); interference of major shareholder that prevented new investments (O); financial claims and lawsuit by two major customers (U); declining local market (X)

effectively, pointing to a key problem area. Two firms outgrew their resources and failed to resolve marketing problems and financial problems respectively. Establishing an effective organization structure was another problem that had to be dealt with for growth to continue. Firm X mentioned geographical expansion and a lack of coordination competence. For many firms, the failure to grow was the result of failing to solve problems of relationships with other organizations. In one case problems with a key financial relationship were not solved[8] (O), or problems with dissatisfied customers (U) remained unresolved. Networks are not always beneficial in organizing growth (compare Powell and Smith-Doerr, 1994; Johannisson, 2000). The financial relationship of firm O can be characterized as a lock-in: in the first instance this relationship enabled the growth of the firm with capital inputs and the supply of new customers, but subsequently the interference of this major shareholder made the entry of new external investors impossible and constrained the growth. The environment was mentioned several times, relating to the labour market, shareholders, customers and a declining local market. Thus, as with delayed growth, a combination of factors caused the plateau in each case.

Most evolving firms in our sample solved these problems successfully, leading to a continuation of growth after two or three years, or even entrance into the accumulation phase. For firm Y there were no clear problems to be resolved but the plateau was interrupted only by a few years of growth.

Sometimes firms face severe problems that are not detectable as setbacks in their growth path, for example when success in one business unit compensates for problems elsewhere in the company. For example, one important customer of firm I had a major disagreement about the service delivered, which led to a large financial claim that has constrained the growth of one of its two business units for some years. However, the firm as a whole continued to grow, because the other business unit was not affected by this claim and continued growing steadily.

Only five evolving firms in our research sample went through a growth reversal. For firm C the setback was brought about by the founder's lack of managerial skills in combination with the attempt to serve too many market segments. Attracting an experienced owner-manager from outside and a focus on fewer market segments has solved these problems. The setback of firm D was caused by a failed attempt to change the organization structure to a team structure. The problem was solved by the appointment of a new director from within the firm, the introduction of a simpler organization structure, and concentration on fewer market segments. Similar coordination problems also led to the setback of firm H. Firm O has even gone through two setbacks. The entrepreneur gave a direct reason for the first setback: a conflict between the consultancy and development personnel on the strategy of the firm. The founder-entrepreneur had a preference for development activities, and this led to the exit of the consultancy personnel. This firm had not made any profits before the first setback, and this state of affairs was reinforced by the fact that the initial financiers did not want to put any more money into the firm. Only after this first setback did new financial participants invest more money and enable the 'revival' of the firm that resulted in resource generation two years after the setback. However, the financial partners stopped the flow of financial inputs again at that moment, and according to the entrepreneur that was constraining the subsequent development of the firm. Table 4.5 summarizes the reasons mentioned for setbacks.

Inter-organizational relationships relatively often cause growth *difficulties*. The problems can often be (partly) resolved through personal relationships and the support and services of inter-organizational relationships. For example, firms T, U, and W recruited an external mentor to solve

Table 4.5   Reasons for setback

Source of problem	Reasons stated
Internal	Lack of managerial skills of the founder (C); too many market segments (C); organization structure (D and H); conflict between consultancy and development personnel (O)
External	

their problems, firm P was supported by a marketing agency and a corporate identity agency, and firm X sought the support of a regional development agency.

The reasons for delayed growth, stagnation, and setbacks resemble the dominant problems mentioned in other empirical studies on problems during start-up and growth (see Kazanjian, 1988; Terpstra and Olson, 1993). But we want to take this study one step further, with an inquiry into the explanation of growth paths and turning points in the life course of young firms.

6   GROWTH PATHS EXPLAINED

In this section we deal with the third research question that required rich evidence – How can the different growth paths be explained? We used a sub-sample including eight cases within two industries (knowledge services and biomedicals) with contrasting growth paths to answer this last research question. Both industries – knowledge services and biomedicals – are knowledge-intensive and characteristic of the knowledge economy. In this section we will explain why these firms have developed and grown in a different way. The particular growth paths of these case-study firms are shown in Figure 4.3.

Firm B was on an 'ideal' growth curve, not achieved, however, without problems. The initial growth of the firm took place in the form of new (spatial) units with a high level of autonomy. After seven years in development, it went through a major transition. This involved the dissolution of the entrepreneurial team and a transformation of the organization structure from a multidivisional/cells organization into a 'knowledge-based network organization'. The transition was triggered by two developments: first, a divergence within the entrepreneurial team; second, certain business units claimed too much autonomy and paid too little attention to the common good of the firm (a divergence in the productive base). These factors led to a simultaneous and discontinuous shift in strategy, control,

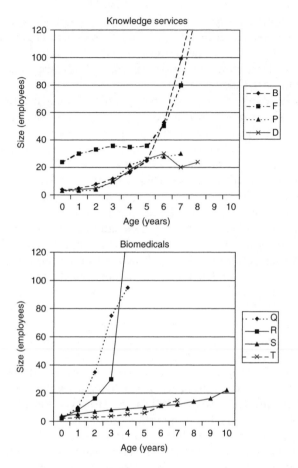

Figure 4.3 Contrasting growth paths of evolving firms in knowledge services and biomedicals

and organization structure. With the help of an external adviser a new strategy process was designed with a new organization structure: a knowledge-based network organization. This specific organization structure promotes the organization of synergy between people and business units, the organization of collectivity, sharing of knowledge, and a less strict division of labour. The consequence of this new organization structure was that the autonomy of the business units became combined with the coordination and sharing of knowledge within the whole system of the firm. This organization structure enabled a persistent growth rate and a way of systematizing the whole organization flexibly and effectively, facilitating the continuous state of reorganization. In addition to these changes in strategy and organization structure, the original entrepreneurial team was disbanded and control in strategic decision-making became more decentralized. This reorientation also led to the start of the accumulation phase (with a robust asset base).

Firm F started as a management buy-out of the Dutch branch of Digital Equipment Corporation, which explains its relatively large start-up size (with a considerable productive and commercial base already in place). It started to grow only after five years, but in a quite explosive way, with an employment growth comparable to firm B at this age. This increased growth was enabled by the shifting focus of the company into Microsoft NT applications for which the demand was booming in the second half of the 1990s. The competence in developing Microsoft NT applications has been built in cooperation with Microsoft Netherlands, later this cooperation also supported competence building in the area of the automation of workflow processes (Microsoft Workflow). In this growth period the firm faced problems with the recruitment of new personnel (productive base): at that moment it was especially hard for relatively small firms to attract skilled ICT personnel. Firm F solved its recruitment problems by initiating retraining projects for new personnel from outside the ICT sector. These projects involved cooperation with the local labour office and led to the start of a new business unit for education within the firm. For knowledge service firms like this one investments in human resources are often the largest 'cost category'.

In its first five years of existence firm P had a growth curve comparable to the other knowledge service ICT firms. However, the growth did not increase after five years, but more or less stagnated. This was caused by a customer group that was too diverse and that could no longer be served in a profitable way (problems in the commercial base). The problems leading to this stagnation triggered a strategic change which is expected to lead to a new growth period in the near future. The entrepreneurs felt the need to make the decision to change the strategy, and to focus on a specific market segment: the knowledge-intensive organizations, including advanced professional service firms and scientific organizations. This did not lead to a changing productive base, but to a changing commercial base. This change has been reinforced with the support of a communication advice agency and a marketing agency, which led to an explicit change in corporate identity and market positioning.

The first five years in the growth curve of firm D were similar to firm B. However, after these five years the growth curve did not increase as much as the one for firm B. Firm D is a medium-sized organization advice company that was started by two serial entrepreneurs. The clients were acquired via the entrepreneurs' existing professional networks (commercial base). Some of the first clients are still important customers. A high level of trust characterizes relationships with these customers: 'Trust is fundamental for realizing organizational change with our customers'; 'selling is nothing less than the construction of trust through which goodwill can arise'. After five years of stable growth, a change in the organization structure failed, and one of the founders left the business. In the sixth year of the firm, there was a setback followed by a transformation. The change from a simple organization structure to a cells structure turned out to be a complete failure, and this was accompanied by the withdrawal of one of the founder-entrepreneurs. This withdrawal also brought about a decrease in the IT orientation and a shift of the firm into consultancy on organizational change trajectories (changing productive and commercial base). The resulting growth syndrome with huge financial losses led to a customer focus on a few industries and a few large customers, rather than trying to take on all the customers who could be reached.

The biomedical firms Q and R stand out because of their extremely steep growth curves. They also stand out in a developmental way, as they generate almost no marketable output (no commercial base), and certainly not any large profits.

Firm Q is a fast-growing biomedical firm specializing in substitution medicine and tissue engineering. Two professors in biomedical sciences started the business activities of firm Q (compare Zucker et al., 1998). They were pushed into entrepreneurship because the University of Leiden was putting increasing financial constraints on their Biomaterials Research Group. They had previous experience of starting two other biotech firms. They sold their last firm for a substantial sum and used the proceeds to fund this firm. So they both came out of the academic research group and can be seen as serial entrepreneurs. The first employees were attracted in the first year. The firm has been financed by several venture capitalists and realized an initial public offering (IPO) four years after its start-up (external inputs to the asset base). Firm Q has become the market leader in tissue engineering in Europe. Only a few research groups and biotech firms are active in this market. It is an R&D-driven organization with an extensive intellectual property portfolio and a wide range of (yet to be commercialized) products. Some products have been sold on the final market, delivering some modest returns. It is expected to make some profits within a few years. During its life course the firm has increased the number of R&D agreements with academic research and clinical institutes all over the world. The firm was transformed from an academically oriented research institute into a stock listed company very quickly. The transformation was facilitated by the entrepreneurial abilities of the two founders, who had already founded and developed two similar firms.

Firm R is a biomedical firm focused on the discovery and development of therapeutics based on fully human monoclonal antibodies. The plan of a new firm had already been initiated more than a year before the formal start-up. The foundation of the start-up was the approval of a patent application in 1995. The idea for this patent was an opportunity recognized by one of the founders at a scientific conference in San Diego. The patent application led to discussions with the chairman of the local university and the president of the academic hospital in which both the founders worked. At that time it was not clear if and how a biomedical spin-off could be commercialized. Two professors of Utrecht University founded the firm, with the academic organizations Utrecht University and the University Medical Centre Utrecht as external shareholders. The Dutch Ministry of Economic Affairs also subsidized the start-up. The firm was incubated within the academic hospital. At its start, collaboration with Novartis (a world leader in pharmaceuticals) had already been initiated, and this proceeded in the next few years. In its second year, the firm reinforced its intellectual property base through agreements with two US pharmaceutical companies. In the third year, a CEO was appointed and the first venture capital round took off. This substantial venture capital investment (asset base) allowed the firm to continue fundamental research and prepare for clinical testing of the lead product candidates (productive base). In the fourth year, closer cooperation was started with another Dutch biomedical firm that had developed a little further than firm R, although in a complementary manner. Potential cooperation problems with this firm and some other operational problems in firm R led to the merger with this other Dutch biomedical firm. The merger of the two companies led to the creation of a 'new' firm with 150 employees. The founder-entrepreneur of firm R did not become CEO, but served instead as Chief Scientific Officer for the new firm. According to the entrepreneur of firm R, the merger 'has enormous strategic value for both companies, and it will enable us to accelerate the development of our products'. Neither the initial firm R nor the new merged firm made any profits. There was some income from the licence of its core technologies to commercial partners and entry into strategic alliances in exchange for fees, milestone payments, and royalties on products developed using their technologies. In the same year, the new firm realized an IPO that had already been planned by the other firm. Firm R had also planned an IPO, only over a longer term, which was thus accelerated by this merger (merger of the productive base led thus led to substantial growth of the asset base).

Firms S and T – both producing and selling diagnostic tests – grew hardly at all during their first years, and only slowly after this initial steady period. In contrast to firms Q and R, these firms did produce some profitable products, that is, they had a moderate commercial base. However, these firms did not have such a promising technology or biomedical product (productive base) that they could attract enormous sums of investment capital (asset base). They did attract some venture capital, but had to survive mostly on their own commercialized products, which they did with moderate success. Both mention that their commercial base is still not sufficiently developed, although they are investing quite heavily in their corporate identity and marketing skills (with market research and the support of external marketing advisors) in addition to their 'normal' investments in product development. After several years they both changed their firm into a more market-oriented firm, due to lagging profits, with a changed organization structure and more focused marketing efforts.

The solution of the problems during the early life course often involved learning and sometimes even the development of a firm-specific competence. Without the development of these firm-specific competences it would be impossible for these firms to continue to grow during their life course.

7 DISCUSSION

We already knew that most new firms never reach a substantial size (see, for example, Storey, 1997). However, we did not know that the few new firms that manage to grow to a substantial size often do not grow in a continuous way. Our empirical study revealed that even in an elite sample of young fast-growing firms, most firms face turning points in their life course (compare Garnsey et al., 2006). These turning points are often caused by problems that constrain growth and force the firm to focus again after a resource or competence shortage. However, these turning points also enable growth: in the short run – after delayed growth – and in the long run, when competence is developed in the problem-solving process.

The case studies revealed that quantitative growth indicators do not always reveal growth problems that have been faced by new firms. Some problems did not negatively affect the employment growth of the firm, and other problems were solved before growth stagnated. The qualitative analysis showed that young firms are almost always in disequilibrium: there is almost never a perfect match between the constituents of their resource base, between input resources and requirements for expansion. This explains why continuous growth is so unlikely. The qualitative analysis also showed that certain growth mechanisms are more important in certain industries than others. For example, the early growth in the asset base of knowledge service firms was realized in a resource generation process with close ties to customers, while for biomedical firms this was mainly realized by acquiring financial resources from investors. However, in the long run, the biomedical ventures also have to generate adequate resources from a product market, or they may be taken over or abandoned by their investors before this occurs.

In contrast to the stage models of growth we did not find evidence for a universal sequential progress in the life courses of the studied firms. But although every firm seems to grow in a unique manner, there is evidence for the presence of a limited set of necessary mechanisms for the growth of (new) firms, which work out in particular ways given the specific context and history of these firms.

8   CONCLUSION

The growth paths of young firms is a topic that has received comparatively little attention in the literature, where cross-sectional methodologies dominate. Yet it is only by examining the unfolding processes through which growth takes place that we can understand the constraints and success attributes so often cited in the literature. This study has shown that although each firm is unique, there are common processes that bring about development and common problems that have to be resolved if this is to occur. Because the requirements for survival and growth are experienced in common, there are common features to development. We found that certain growth paths are more common than others and reflect the relative success of new firms in solving problems they all face.

How and why new firms develop has been a central issue in this chapter. A coherent answer to this question involves a developmental approach. Here the development of the firm is conceptualized in terms of processes that include opportunity recognition, resource mobilization, resource generation and resource accumulation, which lead to the development of competences and capital in a base made up of productive, commercial and financial resources. Problems originating within or outside the firm may deplete the productive, commercial and asset base, leading to turning points in the life course of these firms. These have negative consequences when problems are not solved, but positive consequences when they lead to new solutions and the development of new competence (Hugo and Garnsey, 2005).

Evidence of this kind points to the micro-diversity that underlies aggregate trends, evidence that is lost if growth rates are averaged out and firms characterized by rate of growth, as in much of the 'enterprise monitoring' that currently takes place. Policies of support and strategies for growth operate in the dark unless evidence of this kind is examined and the causal processes underlying development are analysed. Further work of this kind is needed to integrate qualitative and quantitative approaches.

NOTES

1. Some authors have argued that evolutionary economic theories can be regarded as a subset of competence-based theories of the firm (Hodgson, 1999: 247). Other authors have argued that competence-based theories (for example, the dynamic capabilities approach, compare Teece et al., 1997) are built on evolutionary economics (Foss, 1997: 352).
2. Although the developmental approach sketched here differs from current evolutionary economics (Nelson and Winter, 1982), it shares the major building blocks and key assumptions of evolutionary economics including 'dynamics first', bounded rationality, heterogeneity of agents, novelty, selection mechanism, and emergent properties (compare Dosi, 1997; Hodgson, 1999). In an explanation of why firms differ, Nelson (1991) states that an evolutionary theory of dynamic firms consists of the concepts of strategy, firm structure and core capabilities. The developmental approach sketched here is in line with what Cohendet and Llerena (1998: 10) have defined *an* evolutionary theory of the firm, namely 'a theory which explains the structure and behaviour of a firm as an emergent property of the dynamics of interactions of both its constituent parts among each other and of the firm itself with its environment'. These firms do not develop in isolation, but their fates are closely connected to their (local) environments. Although in order to abstract from contingent conditions, the focus in this chapter is more on internal than on external dynamics.
3. These can also be called 'marketing capabilities', which capture and reflect 'how well a firm performs each key customer-connecting process . . . and in designing and managing subprocesses within the customer relationship management process . . .' (Srivastava et al., 2001: 783).
4. This theory of new venture growth has many similarities with the organizational capabilities approach, but it is more process-oriented. The organizational capabilities approach is also more concerned with the properties and products of a problem-solving process (compare Foss, 1997; Hugo, 2002).
5. Routines are 'patterns of interactions that represent successful solutions to particular problems' (Teece et al., 1997), which are resident in organizational behaviour. Next to this behavioural definition of routines, routines can also be interpreted as cognitive regularities (Becker, 2004).
6. There might be a selection bias, since not all the firms were studied for the full ten years.
7. At first glance these firms resemble micro firms that stay small during their life course. However, most entrepreneurs of the micro firms are satisfied with their current business. They are independent and do not want the complexity involved in a growing business, especially that of becoming an employer. These entrepreneurs do not consider expansion, because they are not looking out for opportunities, or they do not have the capacity to manage growth, or they lack the willingness to grow.
8. Cf. Vohora et al. (2004) for similar conflicts of interest.

REFERENCES

Autio, E. and E. Garnsey (1997), 'Early Growth and External Relations in New Technology-Based Firms', Helsinki University of Technology, Espoo, Finland.

Barney, J. (1991), 'Firm Resources and Sustained Competitive Advantages', *Journal of Management*, **17**: 99–120.

Becker, M.C. (2004), 'Organizational Routines: A Review of the Literature', *Industrial and Corporate Change*, **13**(4): 643–77.

Bell, G.C. and J.E. McNamara (1991), *High-Tech Ventures. The Guide for Entrepreneurial Success*, New York: Addison Wesley.

Bhidé, A. (2000), *The Origin and Evolution of New Businesses*, New York: Oxford University Press.

Chell, E. and L. Pittaway (1998), 'A Study of Entrepreneurship in the Restaurant and Café Industry: Exploratory Work Using the Critical Incident Technique as a Methodology', *Hospitality Management*, **17**: 23–32.

Churchill, N.C. and V.L. Lewis (1983), 'The Five Stages of Small Business Growth', *Harvard Business Review*, **61**: 30–50.

Cohendet, P. and P. Llerena (1998), 'Theory of the Firm in an Evolutionary Perspective: A Critical Development', paper presented at the Conference 'Competence, Governance and Entrepreneurship', Copenhagen.

Cope, J. and G. Watts (2000), 'Learning by Doing. An Exploration of Experience, Critical Incidents and Reflection in Entrepreneurial Learning', *International Journal of Entrepreneurial Behaviour & Research*, **6**: 104–24.

Coriat, B. and G. Dosi (1998), 'Learning How to Govern and Learning How to Solve Problems: On the Co-evolution of Competences, Conflicts and Organizational Routines', in A.D. Chandler, P. Hagstrom and O. Solvell (eds), *The Dynamic Firm: The Role of Technology, Strategy, Organization, and Regions*, New York: Oxford University Press, pp. 103–33.

Cyert, R.M. and J.G. March (1963), *A Behavioral Theory of the Firm*, Englewood Cliffs, NJ: Prentice-Hall.

Delmar, F., P. Davidsson and W.B. Gartner (2003), 'Arriving at the High-growth Firm', *Journal of Business Venturing*, **18**: 189–216.

Dierickx, I. and K. Cool (1989), 'Asset Stock Accumulation and Sustainability of Competitive Advantage', *Management Science*, **35**: 1504–11.

Dosi, G. (1997), 'Opportunities, Incentives and the Collective Patterns of Technological Change', *Economic Journal*, **107**: 1530–47.

Dosi, G., R. Nelson and S.G. Winter (2000), *The Nature and Dynamics of Organizational Capabilities*, Oxford: Oxford University Press.

Eisenhardt, K.M. (1989), 'Building Theories from Case Study Research', *Academy of Management Review*, **14**: 532–50.

Eisenhardt, K. and J.K. Martin (2000), 'Dynamic Capabilities: What Are They?' *Strategic Management Journal*, **21**: 1105–21.

Foss, N.J. (ed.) (1997), *Resources, Firms and Strategies: A Reader in the Resource-based Perspective*, Oxford: Oxford University Press.

Garnsey, E. (1998), 'A Theory of the Early Growth of the Firm', *Industrial and Corporate Change*, **7**: 523–56.

Garnsey, E. and P. Heffernan (2003), 'Growth Setbacks in New Firms', University of Cambridge, Cambridge.

Garnsey, E., E. Stam and P. Heffernan (2006), 'New Firm Growth: Exploring Processes and Paths', *Industry and Innovation*, **13**(1): 1–24.

Greiner, L.E. (1972), 'Evolution and Revolution as Organizations Grow', *Harvard Business Review*, **50**: 37–46.

Hanks, S.H., C.J. Watson, E. Jansen and G.N. Chandler (1993), 'Tightening the Life-cycle Construct: A Taxonomic Study of Growth Stage Configurations in High-technology Organizations', *Entrepreneurship: Theory and Practice*, **18**: 5–31.

Hodgson, G.M. (1999), *Evolution and Institutions: On Evolutionary Economics and the Evolution of Economics*, Cheltenham, UK and Northampton, MA, USA: Edward Elgar.

Hugo, O. (2002), 'Understanding New Venture Growth as a Development Process', unpublished PhD dissertation, University of Cambridge, Cambridge.

Hugo, O. and E. Garnsey (2002), 'Investigating the Growth Path of Young Technology-based Firms: A Process Approach', Centre for Technology Management, University of Cambridge, Cambridge.

Hugo, O. and E. Garnsey (2005), 'Problem-solving and Competence Creation in new Firms: Turning Obstacles into Opportunities', *Managerial and Decision Economics*, **25**: 139–48.

Johannisson, B. (2000), 'Networking and Entrepreneurial Growth', in D.L. Sexton and H. Landström (eds), *The Blackwell Handbook of Entrepreneurship*, Oxford: Blackwell, pp. 368–86.

Kazanjian, R.K. (1988), 'Relation of Dominant Problems to Stages of Growth in Technology-based New Ventures', *Academy of Management Journal*, **31**: 257–79.

Levie, J. and M. Hay (1998), 'Progress or Just Proliferation? A Historical Review of Stages Models of Early Corporate Growth', London Business School, London.

McGrath, R.G. (2002), 'Entrepreneurship, Small Firms and Wealth Creation: A Framework Using Real Options', in A.M. Pettigrew, H. Thomas and R. Whittington (eds), *Handbook of Strategy and Management*, London, Sage: pp. 101–13.

Metcalfe, J.S. (1998), *Evolutionary Economics and Creative Destruction: The Graz Schumpeter Lectures 1*, London: Routledge.

Miller, D. and P.H. Friesen (1984), 'A Longitudinal Study of the Corporate Life Cycle', *Management Science*, **30**: 1161–83.

Nelson, R.R. (1991), 'Why Do Firms Differ, and How Does It Matter', *Strategic Management Journal*, **12**: 61–74.

Nelson, R.R. and S.G. Winter (1982), *An Evolutionary Theory of Economic Change*, Cambridge, MA: Belknap Press.

Penrose, E.T. (1995), *The Theory of the Growth of the Firm*, Oxford: Oxford University Press (first published in 1959).

Pettigrew, A.M. (1995), 'Longitudinal Field Research on Change: Theory and Practice', in G.P. Huber and A.H. Van de Ven (eds), *Longitudinal Field Research Methods: Studying Processes of Organizational Change*, London: Sage.

Powell, W.W. and L. Smith-Doerr (1994), 'Networks and Economic Life', in N.J. Smelser and R. Swedberg (eds), *The Handbook of Economic Sociology*, Princeton, NJ: Princeton University Press, pp. 368–402.

Rathe, K. and U. Witt (2001), 'The Nature of the Firm – Static versus Developmental Interpretations', *Journal of Management and Governance*, **5**: 331–51.

Richardson, G.B. (1972), 'The Organization of Industry', *Economic Journal*, **82**: 883–96.

Romanelli, E. and M.L. Tushman (1994), 'Organizational Transformation as Punctuated Equilibrium: An Empirical Test', *Academy of Management Journal*, **37**: 1141–66.

Sayer, A. (1992), *Method in Social Science*, London: Taylor & Francis.

Sorenson, O. (2003), 'Social Networks and Industrial Geography', *Journal of Evolutionary Economics*, **13**: 513–27.

Srivastava, R.K., L. Fahey and H.K. Christensen (2001), 'The Resource-based View and Marketing: The Role of Market-based Assets in Gaining Competitive Advantage', *Journal of Management*, **27**: 777–802.

Stam, E. (2003), 'Why Butterflies Don't Leave. Locational Evolution of Evolving Enterprises', Utrecht University, Utrecht.

Steindl, J. (1952), *Maturity and Stagnation in American Capitalism*, Oxford: Blackwell.

Storey, D. (1997), *Understanding the Small Business Sector*, London: Thomson International Business Press.

Teece, D.J., G. Pisano and A. Shuen (1997), 'Dynamic Capabilities and Strategic Management', *Strategic Management Journal*, **18**: 509–33.

Terpstra, D.E. and P.D. Olson (1993), 'Entrepreneurial Start-up and Growth: A Classification of Problems', *Entrepreneurship: Theory and Practice*, **17**: 5–19.

Tushman, M.L. and E. Romanelli (1990), 'Organizational Evolution: A Metamorphosis Model of Convergence and Reorientation', in B.M. Staw and L.L. Cummings (eds), *The Evolution and Adaptation of Organizations*, Greenwich, CT: JAI Press, pp. 139–90.

Vaessen, P.M.M.V. (1993), 'Small Business Growth in Contrasting Environments', Catholic University of Nijmegen, Nijmegen.

Van Geenhuizen, M.S., P. Nijkamp and P.M. Townroe (1992), 'Company Life History Analysis and Technogenesis', *Technological Forecasting and Social Change*, **41**: 13–28.

Vohora, A., M. Wright and A. Lockett (2004), 'Critical Junctures in the Development of University High-tech Spinout Companies', *Research Policy*, **33**: 147–75.

Zucker, L.G., M.R. Darby and M.B. Brewer (1998), 'Intellectual Human Capital and the Birth of US Biotechnology Enterprises', *American Economic Review*, **88**: 290–306.

5. The coordination and codification of knowledge inside a network, or the building of an epistemic community: the Telecom Valley case study

Nathalie Lazaric and Catherine Thomas

INTRODUCTION

In the telecommunications industry, which is characterized by science-based technologies, cooperation is driven by the needs of accelerating innovation and by joining complementary technological assets and competencies. In this process, formal and informal agreements are implemented and most of the time they are characterized by vertical integration for producing 'subsystems' such as internet access, service providers and so on (Fransman and Krafft, 2002).

Literature has given evidence – beyond economic coordination – of the importance of social links in local networks (Granovetter, 1985; Kogut, 2000) for the emergence of rules, for trust building (Lazaric and Lorenz, 1998) and for structuring cooperation between partners (competing and/or complementary). Rules are important in generating suitable types of competition and in order to avoid jeopardizing resources and capabilities between network members (Avadikyan et al., 2001; Kogut, 2000). The creation of shared rules, beliefs and language could be sustained by an 'epistemic community' which according to Haas (1992) plays an important role in creating a procedural authority, based on recognized expertise and competence in a particular domain. This authority plays a crucial role in selecting practices, in validating some of them and in generating rules in order to diffuse knowledge inside and outside the network (Haas, 1992; Cohendet and Llerena, 2001; Lazaric, 2003).

Inside the Sophia-Antipolis network, many non-profit business-driven associations play a significant role in the production, distribution and use of knowledge inside and between firms. We have focused our attention on 'Telecom Valley', a non-profit, business-driven association founded in 1991 by eight leading actors in the telecommunications industry. Recently,

Telecom Valley launched a project to create an innovative 'Knowledge Management Solution', leading to a process of articulating and codifying knowledge among the association's members, transforming it into a kind of epistemic community. Thus, this project provides a valuable opportunity to observe knowledge-sharing and knowledge-diffusion inside a network. Indeed, in the network configuration, the codification process appears to be more complex than in other organizational designs. This means that it is necessary to create a context in which there are enough incentives to produce and to share collective knowledge and enough energy to overcome the reluctance due to possible misunderstandings between firms during the codification process. Within the network, this tool may have different structuring effects reinforcing the epistemic community: sharing a common entrepreneurial vision, favouring the synergy of individual varieties and creating a better understanding of implemented practices.

In Section 1, we propose to establish a theoretical framework to understand the delicate problem of knowledge sharing and knowledge codification inside a network. In Section 2, we will present our case study and the Telecom Valley project. In Section 3, we will discuss triggers and difficulties in the building of an epistemic community.

1 KNOWLEDGE SHARING AND KNOWLEDGE CODIFICATION INSIDE A NETWORK

After having briefly defined and reviewed problems related to the notion of articulation and codification, we will explain why, according to us, this problem includes both political and cognitive aspects. We will see more precisely the implication of this issue in the network design where problems related to the disclosure of knowledge are far from being obvious and easy to implement.

1.1 Articulation and Codification and their Limits in the Transfer of Knowledge

A lot of recent economic and managerial literature has focused attention on the codification debate (see, for example, Cohendet and Steinmuller, 2000; Cowan and Foray, 1997; Cowan et al., 2000). The debate, which has been very controversial, is open to a variety of interpretations, as indeed are its implications (see Knudsen, 2000; Nightingale, 2001; Johnson et al., 2002).

Cowan and Foray (1997) see the process of codification as including three aspects: model building, language creation and writing the message. They think that technological change can create some dynamic tendencies in the process of codification by decreasing the costs of this process. Nevertheless, for them and for some others (Cowan et al., 2000), the problem of codification resides in the model creation and more precisely in the capacity to articulate knowledge in order to codify it, as well as in the development of language for building a shared and generic language that goes beyond local jargons. Needless to say, investments are very high in this process because the diffusion of codified language depends on the capacity of implementing investments for building a community able to read the codes.

A small but important difference lies in the way this process is conceived. For Cowan et al. (2000) the problem is related to a problem of incentives and costs. These authors are also quite sceptical about the interest of tacit knowledge, seeing it as a brake on this process. On the other hand, for Winter (1987) and other authors (Johnson et al., 2002, Lazaric et al., 2003), tacit knowledge and codified knowledge are not opposed but complementary because these two kinds of knowledge are the intrinsic parts of the codification process. Codified knowledge has little added value without human intelligence and human judgement for making sense and for activating codes in an innovative way (Håkansson, 2002). This problem has been examined in many case studies of the introduction of expert systems. In this case, tacit knowledge still remains and is still important for maintaining and for updating diverse forms of knowledge, notably codified ones (Lazaric et al., 2003).

If, for some authors, tacit knowledge is an obstacle to the replication process and has to be domesticated (Foray and Steinmuller, 2001), for us, tacit knowledge is not seen in a pejorative way and we consider it to be essential for creativity and innovation (Håkansson, 2002). According to us, codes are typically incomplete and the codification in itself does not guarantee the transfer of knowledge because this relies on the relationship between the recipient and the receptor. That is to say that the modes of conversion of knowledge are far from being neutral: 'in this respect, codes, and especially languages are not neutral to transmit knowledge. They include intrinsically a representation of the real world and mobilize different amounts of cognitive resources, both for the emitter and for the receiver' (Ancori et al., 2001: 268).

This means that the process has to be solved in collective and iterative dimensions between the emitter and the receiver in order to obtain some suitable forms of codified knowledge, acceptable for both parts in their content, precision and depth (Lazaric et al., 2003).

This point is far from being trivial as the articulation and codification processes transform the way in which communities habitually represent knowledge and share it between their members at different levels: new knowledge representations come into play at both the individual and the collective levels, while new objectives concerning knowledge creation, accumulation and preservation enter the organizational level. This leads to potential tensions inside communities in order to obtain legitimacy, authority and power in the building of new knowledge. This point has been very well illustrated by the Linux community where disputes are frequent (Muller, 2004; Von Krogh et al., 2003).

Any process of articulation and codification inevitably results in an extraction of knowledge that goes well beyond the remit of the preliminary exchange. Let us define more precisely these terms. We define knowledge as being 'articulated' when the knowledge of a person or an organization has been made explicit by means of natural language. It follows that 'articulable knowledge' is any knowledge that can be rendered explicit through ordinary language. Language in this context refers to a system of signs and conventions that facilitates the reproduction and storage of knowledge in such a way that it can be communicated to, and transferred between, individuals. Articulation is more concerned with the stage of 'explication' through natural language and metaphors (see Nonaka and Takeuchi, 1995, for more details) and codification is more oriented through the diffusion of knowledge via technical tools (see also Winter, 1987; Mangolte, 1997; Divry and Lazaric, 1998; Lazaric et al., 2002; Håkansson, 2002). Articulation, however, is distinct from knowledge codification and may be considered to be a product of this preliminary step: 'Knowledge codification, in fact, is a more restrictive notion with respect to knowledge articulation processes. The latter is required in order to achieve the former, while the opposite is obviously not true' (Zollo and Winter, 2001: 17).

In general, articulation of knowledge increases the vulnerability of the members of the firm notably towards hierarchy. In fact, any extraction of knowledge implies a process of knowledge disclosure on behalf of the different 'communities of practice'. This sense of vulnerability and uncertainty is enhanced by the loss of control over well-established routines. The problem of articulation and codification may even be perceived as crucial and risky in a network of firms exchanging knowledge (as we can see in the following section). That is the reason why the state of confidence and trust between firms and inside the organization is crucial, otherwise this process will be confronted with a lack of real willingness to participate, and consequently with a lack of knowledge exchange (Lazaric, 2003).

1.2 Coordination and Codification of Knowledge inside a Network: Some Challenging Issues

The network structure is a key issue for supporting knowledge creation by offering the benefit of both specialization and variety generation but it entails deep problems of coordination and appropriability in the absence of an authority (Kogut, 2000). A lot of studies on codification inside a network insist on some difficulty of the process as some partners may be reluctant to codify all the knowledge they have jointly produced even if some internal culture may create incentives for a codification process: 'Overall, a significant amount of knowledge produced during this project appears to be codified but only a limited amount of it is really transparent to the partners. This is mostly due to strategic reasons rather than technical obstacles' (Grimaldi and Torrisi, 2001: 1438).

The network, of course, is an organizational form quite distinct from hierarchy, where complexity is increased due to the presence of diverse organizational entanglements: the individual, the corporate, the network and the regional (local institutions) levels and so on.

The driving forces and the dynamic of the codification process
It is important to underline that the codification process is based on two dimensions: the political or regulating dimension, which enables the object of codification to be delimited, and the cognitive dimension, which is influenced by the medium and the way this medium changes the individual and collective representation inside the network. These two aspects are two sides of the same coin because the political dimension could accelerate the codification process with the risk of losing some crucial actors and of not having the time for infusing new collective and cognitive representation emerging from this process. In this context the two facets should co-evolve to ensure the viability of this dynamic.

The content of the codification and its depth have to be negotiated by the actors in the process in order to ensure its suitability. This means that at an early stage, the content of the process could be restricted so as to avoid creating confidentiality problems for some of the network's members. This leads us to define two types of knowledge that could be codified and to examine closely their meaning for the scope of the codification process.

The regulation of such a process inside the network depends strongly on the existing divisions of labour between firms and their previous experience in knowledge sharing inside their own organization:

> The division of labour erects boundaries within firms; it also produces extended communities that lie across the external boundaries of firms. Moving knowledge among groups with similar practices overlapping memberships can thus sometimes be relatively easy compared to the difficulty of moving it among heterogeneous groups within the firm. (Brown and Duguit, 1998: 102)

Epistemic communities offer a means for structuring and regulating such an exchange of knowledge across organizations with some intentionality and some explicit goals. In this context, the role assumed by this community is quite distinct from the traditional 'communities of practice' described by Brown and Duguit (1991) and Wenger (1998). The epistemic community's cognitive function is not limited to the exchange of tacit knowledge but extends to the validation and dissemination of this knowledge to the group of practitioners. It is this fundamental difference between knowledge exchange and knowledge validation that, in our view, distinguishes a community of practice from an epistemic community. In fact:

> An 'epistemic community' is a network of professionals with recognized expertise and competence in a particular domain and an authoritative claim to policy-relevant knowledge within domain or issue-area . . . This network has (1) a shared set of normative and principled beliefs, which provide a value-based rationale for the social action of community members; (2) shared causal beliefs, which are derived from their analysis of practices leading or contributing to a central set of problems in their domain and which then serve as the basis for elucidating the multiple linkages between possible actions and desired outcomes; (3) shared notions of validity, that is, inter subjective, internally defined criteria for weighing and validating knowledge in the domain of their expertise; and (4) a common policy enterprise, that is, a set of common practices associated with a set of problems to which their professional competence is directed, presumably out of the conviction that human welfare will be enhanced as a consequence. (Haas, 1992: 3)

The epistemic community has an important role to play as it has substantial authority and can therefore exert significant pressure on any attempt to validate or invalidate some particular practice inside a network. Such pressure is present at different levels: at an organizational level, it can affect the selection of particular practices by reviewing them and acknowledging them as relevant to both the company and its organizational memory; on the other hand the pressure is also evident at an individual level, as this community can play a role in the selection of the shared beliefs and values that evolve through the use of a particular technology and by generating a new episteme inside the network. Nevertheless the presence of specific actors, like lead users (von Hippel, 1987; Albino et al., 1999), can orient such a process by promoting a specific firm for regulating the process, which has to be accepted collectively by the entire network, notably the scope of codification and its content. The building of such community rules of codification is certainly one of the most crucial problems, as we will explain later.

Authority, legitimacy and the regulation of communities

The main distinction between a community of practices and an epistemic community resides in the possibility for the latter to exercise its authority. The 'epistemic community' plays a significant role in validating or invalidating practices by reviewing them and acknowledging those which are judged particularly relevant inside the network. This could generate some tensions and distrust if the codification process is not perceived as legitimate. In this case, the process of articulation, which is the first step, could be ineffective and impede a real codification. This demonstrates that the design of the project and its rules are important for trust-building and for creating a real legitimacy inside the epistemic community which has not to be created ex nihilo but has to emerge slowly, even if contestation or disputes are inevitable in such building of leadership (see especially Hirschman, 1970; Lazaric and Lorenz, 1998). In effect, the way diverse communities relate to the technology affects the degree to which they are likely to accept the diffusion of their private knowledge (itself a part of local knowledge) and co-operate in the codification process. However, this relation can also be affected by the organization itself and the communication rules that prevail inside the network. Given that articulation and codification can never be complete, because they are based on live expertise that cannot be entirely codified, the epistemic community plays an important role in determining certain 'reliable beliefs' but also in preventing knowledge fossilization. The way in which articulation is perceived at the beginning of the process can lead to a number of minor events that increase in importance during codification. That is the reason why the building of organizational rules is crucial: firstly, for achieving some political and cognitive compromise during codification (Lazaric, 2003) and second, for building a legitimate procedural authority inside the epistemic community.

2   THE TELECOM VALLEY CASE STUDY

Sophia-Antipolis, on the French Riviera, is a highly-publicized technology park, combining establishments of multinational corporations, small and medium-sized firms, and large public research centres and universities (Castells and Hall, 1994). Recently this network has attempted to reinforce links between firms in order to coordinate their knowledge bases. As noted earlier, we focus on Telecom Valley and its role in structuring the network of cooperation by formal or informal rules as well as by codification of knowledge between its members.

2.1   The History of Sophia-Antipolis

Sophia-Antipolis is a regional development project based on R&D and high technologies, located in an area with neither a strong industrial base or a university. Its development was driven by institutions and politicians, who decided, as early as 1969, to promote R&D activities and training in this specific area. The project has benefited, on the one hand, from the significant investments made by France Telecom in cutting-edge technologies, which allowed nodes of national and international networks to be located on the site; and on the other hand, from the decentralization policy initiated by the French government (Longhi, 1999).

During the development of the Sophipolitan project, processes of collective inter-firm learning and spin-off phenomena were absent. Thus, the development of Sophia-Antipolis has been very different from other clusters based on regional collective learning processes since it was characterized until recently by the weakness of local interactions. In these conditions, it is interesting to understand how Sophia-Antipolis has been able to grow into one of the most important centres of high technology activity in Europe.

The development of Sophia-Antipolis has been closely linked to the establishment of large national and international firms (Digital Equipment in 1980, Dow Chemical in 1981, Thomson Sintra in 1982, Matra Communication in 1985, Atos Origin in 1985, VLSI Technology in 1986, Amadeus in 1988 and so on) as well as various public research institutes (Ecole des Mines de Paris in 1976, CNRS in 1976, INRIA in 1982 and so on). This process has led to the formation of three sets of technological activities: energy and environment, life and health sciences, and information technology and telecommunications. From the beginning, the latter has been the growth engine of this cluster. Indeed, the Sophipolitan competences in the domain of telecommunications are now recognized all over Europe (with 727 companies, €3.88 billion of annual turnover and 20 380 jobs).

Nowadays, the Sophipolitan telecom network is becoming a real 'innovative milieu' and this evolution is supported by the firms:

- The accumulation of technological activities in the domain of information technology and telecommunications has generated the creation of a multitude of small service firms (for example, in 1999, 90 new enterprises) and the establishment of standards institutes (European Telecommunications Standards Institute, ETSI, in 1988; World wide Web Consortium, W3C, in 1994).
- From the early 1990s, the crisis in information technology activities has led the firms to develop local links in order to benefit from geographical proximity and implement collective innovative projects.

2.2   The Sophipolitan Telecom Cluster

Cooke and Huggins (2003) offered a definition of cluster considered useful by many scholars (Nooteboom and Woolthuis, 2003) and which we will employ: 'Geographically proximate firms in vertical and horizontal relationships involving a localized enterprise support infrastructure with shared development vision for business growth, based on competition and cooperation in a specific market field.'

In the Sophipolitan telecom cluster, firms are evolving in a multitechnological context covering a wide range of industries from computing and multimedia to space, information processing, online services and networking, and microelectronics. A cluster often includes different value chains (Nooteboom and Woolthuis, 2003). In collaboration with local actors, we have illustrated the main global value chain representative of the telecom Sophipolitain cluster (Figure 5.1).

The characteristics of the corporate interrelationships found in Sophia Antipolis can be summarized in the following way (and see the telecom value chain in Figure 5.1):

- Vertical cooperation set up to take advantage of complementary assets within the labour force (between IT and telecommunications firms) or vertical relations set up to hire strategic competencies, such as manpower in strategic projects.
- Horizontal cooperation between firms to diffuse information between different communities of practice (for example quality practices or industrial relations, in which cooperation should lead to benefits arising from geographical proximities in the labour markets).

Firms and subsidiary companies that are present inside the cluster mainly develop R&D and technological marketing activities and are not directly involved in the productive area. They are for this reason very sensitive to uses' approaches.

The telecom value chain shows the economic exchanges that take place between different poles or value creation nodes. Indeed, starting with the end-user consumer (1), the value chain leads to seven nodes, which are main sources of value creation. These are: Internet access and service providers (2); the value-added re-sellers (3), the distributors that play an active role between the end-user consumer and the terminal device (especially in guaranteeing information exchange); the content providers (4); the network operators and telecom service providers (5); the terminal device manufacturers (6); the network infrastructure providers (7); and finally the application developers (8). The actors located in Sophia Antipolis belong

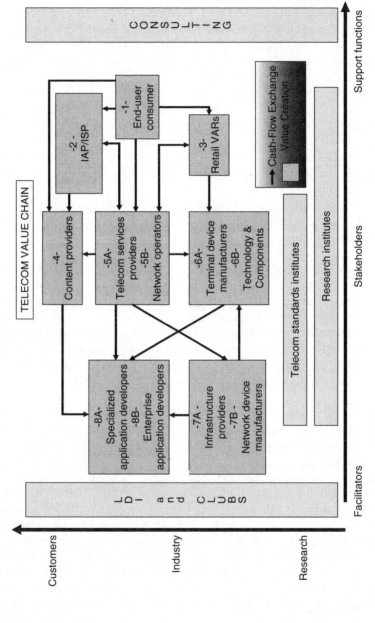

Figure 5.1   The Sophipolitan telecom cluster

essentially to nodes 5, 6, 7 and 8, though some start-ups have begun developing node 4 software applications. Actors are placed on the chain according to the nature of their local activity, a position that can be very different from the generic situation of the group to which a local actor belongs. For instance, the local subsidiary of Hewlett-Packard (formerly Compaq) designs and markets telecom network infrastructure solutions while the parent company is generally known for the design and manufacture of computer devices and solutions.

Given that some important nodes in the telecom value chain (such as terminal device manufacturers (6A)) are under-represented in Sophia-Antipolis and given the strong links between local firms and their parent companies (located elsewhere), the Sophipolitan cluster has always developed strong external links.

The way the value chain is managed is also typical of a technopole in that:

- It combines local and modular logic (indeed some of the cluster's firms produce products and/or services that are integrated in wider-scale solutions);
- At the local level, the cluster's dynamics rely on the social interaction of several communities, associations, clubs and so on.

This is the reason why we included the following elements in Figure 5.1:

- Local development institutes (LDIs) charged with promoting the cluster abroad and attracting foreign investment and companies. Clubs and associations charged with reinforcing the exchange dynamic of the cluster (as we have already mentioned). These are considered to be the facilitators of the relationships established between academia, industry and consumers.
- Research institutes and telecom standards institutes, considered to be stakeholders, in so far as research institutes benefit from partnerships with industrial actors and telecom standards institutes see themselves as the interface between industry and the research institutes and implement telecom standards with them.
- Consulting activities in the domains of law, finance and management, considered to be the elements of support, allowing for a more efficient management of the economic and non-economic links of the telecom value chain.

Recently an increasing number of links between industrial (boxes 5, 6, 7 and 8) and public research institutes have developed. These R&D alliances are essentially focused on technological knowledge. But, in this specific high-velocity industry, increasing technological knowledge requires the capability to reduce mismatches between the production and demand sides (Antonelli et al., 2001). Recently, in 2003, a research laboratory focused on the 'uses' of ICT, was created in Sophia-Antipolis by industrial and public research centres: the university of Nice, CNRS (Centre National de la Recherche Scientifique), the GET (Groupement des Ecotes de Télécommunications) and the INRIA (Institut National de la Recherche Informatique Appliquée).

2.3   Telecom Valley: The Role of Associations

Inside the Sophia-Antipolis cluster, many non-profit, business-driven associations play a significant role in knowledge production, distribution and use inside and among firms.

The emergence of clubs and associations in the 1990s

Numerous clubs and associations have been created in order to facilitate exchanges and prospective thinking in the science park. These include: the Sophia-Antipolis Foundation (1984); Telecom Valley (1991); Club Hi' Tech (1992); PERSAN (1992); Data Base Forum (1994); PMI (1999); Sophia Start-Up Club (2000); InTech'Sophia (2001) and so on.

The objective of the Sophia-Antipolis Foundation (FSA), created in 1984 on the initiative of the local public authority, is to develop scientific and cultural exchanges within the science park and to facilitate partnerships and innovation. The FSA is at the origin of the creation of different associations and clubs which dynamize the cultural, human and economic life of the Sophia-Antipolis science park as, for example, Artsophia Association (for cultural activities), Association for the Inhabitants of the Sophia-Antipolis Park (for leisure activities) or the Start-Up Club (for economic activity). These associations not only unite their members around the same interests, but also have as an objective to stimulate inter-community exchanges within the science park. The FSA, for example, organizes different forums and thematic breakfasts, edits a newsletter, receives international delegations and organizes annual meetings of all local professional clubs and associations.

The FSA's activity and the crisis of the 1990s resulted in the formation of numerous professional clubs, expressing the growing need for communication among the scientific and economic actors of the high-tech industries of this region. For example, as one of its delegates indicates, the objective of the Sophia Start-Up Club is:

> to federate, to bring together firms and to organize regular events. Every second Monday, for a duration of four hours we bring together entrepreneurs, owners

of start-ups, top managers of other firms, investors. In fact, the objective of the Sophia Start-Up Club is to connect firms located not only in the Park but all over France, or even European or international ones, and to help them create relationships with investors, lawyers, and with all the actors who should and do get to know each other during these meetings.

Recently, initiatives which aim at reinforcing the links between public and private research have multiplied. In 2001 for example, INRIA launched a scientific and technical club, InTech'Sophia, whose main objective is to bring together industrial actors and INRIA researchers in order to help them exchange and share experience. These different communities facilitate inter-community endogenous and/or exogenous exchange dynamics within the science park, by responding to a general desire to open borders of the different communities. This corresponds to the principle of cross-fertilization. Beyond being capable of acquiring information on a given theme or a shared interest, these communities continue to open themselves and thus create an environment which favours exchanges.

Telecom Valley: the emergence of a uses-oriented community of interests
Telecom Valley[1] (TV) is a non-profit, business-driven association founded in 1991 by eight charter members, Aerospatiale Satellites (now Alcatel Space Industries), AT&T Paradyne, Digital Equipment (now Hewlett-Packard/Compaq), ETSI (European Telecommunications Standards Institute), France Telecom, IBM, Rockwell International and Texas Instruments.

Today TV brings together close to 80 members representing locally over 8000 employees and €3 billion of annual turnover. It is a group of firms which operate in the same domain of telecommunications (in the broad sense of the term) and local institutions which have competed against each other or cooperated together. All these actors share a common ambition:

> to become one of the most significant communities anticipating, developing and promoting the use, services and technologies which will constitute the future of the 'Information Society'.

For this reason TV tries to connect diverse industries (micro-electronics, information technology and telecommunication and so on) in order to create some generic and shared knowledge about the future evolution of the telecommunications uses and services. This role is essential to maintaining a better coordination of investments inside R&D and for joining investments inside specific technological trajectories and market niches. Additionally, TV wishes to become a European or a global leader in certain domains of expertise, such as intelligent networks, wireless communication, the development of data transmission software and so on.

To this end, TV organizes four commissions: 1) training, 2) research and development, 3) communication and 4) partnerships, directed by a steering committee. The activity of these commissions is oriented towards a double objective: (i) to obtain a global reputation in these domains and (ii) to structure the interactions between its members in order to facilitate exchanges and cross-fertilization processes. In the first case, the different activities include attracting new firms, providing advice to institutional decision-makers and training organisms, and organizing exhibitions of innovative technologies. The second objective presupposes the existence of a real procedural authority for the entire community to progress towards its objective of knowledge creation. Thus, 'rules of good behaviour' within the community have progressively emerged thanks to diverse prizes such as 'CLIPSAT' CLIent Partenaire SATisfait Trophy (which rewards a sub-contractor rated best by customers on the basis of an enquiry realized each year) – or the 'Innovation Prize' (which rewards the most original project in the domain of telecommunications or related services). Moreover, TV elaborates, in a more or less official manner, the membership rules. As a result, certain SSII have been excluded because their practices were evaluated by the Partnership Commission as being disloyal. The role of the prizes is far from trivial here because they create a form of legitimization of TV for regulating the network by the implementation of certain organizational rules. This also generates a climate for trust-building between firms by an acknowledgement of specific capabilities and competencies. It also leads to the emergence of a specific cluster's identity which tends to favour exchanges and combinations of knowledge. Thus, Telecom Valley tries to structure the network of cooperation by formal or informal rules as well as by codification of knowledge between its members.

3 CODIFICATION AND STRUCTURATION INSIDE THE SOPHIPOLITAN TELECOM NETWORK: THE BUILDING OF AN EPISTEMIC COMMUNITY

At the beginning of the 2000s, it is becoming crucial for global firms not only to benefit from external links with partners and parent companies, but also to establish strong regional links in which local high-tech SMEs and research institutes play a key role for sustaining innovative capabilities.

The KMP Project[2] launched in 2002 is illustrative of this evolution. Indeed, the objective of this project is to propose an innovative 'knowledge management solution' including a map of competencies present in Telecom Valley. The building of this web service also entails a process of knowledge articulation and codification between its members, transforming Telecom Valley into an epistemic community.

3.1   The KMP Project and the Building of a Map of Competencies

KMP is an experimental ICT infrastructure: a semantic web service of competencies. The goal is to have a better identification of actors and projects while facilitating the cooperation and the creation of a shared language between its members. Telecom Valley's objective has been to increase innovation and technical knowledge by sustaining collaborative agreements between academic and industrial actors. This objective has emerged because of the perception of a lack of connections inside the cluster generated by a lack of mutual understanding linked to the multi-technological context of this cluster. Contrary to industrial districts, communities of practices inside the Telecom Valley are distributed along diverse professions which lacked some similar vision of the world and some shared codes for communicating and for implementing innovative projects.

In this perspective, the aim of the KMP project can be observed as follows:

- a description of firms' competencies (technical, managerial and relational ones) in order to increase mutual understanding;
- the building of a shared language for facilitating the exchange and the combination of competencies;
- the elaboration of a shared vision of business including an understanding of market characteristics and customer needs in order to build a suitable representation of innovation opportunities.

In order to meet all these goals, a competence mapping tool has been initiated for increasing the portfolio of competencies inside the network including industrial partners and academic ones. The principal aim is not to disclose the content of competencies but to offer some visibility of them in order to accelerate exchanges and combination inside the network. In effect:

> firm-based competences and capabilities ... are not simply 'in the air' or 'untraded'. They are real factors which emerge from, and are reproduced through, the interaction of agents where some systems of interaction are better or more competent, at facilitating some kinds of outcome than are others. (Lawson, 1999)

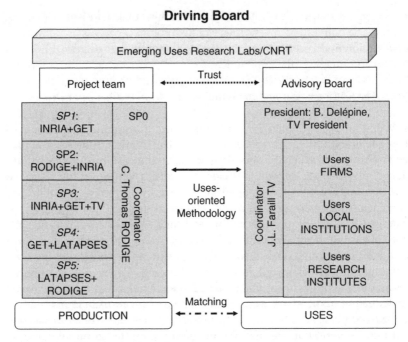

Figure 5.2　The driving board

The methodology of the KMP project is uses-oriented and based on:

● the co-conception of the prototype with the Telecom Valley users;
● the co-evolution of the prototype services and the uses.

The users are involved in the advisory board and are in permanent inter-action with the project team, drawn from diverse academic fields (econom-ics Latapses/GET, management Rodige/GET, computer science INRIA/GET, ergonomy INRIA). The main role of the advisory board is to build a collective validation at each stage of the prototype conception. This project organization is summarized in Figure 5.2.

In this context, uses are not given ex ante but are the result of a perma-nent co-evolution between the project team and the Telecom Valley advi-sory board. For example, at the beginning Telecom Valley's request about the KMP project was the identification of competencies in order to find a partner, but progressively a new demand emerged which was more oriented to the identification and analysis of clusters.

This project is particularly interesting for observing knowledge sharing and diffusion inside a network. Indeed, in the network configuration, the

Table 5.1   Methodological issues for implementing codification

Principles of organizational	Aristotelian causes competences	Categories/codes
Action principle	Efficient cause	Action
Final principle	Final cause	Beneficiary (for whom)
		Business activity (for which kind of market)
Visibility principle	Formal cause	Deliverable (for what result)
Systemic principle	Material cause	Resources (technological and managerial)

codification process appears to be more difficult than in other organizational designs because each member has to evaluate which part of knowledge has to be protected and which part can be shared and transformed into a collective or a public good. This means that it is necessary to create a context in which there is enough incentive for producing and sharing collective knowledge and enough energy to overcome the reluctance due to possible misunderstandings between firms during the codification process.

This tool may have different structuring effects within the network, such as developing the 'epistemic community', sharing of an entrepreneurial vision, favouring the synergy of individual varieties and creating a better understanding of implemented practices. In a long-term perspective, the aim of this infrastructure is to enhance the social learning cycle inside the cluster by reinforcing and creating links inside and outside Sophia-Antipolis.

3.2 The Process of Codification in Practice

The codification process includes diverse stages: model building, language creation and the writing of messages. These stages are not sequential but iterative ones implying the co-evolution of diverse forms of knowledge (tacit, articulated and codified).

Starting from the Trivium[3] methodology, an abstract representation of competences based on five points – action, deliverable, business activity, beneficiary and key resources (organizational or technical ones) – has been proposed. These five categories constitute the model of competencies based on the managerial literature on organizational competencies and the four Aristotelian causes (Rouby and Thomas, 2004). They are presented in Table 5.1.

These categories constitute an abstract level of codification allowing for the creation of codes. These codes permit the location of competencies and their comparison, depending on the interest and vision of the actor, who is able to choose the appropriate combination of relevant points. These first points for representing competencies are still being used and absorbed by actors. They constitute the first codes shared by the community and the first bricks for building the shared language. This shared language is based on the elaboration of specific ontologies for each category (action, beneficiary, business activity, deliverable and resources). An ontology[4] defines worlds constituting the area in which the knowledge will be represented by the diverse actors involved. In the KMP project, the resource ontology is very difficult to build because of the multi-technological context of actors present in the network.

Once competencies are identified and located, a precise description is suggested, including a description of the problem solved by the competency (for instance the storage of data on chips) and the way in which this problem is solved (the know-how, skills, equipment on the building of chips). This description is made without the precision of categories, allowing each firm to be more or less precise on this strategic aspect and to use informal language for this purpose.

Two levels of codification are present in the KMP model:

- An abstract level allowing the identification of the minimum number of categories necessary for modelling competencies. At this level a formal language is required notably through ontology.
- A more concrete level allowing to each firm to present its own competencies according to their communicative strategies.

The first abstract level provides the scope of competencies and allows their localization and their potential comparison. The second, concrete, level illustrates the depth of codification for each competency. The depth of codification should enable the evaluation of the potential value of the combination of competency with a partner for building collaboration.

3.3   Content of Codification and Driving Forces

The content of the codification and more precisely its scope and its depth are driven by the objectives of the process and the willingness of actors involved. The motivation and commitment of actors has been progressively fostered by the 'uses-oriented' methodology. Three main driving forces have been identified: first the lead users, second the increased interest of partners, third the cognitive dimension and the non-neutrality of the codification process.

The role of lead users
At the beginning of the project only a limited number of lead users were really involved in its elaboration and launch. We can identify three types of

lead users, two of them belonged to the corporate level and a third to the individual level:

- Firms which have important collaborative agreements and see in the KMP Project an immediate way of reducing their transactions costs.
- Firms that were still engaged in knowledge management practices at a corporate level which were consequently sensitive to codification and saw in the longer term the direct value of this tool for their company.
- Individuals involved in order to increase their social capital and their potential mobility inside the network.

The role of firms was crucial because of the identity and the size of these firms (the subsidiaries of world leaders in their respective fields). The involvement of these firms has given some credibility to the KMP Project and has created some bandwagon effects. These firms have encouraged some suppliers to enter the project and also to become lead users. At the pre-launch stage, five firms and one regional institution were clearly involved allowing for the establishment of the project, its funding and launch. This stage highlights the political dimension of codification based on market power.

The role of individuals is quite distinct but also essential, as they participate actively in the KMP dynamic and the design of the tool. Many scholars have underlined the influence of key individuals in the success of ICTs – for playing the role of 'coaches' and for being engaged in technology–user mediation (Roberts, 2000).

The increased interest and the progressive enlargement implication of actors

Since the launch of the first advisory board, open to all the members of Telecom Valley, a large number of firms have announced their intentions to join the KMP Project. Today, ten firms, two regional institutions and three research institutions belong to the advisory board. These actors create some significant 'network externalities' for the development and the diffusion of the project. The effective launch of KMP and the presentation of some tangible results (such as the identification of codes to describe competencies) have enlarged the implication of users by a better understanding of its aim.

Indeed the codification of competencies is linked to a growing interest of actors involved in the process. The codification entails a dynamic of collective representation concerning the portfolio of competencies inside the network, allowing the actors to evaluate their position and their action capacity. In a network diverse individual and collective interests are present:

- Find a suitable way to add value via individual corporate competencies.
- Find a partner for solving problems in areas where internal competencies are lacking.
- Have a better understanding of partners' needs for improving the demonstration of internal competencies.
- Share some joint resources for achieving a better exploitation of the network competencies.
- Create some shared vision of the market for developing present and future projects.

One way to achieve these aims is to build a collective representation of the territory and an interactive representation of it through an evolutionary map of competencies. This structure is both the prerequisite and the result of actors expressing their own and collective interests. The global aim is not to codify know-how for its own sake but to codify competencies in order to combine them more accurately.

The step-by-step approach, developed by the uses-oriented methodology, allows for a progressive involvement of actors in sustaining a process of adoption/adaptation in the prototype-building (Latour, 1989) and for generating trust among all the partners of the project (Lazaric and Lorenz, 1998).

The cognitive dimension and the non-neutrality of the codification process
Interest in the project is also linked to diverse cognitive factors:

- The perception of the non-neutrality of the codification process. For example, in the application developers' segment of the value chain ((8) in Figure 5.1) where competition is high between firms, the lead users have asked to create a team in order to develop a mutual understanding about the building of the same part of the technological ontology. The creation of this shared language constitutes a crucial stage for the project development and trust-building between competitors. They also find a compromise about the depth of description at the concrete level.
- All these interactions around the prototype design increased the amount of articulated knowledge inside Telecom Valley, generating not only input for the codification project but also some knowledge externalities by reinforcing potential combinations between members of the network (Håkansson, 2003).

● These interactions are producing some shared knowledge about the understanding of market characteristics and the innovation opportunity, reinforcing the effectiveness of the firms' development strategies.

These three points show the codification in its political and cognitive dimensions. These two dimensions are intertwined. For example the cooperation of firms belonging to (8) in Figure 5.1 for the building of technical ontology has transformed their industrial relationships, showing them that cooperation could be useful notably for their participation in European contracts.

Consequently our case study shows the importance of negotiation on the content, depth and precision of forms of codified knowledge, leading to the creation of new collective representation inside a cluster. This negotiation is not only based on the political dimension (for obtaining a voluntary commitment of members to the economic aims of the project) but also on the cognitive dimension, for building ontologies enabling the representation of competencies and knowledge. If lead users and existing division of labour inside the cluster are important triggers for the beginning of the codification process, more important are the collective negotiations that create belief in the codification process and pave the way for positive convictions on its outcomes.

3.4   The Progressive Legitimization of TV as an Epistemic Community

The active involvement of TV in the process of competencies codification via the KMP Project legitimizes its role in the production of knowledge and in the regulation of the cluster, transforming this association into a real epistemic community.

Knowledge creation and leadership of the regional telecommunication cluster

Created by the major telecommunication companies, Telecom Valley started as a lobbying association. Its role has been progressively enriched by the creation of four commissions, but as each firm was aiming to preserve its own autonomy, informal relationships prevailed, impeding the creation of specific assets inside TV, for example, human assets dedicated to maintaining and regulating the social network. The KMP Project and the codification involved have transformed the function of TV which has been consequently legitimized in this role of knowledge creation and regulation. Recently this new role has been accepted by all the members of TV, and the association is now looking at ways of developing KMP in a more extensive way. That is to say, including its extension to all the members of the Sophipolitan telecom cluster and then to all the regional members of the telecom cluster. This change is crucial because it acknowledges the role of TV in the creation and the regulation of knowledge by the hiring of specific human assets dedicated to the project. Having acquired a specific competency in codification and knowledge regulation, TV aims to diffuse its methodology outside the Sophia-Antipolis area in order to expand its leadership inside the PACA region.[5]

The regulation of knowledge and leadership in the Sophipolitan area

An important outcome of the KMP Project has been to convey the nature of the diversity of existing competencies, in other words, their similarity and complementarity, according to Richardson's terminology (1972). 'Similarity' in the KMP Project related to competencies sharing the same 'action' and 'resources' whereas 'complementarity' was about competencies found within the same 'business activity' which could be combined if belonging to different organizations.

Inside the Sophia-Antipolis area, many non-profit, business-driven associations play a significant role in knowledge production, distribution and use within and between firms. The 1990s were characterized by the creation of a number of associations, as we mentioned earlier. This form of governance was the main vector used by the actors to collectively face the constraints induced by changes. However, their proliferation has also been a source of problems. It has led to 'congestion effects' and to visibility problems with respect to the organization of the socio-economic relations of Sophia-Antipolis.

Similarity and complementarity concepts have also had some structural effects within the whole territory of Sophia-Antipolis. SAME (Sophia-Antipolis Micro Electronics) is an association set up recently in order to reinforce R&D policy within the micro-electronic sector. This initiative was perceived by other associations as representing a potential obstacle to visibility within the territory. For example the Hi' Tech club argued that different associations could impede the fostering of interactions (by introducing an overly fragmented new division of labour within the cluster). This dispute was finally solved by TV, which proposed to clearly distinguish between the different roles that associations have within the cluster. Consequently associations like SAME play a crucial role by promoting technological innovations in clustering firms which have similar competencies. Other associations, such as Club Hi' Tech or Telecom Valley, have more of a horizontal role, orienting markets and defining the future uses of different technological areas. Consequently these two associations are clustering firms which have complementary competencies.

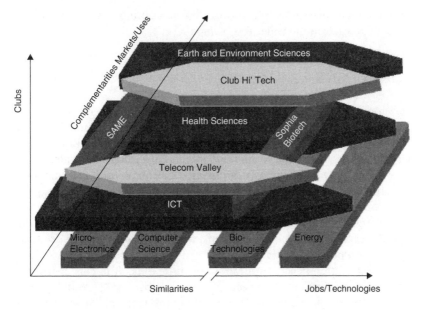

*Figure 5.3   Similarity and complementarity as structuring the
          Sophipolitan area*

Thus, the KMP Project has given rise to a process of knowledge articulation and codification between its members, structuring the Sophipolitan area and transforming the role of the different associations or clubs by delimiting their specific role in supporting innovation or in orienting the long-term strategy of firms more clearly (see Figure 5.3).

Recently TV has suggested that all clubs and associations should locate their role in terms of fostering complementarities (market-oriented) or similarities (technological innovation-oriented). This result has to be shown in the very important event regulating Sophia-Antipolis – the annual 'Club's Day' – where all associations and clubs have to present a map illustrating and promoting their specific role. The diffusion of the KMP methodology beyond the telecom cluster shows the increasing leadership of TV:

The extension of this leadership is reinforced in two ways. First, by an internal legitimization of the association by its members of its ability to regulate and validate the codification process based on the collective negotiation process. This legitimacy has generated important trustworthiness effects crucial for generating knowledge transfer and for articulating knowledge (Szulanski et al., 2004). Second an external legitimization of the TV association by firms outside the Sophipolitan cluster and by regional actors for extending the codification process and for selecting future innovative research projects in the wider PACA region.

CONCLUSION

This codification process highlights the role of Telecom Valley for coordinating and guiding the activities of diverse actors by providing them with information about future innovative opportunities inside and outside the network. A real epistemic community is emerging as Telecom Valley paves the way for knowledge articulation by the creation of codification boundaries and limits. Telecom Valley could be seen as what Haas (1992) called a 'procedural authority', reducing 'cognitive distance', reinforcing proximity and giving sense to the codification process. Such a community, sharing both the explicit and tacit elements of knowledge, facilitates the exchange of ideas and possibly innovatory combinations (Håkansson, 2003).

The codification process appears to be more difficult in clusters than in other types of organizations because each member has to evaluate which part of the knowledge has to be protected and which part can be shared and transformed into a collective or public good. This means that it is necessary to create a context providing sufficient incentive to produce and share collective knowledge and enough energy to overcome the reluctance arising from possible misunderstandings between firms during the codification process.

Consequently, a web service of competences is a social construction, based on cognitive and political dimensions. It has to be built by and for the actors themselves in a process of co-evolution. This codification could not be driven by external actors such as regional institutions. The methodology of both conception and step-by-step implementation guarantees trust-building inside the codification process and between the behavioural attitudes of partners with diverse goals toward the KMP project. Trust-building is a prerequisite for the successful transfer of tacit knowledge (Szulanski et al., 2004). Moreover, it also allows for the codification process to go beyond the initial restricted objectives.

Trustworthiness is crucial because inter-community knowledge diffusion presupposes, as we have seen before, the elaboration of a common language and of a shared frame of reference as well as of a clearly defined objective of knowledge creation, recognized and validated beyond the frontiers of the initiating community. Our case study underlines the importance of the collective negotiation involved in the codification process allowing the emergence of a procedural authority crucial for the creation and regulation of knowledge inside a cluster (Haas, 1992).

These elements are characteristic of an epistemic community. It is therefore interesting to note that by pursuing their 'exchange' objective, certain communities of interest become true epistemic communities.

NOTES

1. Further information is available at: http://www.telecom-valley.fr.
2. KMP Project 'Knowledge Management Platform' – part of the Minister of Telecommunication's 'RNRT' French Telecom programme called 'Réseau National de Recherche en Telecommunication', implemented between academic partners and industrial partners, http://www.telecom.gouv.fr/rnrt/projets/res_02_88.htm.
3. See the project 'Connaissance 2001', Partners (CEA, Urfist, Trivium), http://www.urfist.cict.fr.
4. 'An ontology is an object capturing the expressions of intentions and the theory accounting for the aspects of the reality selected for their relevance in the envisaged applications scenarios' (Gandon, 2001).
5. The PACA acronym comes from Provence-Alpes-Côte d'Azur, a French *region* which ranges from Marseilles to the Italian border.

REFERENCES

Albino, V. and A.C. Garavelli (1999), 'Knowledge Transfer and Inter-firm Relationships in Industrial Districts: The Role of the Leader Firm', *Technovation*, **19**: 53–64.

Albino, V., A.C. Garavelli and G. Schiuma (2001), 'A Metric for Measuring Knowledge Codification in Organisation Learning', *Technovation*, **21**(7): 413–22.

Ancori, B., A. Bureth and P. Cohendet (2001), 'The Economics of Knowledge: The Debate about Codification and Tacit Knowledge', *Industrial and Corporate Change*, **9**(2): 255–87.

Antonelli, C., J.L. Gaffard and M. Quéré (2001), 'Interactive Learning and Technological Knowledge: The Localized Character of Innovation Processes', *Conference 'Nouvelle économie'*, Sceaux, May 17–18.

Avadikyan, A., P. Llerena, M. Matt, A. Rozan and S. Wolff (2001), 'Organisational Rules, Codification and Knowledge Creation in Inter-organisation Cooperative Agreements', *Research Policy*, **30**(9): 1443–58.

Brown, J.S. and P. Duguit (1991), 'Organizational Learning and Communities of Practice: Towards a Unified View of Working, Learning and Innovation', *Organization Science*, **2**: 40–57.

Brown, J.S. and P. Duguid (1998), 'Organising Knowledge', *California Management Review*, **40**(1): 90–111.

Castells, M. and P. Hall (1994), *Technopoles of the World*, London: Routledge.

Cohendet, P. and P. Llerena (2003), 'Routines and Incentives: The Role of Communities in the Firm,' *Industrial and Corporate Change*, **12**(1): 271–97.

Cohendet, P. and W.E. Steinmuller (2000), 'The Codification of Knowledge: A Conceptual and Empirical Exploration', *Industrial and Corporate Change*, **9**(2): 195–209.

Cohendet, P. and P. Llerena (2001), 'Routines, Communities and Organizational Capabilities', paper presented to the DRUID Conference in Honour of Richard R. Nelson and Sidney G. Winter, Aalborg, Denmark, 12–15 June.

Cooke, P. and R. Huggins (2003), 'High Technology Clustering in Cambridge', in F. Sforzi (ed.), *The Institutions of Local Development*, Aldershot, UK: Ashgate, pp. 51–74.

Coombs, R. and R. Hull (1998), 'Knowledge Management Practices and Path-dependency in Innovation', *Research Policy*, **27**(3): 239–55.

Cowan, R. and D. Foray (1997), 'The Economics of Codification and the Diffusion of Knowledge', *Industrial and Corporate Change*, **6**(3): 595–622.

Cowan, R., P.A. David and D. Foray (2000), 'The Explicit Economics of Codification and Tacitness', *Industrial and Corporate Change*, **9**(2): 211–53.

Divry, C. and N. Lazaric (1998), 'Mémoire organisationnelle et codification des connaissances', *Revue Internationale de Systémique*, **12**: 3–11.

Foray, D. and W.E. Steinmuller (2001), 'Replication of Routine, the Domestication of Tacit Knowledge and the Economics of Inscription Technology: A Brave New World?', paper presented to the DRUID Conference in Hounour of Richard R. Nelson and Sidney G. Winter, in Aalborg, Denmark, 12–15 June.

Fransman, M. and J. Krafft (2002), 'Telecommunications Industry', *The Handbook of Economics, International Encyclopedia of Business and Management*, W. Lazonick (ed.), London: Thomson.

Gandon, F. (2001), 'Engineering an Ontology for a Multi-agents Corporate Memory System', INRIA Research Report, INRIA, France: http://www.inria.fr/rrrt/rr-4396.html.

Grandori, A. and B. Kogut (2002), 'Dialogue on Organization and Knowledge', *Organization Science*, **13**: 224–31.

Granovetter, M. (1985), 'Economic Action and Social Structure: The Problem of Embeddedness', *American Journal of Sociology*, **91**: 481–510.

Grimaldi, R. and S. Torrisi (2001), 'Codified-Tacit and General-Specific Knowledge in the Division of Labour among Firms: A Study of the Software Industry', *Research Policy*, **30**: 1425–42.

Haas, P.M. (1992), 'Introduction: Epistemic Communities and International Policy Coordination', *International Organization*, **46**(1): 1–35.

Håkansson, L. (2002), 'Creating Knowledge – the Power and Logic of Articulation (What the Fuss is All About)', paper presented at the Oslo LINK conference, Norway, 1–2 November.

Håkansson, L. (2003), 'Epistemic Communities and Cluster Dynamics: On The Role of Knowledge in Industrial District', DRUID Summer Conference: Creating, Sharing and Transferring Knowledge, Copenhagen, 12–14 June.

Heflin, J., R. Volz and J. Dale (2002), 'Web Ontology Requirements', Proposed W3C Working Draft, February: http://km.aifb.uni-karlsruhe.de/owl/index.html.

Hirschman, A.O. (1970), *Exit Voice and Loyalty*, Cambridge, MA: Harvard University Press.

Johnson, B., E. Lorenz and B.-Å. Lundvall (2002), 'Why all this Fuss about Codified and Tacit Knowledge?', *Industrial and Corporate Change*, **11**(2): 245–62.

Knudsen, T. (2000), 'Why Tacit Knowledge Protects the Firm's Evolutionary Potential and Why Codification Does Not?', working paper presented for the workshop 'Cognition and Evolution in the Theory of the Firm', Max Planck Institute, Jena.

Kogut, B. (2000), 'The Network as Knowledge: Generative Rules and the Emergence of Structure', *Strategic Management Journal*, **21**: 405–25.

Latour, B. (1989), *La science en action*, Paris: Gallimard.

Lawson, C. (1999), 'Towards a Competence Theory of the Region', *Cambridge Journal of Economics*, **23**, 151–66.

Lazaric, N. (2003), 'Trust Building inside the "Epistemic Community": Some Investigation with an Empirical Case Study', in F. Six and B. Nooteboom (eds), *The Process of Trust in Organizations*', Cheltenham, UK and Northampton, MA, USA: Edward Elgar, pp. 147–67.

Lazaric, N. and E. Lorenz (1998), 'The Learning Dynamics of Trust, Reputation and Confidence', in N. Lazaric and E. Lorenz (eds), *Trust and Economic Learning*, Cheltenham, UK, and Northampton, MA, USA: Edward Elgar, pp. 1–20.

Lazaric, N., P. A. Mangolte and M.L. Massué (2002), 'Capitalisation des connaissances et transformation de la routine organisationnelle: le cas Sachem', *Revue d'Economie Industrielle*, **101**, 4 ème trimestre: 65–86.

Lazaric, N., P.A. Mangolte and M.L. Massue (2003), 'Articulation and Codification of Collective Know-how in the Steel Industry: Evidence from Blast Furnace Control in France', *Research Policy*, **32**: 1829–47.

Longhi, C. (1999), 'Networks, Collective Learning and Technology Development in Innovative High Technology Regions: The Case of Sophia-Antipolis', *Regional Studies*, June, **33**(4): 333–42.

Lundvall, B.-Å. and B. Johnson (1994), 'The Learning Economy', *Journal of Industry Studies*, **1**(2): 23–42.

Mangolte, P.A. (1997), 'La dynamique des connaissances tacites et articulées: une approche socio-cognitive', *Economie Appliquée*, **L**(2): 105–34.

Mansell, R. and E. Steinmuller (2000), *Mobilizing the Information Society*, Oxford: Oxford University Press.

Muller, P. (2004), 'Autorité et gouvernance des communautés intensives en connaissances: une application au développement du logiciel libre' ('Authority and the governance of knowledge-intensive communities: an application to the development of open source software'), *Revue d'Economie Industrielle*, **106**(2): 49–68.

Nightingale, P. (2001), 'If Nelson and Winter are Only Half Right about Tacit Knowledge, Which Half? A Reply to David, Foray and Cowan', paper presented to the DRUID Conference in Honour of Richard R. Nelson and Sidney G. Winter, Aälborg, Denmark, 12–15 June.

Nonaka, I. and H. Takenchi (1995), *The Knowledge Creating Company: How Japanese Companies Create the Dynamics of Innovation*, New York: Oxford University Press.

Nooteboom, B. and R.K. Woolthuis (2003), 'Cluster Dynamics', to be published in a farewell volume for Jan Lamboog, Kluwer.

Polanyi, M. (1958), *Personal Knowledge Towards a Post-critical Philosophy*, London: Routledge and Kegan Paul.

Richardson, G.B. (1972), 'The Organization of Industry', *Economic Journal*, **82**(327): 883–96.

Roberts, J. (2000), 'From Know-how to Show How: Questioning the Role of Information and Communication Technologies in Knowledge Transfer', *Technology Analysis & Strategic Management*, **12**(4): 429–43.

Rouby, E. and C. Thomas (2004), 'La codification des compétences organisationnelles: l'épreuve des faits', *Revue française de Gestion*, **149**: 51–68.

Steinmueller, W.E. (2000), 'Will Information and Communication Technologies Improve the "Codification" of Knowledge?', *Industrial and Corporate Change*, **10**(2): 361–76.

Szulanski, G., R. Cappetta and R. Jensen (2004), 'Knowledge Transfer and the Moderating Effect of Causal Ambiguity', *Organization Science*, **15**(5): 600–613.

von Hippel, E. (1987), 'Cooperation between Rivals: Informal Know-how Trading', *Research Policy*, **16**: 291–302.

Von Krogh, G., S. Speath and K.R. Lakhani (2003), 'Community Joining and Specialization in Open Source Software Innovation: A Case Study', *Research Policy*, **32**(7): 1217–241.

Wenger, E. (1998), *Communities of Practice: Learning, Meaning and Identity*, Cambridge: Cambridge University Press.

Winter, S. (1987), 'Knowledge and Competence as Strategic Assets', in D.J. Teece (ed.), *The Competitive Challenge: Strategies for Industrial Innovation and Renewal*, Cambridge, MA: Ballinger, pp. 159–83.

Zollo, M. and S.G. Winter (2002), 'Deliberate Learning and the Evolution of Dynamic Capabilities', *Organization Science*, **13**(3): 339–51.

6. Governance forces shaping economic development in a regional information society: a framework and application to Flanders

Theo Dunnewijk and René Wintjes

INTRODUCTION

Economies differ in the way they are affected by the emerging information society. The information society emerges globally, but the global package of interrelated trends that involves information and communication technology (ICT) emerges in regional economies, which have their own identity. Regional specificity asks and allows for regional-specific responses from policy-makers who want to reap economic benefits from furthering the information society. In this chapter we claim that there is more to be answered in a regional information society than the traditional dilemma: what can be (publicly) planned and what can be left to (private) market forces. Even public–private partnership solutions do not take into account the myriad of governance mechanisms, which shape economic dynamics in a regional information society.

In Section 1 we introduce a conceptual framework that incorporates several governance mechanisms or forces (labelled as 'planning', 'democracy', 'market', and 'serendipity') that shape the conditions as well as the economic dynamics in a regional information society. In Section 2 we apply and test our conceptual framework in developing a better understanding of governance in the regional information society of Flanders.

We lay claim in this chapter to the proposition that a long-term dominance of one or two of the four forces is hampering the development of the information society. Consequently, information society technology (IST) policies should address issues concerning the weakest forces, or worst functioning governance mechanisms. Along with the implementation of IST policies, the use of a force of governance creates momentum elsewhere, so the other forces must be taken into account in the next policy cycle.

1   THE FORCES OF GOVERNANCE IN THE INFORMATION SOCIETY

In the Lisbon strategy the European knowledge economy is seen as capable of using information society technologies to enhance its competitive position in the world economy, thereby increasing the participation and welfare of its citizens. Instead of analysing the governance of knowledge or the knowledge economy we focus on the governance of technologies in which computers and networks are integrated into the everyday environment, rendering accessible a multitude of services and applications.[1] In such a setting, everybody, in everyday life, is confronted with information society technologies. It is indeed the Lisbon strategy, together with the general purpose character[2] of ISTs that necessitates governments – local, regional and national as well as supranational – playing an active role in getting the best out of this technology. As a consequence all EU member states support and maintain the society-wide discourse on governance of the society-wide implementation of ISTs. Although local or regional governments act within the framework of national and EU IST policies, it is the role of the regional government that we wish to elucidate in this chapter.

Governance of the information society is akin to innovation policy. Innovation policy is a sequence of policy actions aimed at enhancing the quantity and efficiency of innovative activities. Innovative activities refer to the creation, adaptation and adoption of new or improved products, processes, or services (Cowan and Van der Paal, 2000). The sequence of policy actions involves stimulating, guiding and monitoring knowledge-based activities within a political jurisdiction of a nation or a region (De la Mothe, 2004). Regarding the information society there is an additional emphasis on society-wide learning including many who in the past were ignored or discounted (Rosell, 1999). We therefore aim at a governance framework that can be applied to a society as a whole and not just to companies or universities as major agents of a regional innovation system. The aim of IST policies is an economic and institutional environment that promotes the creation, dissemination and adaptation and adoption of IST applications and productions that enhance the competitiveness and attractiveness of the regional economy in a collective learning setting.

The framework presented here is an eclectic model because several existing paradigms are incorporated, and it includes many lines of reasoning without providing one simple solution or pointing at a few straightforward hypotheses concerning any of the involved dilemmas. For each part of the framework an extensive literature exists, but in order to arrive at the total picture we propose to put them together in one framework.

The so-called 'planning debate' between Oscar Lange and Friedrich von Hayek began in the early 1930s and revived in the 1970s (Kornai, 1971) in the convergence discussion, because of the increasing intervention in capitalist economies. The discussion ended abruptly with the collapse of the Soviet Union in 1989. Intervention in the management of the capitalist economy gradually shifted into involvement as a main actor in the entrepreneurial economy (Audretsch and Thurik, 2000).

Democracy and the balance between equity and efficiency as important drivers for economic development are what Sen (1999) emphasized, while Minier (1998) pointed to the significance of a democratic state as fertile soil for the impact that public and human capital have on economic growth.

Government became governance as the analysis of politics and policy-making reveals (Pierre, 2000). New political practices emerged after the failures of interventionist and centralized policy-making (Hajer and Wagenaar, 2003). It was the network society that undermined the traditional power of the state. Therefore government turned into governance in a complex networked world and trust became a condition sine qua non (Castells, 2000; Fukuyama, 1995). What remained was the responsibility of the government to act on the societal imbalance regarding inequality, polarization and exclusion (Castells, 2000). Therefore we introduce the market mechanism as a countervailing force to planning in our policy-making framework.

Merton and Barber (2004) drew attention to the significance of 'serendipity' in the search for innovative practices, while Florida (2002) emphasized the role of creative people for innovation. With this fourth force, the force of serendipity, we close the playing field.

That is why the framework starts from these four forces:

- *Planning* as precondition for public policy.
- *Markets* as a precondition for rivalry.
- *Democracy* as a precondition for voice and accountability.
- *Serendipity* as a precondition for creative ideas.

The IST domain in Figure 6.1 is shaped by a combination of these four forces. It is assumed that the actual mix of forces that suits the current IST domain best is different along time and space and elements of all four forces are constantly interacting. Therefore, IST policies can be perceived as constraining or releasing these forces in order to arrive at a favourable mix that suits the IST domain in the region.

Another way to explain the framework is that it distinguishes four different mechanisms by which solutions and decisions concerning policy questions are generated. Questions that are linked for instance to the

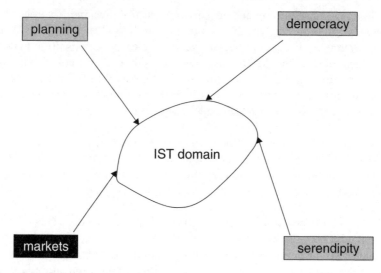

Figure 6.1   The forces of governance

Lisbon strategy or the opportunities of a specific technology are put into perspective by:

- The planning mechanism: let a central public expert decide top-down, follow the leader and go for it.
- The democracy mechanism: discuss it, vote on it and come to agreements and arrangements.
- The market mechanism: let markets value what is economically contestable or not.
- The serendipity mechanism: experiment, let ideas flow and let many flowers blossom.

The next subsection describes the four forces or mechanisms of the framework in more detail and how they relate to the literature.

1.1   Planning

'Planning' in this chapter refers to a strategy of the government, where policy-makers decide on what a region needs and what it has to offer concerning IST developments, for example, which specific technologies or sectors should be supported or protected. The most common rationale for planning is market imperfection or market failure. But, 'notions like market failure cannot carry policy analysis very far, because market failure is ubiquitous' (Nelson and Soete, 1988). Although policy-makers are not perfect in selecting the best thing to do under highly uncertain conditions, planning can nevertheless be very effective to get new things started. For example, public leadership can be very effective concerning investment in infrastructure or selecting technology standards. Regarding the virtue of planning, we also think here of the concomitant and inescapable 'infant industry' argument, which is opportunistic and, by definition, only valid temporarily. Long ago many authors justified premiums from the government to start an activity. Take for example Arthur Dobbs in 'An Essay on the Trade and Improvement of Ireland (1729–31)', Part II:

> . . . premiums are only to be given to encourage manufactures or other improvements in their infancy . . . [and that further help would be in vain] . . . if after their improvement they cannot push their own way.[3]

Planning in complex policy processes, as in the governance of an information society, might be based on different models: a technical bureaucratic model, a political influence model, a social movement model or a collaborative model (Innes and Booher, 2000). So, planning comes in many appearances and intensities: for example, incentives and targets, the promotion of entrepreneurship, subsidies to further innovation and learning, rules and procedures for conflict resolution, redistribution of costs and benefits, and regulation of liability.

But, in whatever way planning is organized, it is a deliberate, wilful act to create a path towards a certain goal, where human agency takes the shape of a hierarchical structure that constitutes a system for action. The virtue of planning as a governance force is in its effectiveness, stemming from powerful and convincing implementation. The major drawback of planning becomes apparent when planning is the dominant mode of governance for a long time. Getting 'locked-in' to the planning force relates to failures in identifying and in addressing alternative solutions that might be (more) successful.

1.2 Markets

Because of the inherent uncertainties attached to new knowledge and information, new technologies, new products or new sectors, markets do not function very well in the valuation of IST developments. Take, for example, the confusing signals from the stock markets over the past decade. These markets are characterized by asymmetric distributed information among the parties and this goes hand in hand with adverse selection. So, buyers and suppliers have different information, especially concerning the exchange of goods and services. The informational poor – mostly 'small' entities like peripheral regions, SMEs and private persons, especially the least well-educated – can be deprived of valuable information, which can lead to 'imperfections' and barriers to competition. For example, dominant telecom operators can have more information or might be more powerful, simply because they are the main network operators and use this power to maintain their dominant position. Countervailing powers are then necessary because of the uncertainties concerning knowledge, caused by the dynamic and immature nature of information and telecom markets.

In the case of ISTs, the external effects of leaving markets 'incomplete' might indeed be quite substantial. In general the market mechanism refers to a basic arrangement through which people can communicate prices, interact with each other and undertake mutually advantageous activities (Sen, 1999). In practice well-functioning markets have to be organized, and a variety of political, institutional and very practical tools, such as finance, may help to overcome some of its imperfections. Action from policy-makers is therefore necessary to accommodate the functioning of markets, for example, in the form of political equity arrangements, competition authorities, market regulators, or legal tools such as intellectual property rights, specific venture capital and complementary business services. National market authorities monitor markets in order that no one can manipulate the market unnoticed. For example, market regulators monitor telecom, insurance and financial markets. Consumer organizations counter asymmetric information. All these actors are trying to get the best out of 'the market mechanism' within the boundaries of their norms and values and no one really controls the market.

In short, markets are powerful constructions to create contestability and rivalry among economic agents, but they have an excluding effect especially when it concerns network technologies. Contestability contributes to welfare, but equity is not automatically guaranteed. Therefore markets and institutional arrangements go hand in hand and these arrangements are shaped and maintained by political ideas that can be quite different among countries.

1.3 Democracy

Policy models are the result of a democratic process and coincide with local governance systems as well (Hesse and Sharpe, 1991). Democracy plays a constructive role in choosing a direction in policies, and IST policy is no exception. Democracy is also helpful in defining local identity or to promote inclusion and it impacts spatial and regional (in)equality and distribution among sectors of the economy.

The strengths and weaknesses of a local society are challenged by the emerging information society and this requires a community-wide answer. Network technologies work as the challengers of local identity because they are appropriation instruments in an economy based on innovation, globalization and flexibility, while they impact social inclusion (Castells, 2000). The value of a network (infrastructure or technology) increases as more people are connected. And creative use of public–private partnerships or alliances within a shared local context opens windows of opportunity to achieve competitive advantages, reinforcing local identity (Dunnewijk and Wintjes et al., 2003).

If policy-makers formulate an information society strategy – as most EU member states and regions have done[4] – and take the lead to implement it, what might be the expected external effects? Besides the social and political arguments, a major economic argument concerns the uncertainty of the welfare loss of the excluded. What are the costs of lost opportunities for the excluded, what are the gains for the included? Public (human) capital formation – as is the objective in education – is a good example, since it seems to have more effect on economic growth in democratic countries than in less democratic countries (Minier, 1998). In his analysis of indicators on national innovation systems, Arundel (2003) found evidence for a relationship between trust, income equality and an innovation index.

In general, democratic structures (in all the above-mentioned senses) are beneficial to the development of an information society. Neither the market nor the policy-maker is perfect in indicating which resources, sectors, regions or technologies will be most vital in the future. In other words: what will be the price of excluding certain people, sectors, regions or technologies? An increase of so-called 'generic policies' versus the decrease of policies targeting specific beneficiaries (whether people, sectors or regions) illustrates the awareness that the price of support focused on specific parts of society may be too high in the end. On the other hand it may also be a sign of increasing risk-aversion among policy-makers. A society can be locked-in in this respect when it is dominated too much and for too long by the force of democracy. That does not mean too much democracy, but it can be an indication of either a lack of decisions, a lack of leadership, (too much) aversion to risk and change, possibly endless discussions in policy-making, slow implementation procedures, and possibly too much influence of vested interests and of the majorities of the past.

1.4 Serendipity

Serendipity concerns the ability of society to solve problems that even policy-makers are not aware of. In this corner of the playing field, creativity, information culture and all kinds of experiments and niches are situated. It is 'the role of change in discovery' and 'the happy accident' in (respectively basic and applied) research that are emphasized by Merton and Barber (2004) in describing the role of serendipity in developing good practices.

Serendipity defined as elements of chance – or, as Louis Pasteur, wrote 'chance favours only the prepared mind'[5] – might be crucial for IST's role in enhancing the competitive advantage of regions. Preparedness must be understood very dynamically because as networks evolve, new answers are necessary not only once upon a time, but steadily (Meyer and Skak, 2002). In this respect an open mind helps to come to new solutions, as it favours the chance of successful learning-by-doing and learning-by-using.

Florida (2002) argues that the defining feature of economic life is the rise of human creativity, because new technologies, new industries and new wealth are emerging. Decades ago Merton (1965) saw the unanticipated effects of 'standing on the shoulders of giants' as very important drivers for what later became known as endogenous economic growth. This economic vision of ICT spillovers runs from ICT applications and their learning processes to new products and new markets by means of knowledge spillovers. By taking into account the social context in which human beings interact from their own preferences (for example, on how they use their leisure, how they learn, how they organize) the phenomenon of ICT-related spillovers comes to life. This is a crucial point as far as ISTs are concerned because the differences between regions (countries) are huge (SCP, 2001).

The ability – to give an example – to innovate in a local innovation system can have quite different characteristics as a consequence of specific local dimensions. Certain locally-embedded skills, ethics or other intangibles could lead to spatially different pathways of IST developments. Information culture differs widely and can be illustrated in more than one layer, for example, social-cultural, institutional and economic. For the social-cultural dimension indications could be the use of free time. For the economic dimension we could perhaps indicate serendipity and creativity by the size of the business services sector: a sector that consists mainly of SMEs supplying ICT, research, legal, technical, promotional and other services to the local market. These niche players, who are typically risk-taking entrepreneurs who spot new markets before others do, are of major importance in helping others (and society at large) to realize the potential gains from ISTs.

However, mere serendipity hampers the selection and exploitation of the many generated solutions, when they are not subsequently taken up by any of the other governance forces.

1.5 Six Dilemmas Implied by the Forces

Apart from being a force in itself, the forces are related, and possibly opposed to each other. Pairwise confrontation yields the dilemmas of development and they are called dilemmas because we assume that development is hampered if a certain balance is lacking between the four forces. The appropriate balance in this respect is defined as leaving the other dilemmas no worse off.

The corners of Figure 6.2 represent the undifferentiated forces of 'planning', 'democracy', 'serendipity' and 'markets'. The arrows symbolize the dilemmas, while the text placed on these arrows puts the dilemma in a certain perspective. The forces can be seen as four sides of a square that embrace all feasible combinations of forces which support IST policies.

Market – democracy   The classical dilemma 'efficiency versus equity' points at the choice between what is an economic necessity and what is needed for democracy? The issues involved in the choices to be made in IST policy are not very different from policy in general: it is a choice between political freedom and economic needs (Sen, 1999). And therefore, there is room to manoeuvre in finding an answer to the challenges and opportunities of the information society.

One-person one-vote seems the guiding principle for democracy, while in competitive markets enterprises also have one vote, that is, they cannot command prices or quantities. In reality political parties as well as enterprises operating in the markets are often powerful institutions, sometimes

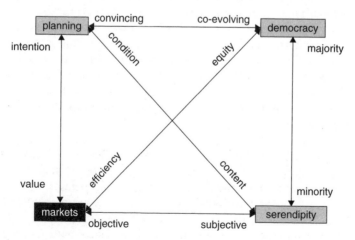

Figure 6.2   The implied dilemmas

even ruling with almost monopoly power (Becker, 1958). Frequently policy-makers are confronted with monopoly power in the information society, for example, because of network effects providing first movers with a winning edge (Shapiro and Varian, 1997). Therefore, the question arises of whether market solutions, in practice, can be regarded as in the interest of the public or not.

Planning – markets   Planning and markets are opposed in the sense that the former tries to materialize an intended effect, while the latter is an immaterial device that assigns value to an economic good or service although no one is able to predict or dictate that value. Intervention can distort the functioning of markets, but markets can be incomplete and prices do not always carry all the information that is needed. Under these conditions some forms of government policy might increase welfare (Greenwald and Stiglitz, 1986).

Planning – serendipity   Planning and serendipity are also opposed in the sense that the latter summons an unexpected content as a solution to an existing but largely unknown problem, while the former doesn't always solve the problems everybody knows, but delivers conditions or a method to deal with decisions and problem-solving in controlled surroundings. But serendipity can also be the lucky result of planning and of 'being prepared'. Anyhow, serendipity is linked to the ability to see and exploit favourable circumstances.

Planning – democracy   Planning and democracy are different in the sense that pure planning is autocratic and convincing because the experts are in charge. So their knowledge is what counts. Pure democracy is in many senses the opposite: everybody has a vote, mere existence as a grown-up is enough to qualify for a vote. The result is quite often that the autocratic 'optimal' solution evolves to take the democratic voice into account without losing contact with the experts. That is why in reality there exist a number of planning styles – from convincing, co-opting and converting to co-evolving (Innes and Booher, 2000).

Markets – serendipity   Pure (neoclassical) markets lead to objective results and do not allow for novelty. Serendipity, on the other hand, is rather subjective. It is like the opposed views on technology development. It can either be deterministic and path-dependent or the result of path creation (Garud and Karnøe, 2001), or even socially constructed (Bijker et al., 1989). Markets are devices or mechanisms allocating what is supplied to what is demanded without surprise while serendipity is unpredictable.

Serendipity – democracy Serendipity is also opposed to democracy, for democracy is not spontaneous. Democracy is deliberate and implies negotiations, convergence of points of view, compromises and alliances, hence the will of a majority. Serendipity may be hampered by compromises and mostly it is the invention of the smallest minority: the individual. However, without democracy (and the other forces) there is only partial diffusion of the invention and the exploitation of the thousand flowers that blossom.

1.6   The Nature of the Model

The presented model is to a large extent eclectic because it incorporates several paradigms[6] and includes many lines of reasoning without providing a simple solution or pointing to a few straightforward hypotheses concerning any of the involved dilemmas.

The Lange-Hayekian planning–market controversy reminds us also of the theory of the firm as set out by Coase, North, and Williamson, focusing on governance mechanisms related to hierarchy and markets to explain the existence of companies.

The four forces and the appreciation of their functioning are to a large extent embedded in societies. Some societies show more trust in markets or in democracy than others and therefore societies emphasize these mechanisms differently.

The embeddedness in society also has policy implications for open methods of coordination, which emphasize the role of identifying and exchanging best practices within Europe. Context-dependency and the large diversity among societies in Europe make simply copying policy practices and institutional qualities problematic. Transnational and interregional policy learning calls for de-contextualization and re-contextualization of policy practices.

Furthering the information society involves an ongoing learning process of finding new balances between the four governance mechanisms, avoiding becoming locked-into or over-emphasizing one or two of them. It also involves addressing the identified dilemmas, because sooner or later the neglected dilemmas will become bottlenecks.

This implies a government role in framing the issues, designing the process, rethinking regulation and building consensus, thereby taking into account the limits of existing institutions. Moreover, engaging society by means of practices that help people processing the issues at stake is essential. In the civic discourse on the Information Society shared values might be discovered and public voice used to solve deadlocks (Rosell, 1999).

This brings us to our main claim that a long-term dominance of one or two of the four forces is the major bottleneck for IST developments.

Consequently IST policies should address issues concerning the weakest forces or worst functioning governance mechanisms. The implementation of IST policies and the use of a force of governance creates momentum elsewhere that must be taken into account in the next cycle of the policy implementation.

In the next section we use this conceptual framework to show the relevance of our main claim that long-term dominance of one or two forces constitutes a bottleneck in the development of a regional information society.

2   THE GOVERNANCE MECHANISMS THAT SHAPE THE INFORMATION SOCIETY OF FLANDERS

In this section we present and interpret empirical findings mainly from a case study on IST developments in the region of Flanders in Belgium (Nauwelaers and Wintjes, 2003). Applying the framework basically means discovering which roles the four forces have played in IST policy in Flanders, and how the policy dilemmas were addressed in Flanders from the 1980s onwards. Since Flanders and its IST policy are embedded in the EU and the EU IST policy, we first describe the three pillars of the IST policy of the EU.

2.1   Multi-level Governance: European and Belgian IST Policy

Since all EU member states have to comply with the EC directives issued in the past, there is no doubt that the IST policy of the EU and national IST policy impacted the situation of Flanders. We therefore start with EU policy and a comparative analysis of the information society of Belgium and three other member states.

Currently the EC's IST policy is based on three interrelated pillars:

- *IST research* is seen as a key to innovation and competitiveness. The budget for IST research for the sixth framework programme is €3.6 bn and is the largest research priority of the EC during 2002–06.
- *The action plan eEurope 2005*[7] launched seven key actions[8] or priorities for IST policy in the EU: (1) the widespread availability and use of broadband networks throughout the Union by 2005 and the development of Internet protocol IPv6; (2) the security of networks and information; (3) *e*Government; (4) *e*Learning; (5) *e*Health; (6) *e*Business; and (7) *e*Inclusion.
- *IST regulation* is aimed at setting the right conditions for competition in the electronic communication sector to reinforce the single market

Table 6.1   Benchmarking Flanders

	Flanders	BEL	EU+	NL	FIN	FRA
Infrastructure	142	153	100	182	109	91
Human resources	92	104	100	171	234	58
eGovernment	93	89	100	77	131	84
ICT usage SMEs	59	100	100	110	105	85
ICT production	112	93	100	82	133	85
R&D in ICT	117	62	100	61	158	81
Internet at home	96	90	100	191	186	56

Source: Dunnewijk et al. (2002).

and to safeguard consumer interests. A liberalized telecommunications industry is seen as a condition sine qua non. Regulation here is essentially a temporary phenomenon: entrants need support from the national regulators and when the desired market conditions have established,[9] regulation can be rolled back. All member states are required to transpose the EU regulatory framework, at least for the core directives.[10]

On the level of the member states the EU IST policy on the one hand implies obligatory transposition of IST regulation, while on the other hand there are opportunities to formulate and implement a specific national IST policy. The same can be said about regions.

So, the question is what is the position of Belgium, with regard to EU IST policy and more specifically what is the position of Flanders? To answer this question we compare Belgium and Flanders with France, The Netherlands, Finland and the EU-15 average. The summary indicators of Table 6.1 are described in Dunnewijk et al. (2002), a study that looks for ways to monitor IST developments in Flanders. The region appears to perform relatively well with respect to ICT production, ICT-infrastructure, and ICT research.

However, in terms of a widespread ICT usage Flanders lags behind. Especially ICT usage in SMEs and the penetration of the Internet in households (see Figure 6.3) which is still surprisingly low compared to many other places in Europe.

2.2   Applying the Framework to Flanders

So far the framework describes the forces statically. However, in general, policy and especially IST policy comes in repeated cycles, not in the least because of (policy) learning effects. This is depicted in Figure 6.4.

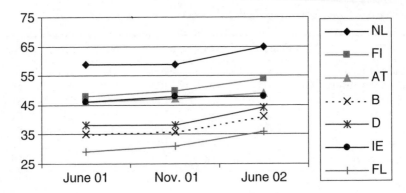

Note: The survey for Flanders was in May 2001 and May 2002.

Source: Flash Eurobarometer 125; and Internetstatistieken Vlaanderen, 3e meting.

Figure 6.3   Internet penetration in households, 2001–02 (%)

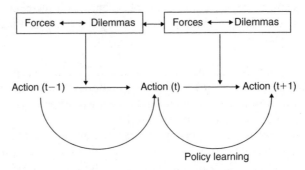

Figure 6.4   Interaction of the policy actions cycles

Applying the framework means assigning the four forces to specific policy actions in Flanders. However, the forces remain under the influence of the dilemmas attached to these forces, as we show below. Evaluation of the policy actions leads to learning and modified policy action in the next policy cycle.

For each of the three pillars of the EC's IST policy we have selected a Flemish policy issue. The issues have been described elsewhere (see Nauwelaers and Wintjes, 2003; Dunnewijk et al., 2002) and they characterize the development of Flanders as an information society, both in terms of public policy and in terms of regional specific strengths and weaknesses.

The first two policy issues must be analysed against the specific regional background of building the identity of Flanders as a technologically advanced 'nation'. The creation of the IMEC research centre and the TV cable operator Telenet respectively relate to the above-mentioned EU topics of 'IST research', and 'IST regulation'. They also relate to the identified strength of Flanders regarding ICT research and ICT infrastructure. A third relevant issue we will address is the relative weakness of Flanders concerning the use of ICTs in households and SMEs. It is largely unknown why the use of ICT in households and companies differs between countries and regions, but there could be a cultural explanation and there is also the possibility of a governance deficit. Before discussing these three specific IST policy issues we discuss the more general development of regional policy in Flanders and the role of the four forces.

2.2.1 Increased regional autonomy generated momentum for public planning in Flanders

Since 1993, Belgium has been a federal state composed of (language) communities and regions. Belgium has three official languages (French, Dutch and German) and they define three communities: the French-speaking community, the Dutch-speaking or Flemish community and a small German-speaking community. In addition, Belgium has three regions: the Flemish region (in the north), the Walloon region (the south) and the small Brussels-Capital region in the centre. Each community and region and the federal state have their own government and parliament (seven in total). Four legal reforms were implemented in 1970, 1980, 1989, and 1993 to reach this federal structure. Within this complex context of federalization, policy-makers in Belgium were for a long time (pre-) occupied with rivalry, bargaining and reaching consensus between regions, communities and the national policy. Within our governance framework this situation can be interpreted as being 'locked-in' to the governance mechanism of democracy. The complex process of federalization of Belgium initially hampered the development of a strong national vision and policy plans concerning the information society. The different regions and (language) communities all had different assets and needs concerning ICT developments. But, with the gained competencies, supported by a strong political will to build on the Flemish identity, a momentum for a strong emphasis on regional planning was created.

Although some deny the existence of a Flemish identity, while others perceive it as just one variant of a Western European identity (Kerremans, 1997), the IST initiatives of the Flemish government were launched within a context of 'nation-building'. With their own full-fledged government, they have formulated their own policies with regard to finance, economics, social welfare, health care, traffic, public works, environment, education and culture. The Flemish government in particular took a high profile with regard to political autonomy. Christian Democratic Chairman Luc Van den Brande was called

'Minister-President', and his executive council was called the 'Government'. The suggestion is that the constitutional reform process has initiated the creation of the Flemish state, not merely an autonomous region within the Belgian Federation. Politicians in the 1980s had chosen 'technology' as the flagship for its new identity and increased autonomy of Flanders: the programmes 'Flanders Technology' and 'Third Industrial Revolution' were launched at gigantic fairs showing the high-tech assets of the regions.

Planning strategies in this nation-building context imply connecting focused or specific IST strategies with public services and promotion. The evidence here is the support for IMEC, the creation of Telenet, and, for instance, the policy to use the public broadcasting services, such as the Flemish Radio and Television (VRT), in the diffusion of ISTs.

2.2.2   Regional public planning for excellence in ICT research: IMEC

IMEC is Europe's leading independent research centre in the field of micro-electronics, nanotechnology, and design methods and technologies for ICT systems. With a budget of €120 million (2001) and a staff of more than 1200 highly qualified people, IMEC performs world-class research, cooperating with 467 partners worldwide. The acronym of IMEC (Inter-university Micro Electronics Centre) reveals how it was founded in 1984 by combining and concentrating the expertise and research activities of a few universities in one centre in Leuven. In the first few years IMEC was heavily dependent on the subsidy from the Flemish government. Today, IMEC generates 76 per cent of its total budget itself; 24 per cent is funded by the Flemish community. Three strategic goals are part of the agreement: to stay a micro-electronic centre of excellence, to increase interactive and multidisciplinary research with universities and enterprises, to include SMEs in Flanders as clients.

Management contracts between the Flemish government and IMEC succeed each other and are discussed in the Flanders parliament. This leads to evolving programmes based on evaluations and impact indicators for a diversity of local spillovers such as the number of spin-off companies, labour mobility and the increased contracts for local companies of which a growing share are in non-ICT industries. Concerning labour mobility it is interesting to note that people working at IMEC are on average very young and employment turnover is high (17 per cent change per year on average). About a third of new talent comes from abroad; while between 65–70 per cent of the people leaving IMEC find new jobs in Flanders. Therefore, many of the globally-attracted talented graduates only work a few years at IMEC and take their knowledge and ideas with them when they leave the company, but remain in Flanders.

Recalling our framework, planning has been the major force used by the Flemish government in creating IMEC. Within the broader and convincing plan to promote technology in Flanders the decision to focus on micro-electronic technology and concentrate in Leuven was a clear sign of public leadership. Over the years the other governance mechanisms (markets, democracy and serendipity) have become more important in the evolution of the public approach to reap benefits for Flanders and increase sustainability.

The government stimulated the search for private research contracts. IMEC managed to develop a good position in the global market, and became less dependent on government subsidies (see Figures 6.5 and 6.6). After the initial selection by Flemish policy-makers of ICT research as a field of priority, the policy-makers have chosen the market mechanism to validate the results and select the most interesting research fields. However, the policy-makers especially asked IMEC to search for clients in Flanders, because such linkages would generate spillovers and enhance embeddedness in the Flemish economy. For many years the income from contract research with Flemish industry was rather limited, but recently the Flemish market has grown considerably (see Figure 6.6).

The force of democracy comes in as the subsidies and the impact on Flanders and the management contracts with IMEC are debated in parliament. The current management agreement with IMEC covers the period 2002–06. The previous one received a positive evaluation in 2002 and therefore the yearly contribution has been increased to €33m, apart from the

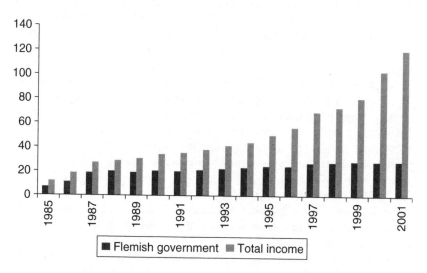

Source: IMEC Annual Reports.

Figure 6.5   Evolution of IMEC's total income, 1985–2001 (€ million)

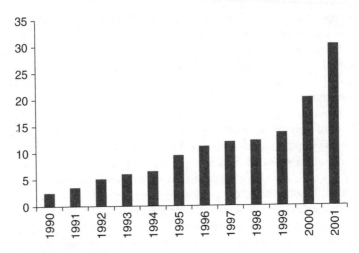

Source: IMEC Annual Reports.

*Figure 6.6   IMEC's total income from contract research with Flemish
industry, 1985–2001 (€ million)*

funding of €37m for set-up which is an investment in a 'clean room'.[11] According to this contract the third strategic goal set for IMEC has been widened to include collaboration with Flemish SMEs within and outside the area of micro-electronics. To meet this target an incubator has been established to stimulate spin-offs from joint research.

An example of the increased importance of serendipity as a mechanism which brings economic benefits from IMEC to spillover to the region is the fact that local clients increasingly are in non-micro-electronic industries, emphasizing the general purpose nature of technologies developed at IMEC. The increased public trust and efforts concerning the force of serendipity can also be witnessed in the emphasis the government has placed on the creation and support by IMEC of spin-off companies.

2.2.3   ICT infrastructure: Telenet

For a long time a comparative advantage of the region concerning ICT infrastructure has been the availability of a dense cable TV network over the whole territory. By the creation of Telenet, Flanders competition in the local loop of the quasi-monopolistic telecom market was introduced and the new technological opportunities could be exploited. Stimulated by the Flemish government the local cable owners in Flanders merged (while in the Walloon region this was not attempted). This merger is, technically speaking, already a success, but from the economic and societal perspective the advantages remain still to be proven. Today, the proportion of broadband users is very high in Flanders, but the lack of cheap access to 'Internet for beginners' might still be a problem concerning the inclusion of notably the poorest and least-aware segments of the population. Even rich populations have their less wealthy citizens and the digital divide is present in Flanders.

The dilemma between market and democracy in our framework touches upon the old dilemma of 'efficiency versus equity'. Concerning the information society we can think of a trade-off between competitiveness of the telecom sector and e-inclusion. Through merging all the small local cable companies Telenet was created, a regional telecom operator exploiting the dense cable network for telephony and data exchanges. With the creation of Telenet we witness the dominance of the force of planning concerning the Flemish ICT infrastructure. The market in fact did not have a chance to select the most profitable local cable companies. The results in terms of penetration of broadband are remarkable in all sub-regions of Flanders, and broadband prices all over Flanders are relatively low. However, the rise of Telenet did not lead to cheaper dial-up connections. This could explain why a saturation point seems to be reached in household Internet penetration at a rather low level.

A new regional strategy is currently being implemented to address this e-inclusion issue, with the development of interactive TV (eVRT). Since almost every household has television and cable, and since television is an even more widely used communication technology than computers, the idea is that developing interactive digital TV will lead to a high level of e-inclusion. Besides the forces of democracy, serendipity entered as a governance mechanism concerning eVRT, since it was publicly promoted as a potential technological test-bed for new developments related to digital TV, for example, concerning the production of content.

The latest management contract introduces iDTV (interactive Digital TV) as well as a role for the eVRT (electronic or e-flemish (Vlaamsche) Radio and TV Broadcasting) as an application service provider (ASP) to unlock the audio-visual archive for the market and public. The digital home platform is a development (pilot) project in 100 participating Flemish households. Set-top boxes deliver digital TV with several applications: interactive games, chat, e-mail, e-banking, e-government, and entertainment. A most remarkable part of eVRT is the building of a new DBVT network (digital video broadcasting – terrestrial). This technology enables the public broadcaster, VRT, to deliver the signal without the incumbent cable monopolist Telenet, which is yet another attempt to increase competition in the local loop.

2.2.4   Relatively low ICT usage in companies and households

In the serendipity corner of the governance framework, creativity, 'info-culture' and all kinds of experiments and niches are situated. Spillovers run from ICT applications to new products and new markets, at least from the economic perspective. Seen from the socio-cultural perspective, human beings interact according to their own preferences (on how they spend their leisure time, how they learn and how they organize and like to communicate) and these preferences impact ICT-related spillovers. The power of serendipity lies in the unpredictable outcome of experiments: 'learning-by-doing' or 'learning-by-using'. Intangible assets embedded in specific preferences and attitudes concerning social interaction and learning generate different pathways of information society developments.

We have noted that besides the effect on e-inclusion, the development of interactive TV is meant to generate many small experiments concerning the development of applications and content based on the force of serendipity.

A broad notion of 'test-beds' is often based on intangible assets, which promote innovative and entrepreneurial behaviour and awareness. These assets can be embedded in specific preferences and attitudes concerning social interaction and learning. For example, the attitude towards entre-preneurship, which in Belgium is rather low compared to most other countries in Europe (Flash Eurobarometer 134, EC 2002).

In the case of Flanders we can also point to the importance of preferences towards modes of communication, since people in Flanders seem to prefer face-to-face communication for social interaction. Such 'info-cultures' can clearly function as 'bottlenecks or accelerators'. So, cultural factors could explain why people in Flanders have taken up IST developments outside work relatively slowly. Again, the eVRT initiative could very well affect this info-culture, bringing IST into every living room in Flanders.

The dimensions of serendipity and regional characteristics with regard to economic development and social-cultural behaviour clearly show that there is probably no strategy that fits all, but these dimensions have to be accounted for in the design of local IST policies.

2.3   Interpretation of the Case of Flanders

The case study on Flanders shows that in the complex context of the many democratic institutions in Belgium, the conflicting interests of regions and communities have prohibited a strong IST policy-push. In the terms of our framework we witness the democracy – planning dilemma (see Figure 6.2). The process of federalization and reform of the democratic institutions hampered the initial development of convincing national policy plans for an information society (as well as co-evolving regional plans). However, the increased regional autonomy generated momentum in which public planning for a 'technological society' evolved into the planning of the information society in Flanders.

Supported by a strong political will to build on the Flemish identity, the region focused on high-tech development. As a form of nation-building the identity-push was a championing strategy to further high-tech industries and provoke spillovers in Flanders (see Shane et. al., 1995). This championing strategy was initiated by the Flemish government under the leadership of its Prime Minister Luc van den Brande and had a pivotal role in convincing others in the region. Policy awareness and numerous convincing and co-evolving programmes have been developed, with IMEC and Telenet as flagships. The linear vision (on technology development) on which these flagships were originally founded induced a strong focus on infrastructures and on the 'hardware' of the information society, rather than on the 'software' aspects and usage and the absorptive capacities for such technological developments of the wider public.

Regarding the telecom infrastructure we conclude that the position of Belgacom is still dominant, but the government's decision to create Telenet, covering all provinces of Flanders, resulted in rivalry concerning the supply and use of broadband connections all over Flanders. In terms of efficiency the force of markets seems to have taken over rather successfully from planning. However, (recalling the markets – democracy dilemma) in terms of equity and inclusion the rise of Telenet has been less successful, because it did not lead to cheaper dial-up connections. With the eVRT initiative the force of serendipity may very well be strengthened, since digital television may indeed become a technological test-bed for new products, services, processes and content.

The developments concerning IMEC show clearly how a development which started out of planning to support a certain technology and sector can have a much wider and more sustainable impact on IST developments in a region, when the other forces take over in terms of governance mechanisms.

So, planning has been the dominant governance mechanism in shaping the information society in Flanders, but soon both the mechanisms of democracy and markets have joined forces. The IST policy became less 'pushy' by incorporating elements of democracy and markets. Most recently, IST policy-makers in Flanders have a special interest in the force of serendipity.

Recent initiatives show a growing attention to users' needs and the recognition of the importance of availability of appropriate applications that could widen the effective usage of ICTs and contribute to regional development in a larger sense. Flanders started IST developments in the planning corner of Figure 6.1, but most recently they have migrated towards the right lower corner of serendipity. Since serendipity is one of the less well functioning mechanisms in Flanders, improvements in this corner will contribute most to finding a new balance of forces.

3   CONCLUSIONS

Returning to the governance framework, we feel confident in saying that all measures, phenomena and capacities in the field of IST-related developments must have a consciously chosen and timely adjusted mixture of the four forces, or governance mechanisms of planning, markets, serendipity and democracy.

Concerning an information society the governance mechanisms of democracy and serendipity help in understanding the relationship between economy, society and technology. In this respect the traditional framework of a dichotomy between the governance mechanisms of public planning and private markets is clearly not sufficient.

The four forces or governance mechanisms and the appreciation of their functioning are to a large extent embedded in societies. This brings us to our main claim that a long-term dominance of one or two of the four forces is the major bottleneck for IST developments, and consequently, that information society policies should address issues concerning the weakest forces, or worst functioning governance mechanisms.

The embeddedness in society also has policy implications in relation to e-Europe and the open methods of coordination, which have emphasized the role of identifying and exchanging 'best practices' within Europe. Because of 'context-dependency' and the large diversity among societies in Europe, copying policy-practices and copying 'institutional qualities' may not have the desired effect. Transnational and regional policy-learning from cases such as Flanders therefore needs de-contextualization and re-contextualization. Improving economic dynamics in a regional information society calls for policy intelligence in managing change in a context of real time and real place, which can be seen as a 'quality in institutionalization'.

Enhancing the benefits of ISTs involves an ongoing learning process of finding new balances between the four governance mechanisms, avoiding becoming locked-into one or two of them, and addressing the identified dilemmas, because sooner or later the neglected mechanisms will become bottlenecks.

NOTES

1. This is the definition of ISTs currently in use in the sixth framework programme of the European Commission. See: http://www.cordis.lu/ist/workprogramme/wp 0506_en/ 1_4.htm.
2. A general purpose technology is extremely pervasive and is defined as a technology that has scope for improvement when actors use it. It has also a wide variety of uses, that is, many other applications are discovered as it evolves. A general purpose technology also has an economy-wide range of use and strong complementarities in the technological sense as well as in the sense of (price) substitutability (Lipsey et al., 1998).
3. Cited in J. Schumpeter (1972), *History of Economic Analysis*, 8th edn, London: Allen & Unwin, p. 349.
4. As in 'eEurope 2005: an information society for all', an action plan to be presented in view of the Seville European Council, Commission of the European Communities, COM(2002) 263, final. Also the existence of national information society strategies in the EU member states is an example of the society-wide planning of the information society.
5. Quoted in H. Eves (1988), *Return to Mathematical Circles*, Boston: Prindle, Weber and Schmidt, p. 87.
6. That is, at least the techno-economic paradigm (Freeman and Soete, 1997) and the socio-economic paradigm (Etzioni, 2001) and implicitly the paradigms of social and cultural capital as formulated by Becker (1974) and Bourdieu (1986).
7. This action plan, which is the continuation of the eEurope 2002 Action Plan adopted at the Feira European Council in June 2000, forms part of the Lisbon strategy whereby the European Union seeks to create the most competitive and dynamic information economy in the world and to improve its employment and social cohesion by 2010.
8. Progress towards the information society is monitored by the so-called open key coordination procedure which means confronting and comparing national results on 23 benchmark indicators with predefined targets with the aim of formulating a policy in this area.
9. That stage is probably reached when incumbent telecom operators regain some of their lost market shares.
10. The framework, access, authorization, universal service and competition directives.
11. A 'clean room' is a room in which a stepper wafer makes silicon disks in the production of chips.

REFERENCES

Arundel, A. (2003), 'National Innovation System Indicators', 2003 European Innovation Scoreboard: Technical Paper No 5. Luxembourg: European Commission – Enterprise Directorate-General. Available at: http://trendchart. cordis.lu/scoreboards/scoreboard2003/pdf/eis_2003_tp 5_national_innovation_s ystems.pdf.

Audretsch, D.B. and A.R. Thurik (2000), 'Capitalism and democracy in the 21st Century: From Managed to Entrepreneurial Economy', *Journal of Evolutionary Economics*, **10**: 17–34.

Becker, G. (1958), 'Competition and Democracy', *Journal of Law and Economics*, **1**: 105–9.

Becker, G. (1974), 'A Theory of Social Interaction', *Journal of Political Economy*, **82**(6): 1063–93.

Bourdieu, P. (1986), 'The Forms of Capital', in J.G. Richardson (ed.), *Handbook of Theory and Research for the Sociology of Education*, New York: Green wood Press, pp. 241–58.

Bijker, W., T. Hughes and T. Pinch (eds) (1989), *The Social Construction of Technological Systems*, Cambridge, MA, and London: MIT Press.

Castells, M. (2000), *The Rise of the Network Society*, 2nd edn, Oxford: Blackwell Publishers.

Cowan, R. and G. van de Paal (2000), 'Innovation Policy in a Knowledge-based Economy', a MERIT study commissioned by the European Commission DG Enterprise, June.

De la Mothe, J. (2004), 'The institutional governance of technology society, and innovation'. *Technology in Society*, **26**: 523–36.

Dunnewijk, T. and R. Wintjes et al. (2003), 'Identifying Factors of Success and Failure in European IST-related National/Regional Developments': fiste.jrc.es/download/eur 20825en.pdf.

Dunnewijk, T., R. Wintjes and H. Hollanders (2002), 'ICT monitor Vlaanderen: Eindrapport van een haalbaarheidsstudie', IWT Observatorium no. 39, Brussels.

EC (2000), European Commission, *Towards a European Research Area*, COM (2000) 6.

EC (2002), European Commission, DG Regional Policy, 2002, *Regional Innovation Strategies under the European Regional Development Fund, Innovative Actions 2000–2002*.

Etzioni, A. (2001), 'Toward a Socio-economic Paradigm': http://www.sase.org/conf2001/abstracts/etzioni_paradigm.html.

Florida, R. (2002), *The Rise of the Creative Class*, New York: Basic Books.

Freeman, C. and L. Soete (1997), *The Economics of Industrial Innovation*, 3rd edn, Cambridge, MA: MIT.

Fukuyama, F. (1995), *Trust: The Social Virtues and the Creation of Prosperity*, New York: Free Press.

Garud, R. and P. Karnøe (2001), 'Path Creation as a Process of Mindful Deviation', in R. Garud and P. Karnøe (eds), *Path Dependence and Creation*, Mahwah: Lawrence Erlbaum Associates Publishers, (pp. 1–38).

Greenwald, B. and J. Stiglitz (1986), 'Externalities in Economics with Perfect Information and Incomplete Markets', *Quarterly Journal of Economics*, **101**(2): 229–64.

Hajer, M.A. and H. Wagenaar (eds) (2003), *Deliberative Policy Analysis: Understanding Governance in the Network Society*, Cambridge: Cambridge University Press.

Hesse, J. and L. Sharpe (1991), 'Local Government in International Perspective: Some Comparative Observations', in J. Hesse (ed.), *Local Government and Urban Affairs in International Perspective*, Baden-Baden: Nomos.

Innes J. and D. Boohe (2000), 'Planning Institutions in the Network Society: Theory for Collaborative Planning', in W. Salet and A. Faludi (eds), *Revival of Strategic Spatial Planning*, Amsterdam: Elsevier/Oxford University Press.

Kerremans, B. (1997), 'The Flemish Identity: Nascent or Existent?' http://www.respublica.be/jaargangen/jaargang 1997%282%29.htm#top.

Kornai, J. (1971), *Anti-Equilibrium*, New York: North Holland/American Elsevier.

Lipsey R., C. Beckar and K. Carlaw (1998), 'What Requires Explanation?', in E. Helpman (ed.), *General Purpose Technologies and Economic Growth*, Cambridge, MA, and London: MIT Press.

Merton, R. (1965), *On the Shoulder of Giants*, New York: Free Press.

Merton R. and E. Barber (2004), *The Travels and Adventures of Serendipity. A Study in Sociological Semantics and the Sociology of Science*, Princeton and Oxford: Princeton University Press.

Meyer, K. and A. Skak (2002), 'Networks, Serendipity and SME Entry into Eastern Europe', *European Management Journal*, **20**(2): 179–88.

Minier, J.A. (1998), 'Democracy and Growth: Alternative Approaches', *Journal of Economic Growth*, **3**: 241–66.

Nauwelaers, C. and R. Wintjes (2003), 'Identifying Factors of Success and Failure in European IST Related National/Regional Developments: The Case of Flanders': fiste.jrc.es/pages/activities/enlargement/docs/Flanders-Final%201-5-2003%20IPTS%20publ.doc.

Nelson, R. and L. Soete (1988), 'Policy Conclusions', in G. Dosi, C. Freeman, R. Nelson, G. Silverberg and L. Soete (eds), *Technical Change and Economic Theory*, London: Pinter.

Pierre, J. (2000), *Debating Governance*, Oxford: Oxford University Press.

Radaelli, C. (2003), 'The Open Method of Coordination: A New governance architecture for the European Union?', SIEPS Report No. 1, March: www.sieps.su.se.

Rosell, S. (1999), *Renewing Governance*, Toronto: Oxford University Press.

SCP (2001), 'The Netherlands in a European Perspective; *Social & Cultural Report 2000*', Social and Cultural Planning Office, The Hague, March.

Sen, A. (1999), *Development as Freedom*, New York: First Anchor Books Edition.

Shane, S., S. Venkataraman and I. McMillan (1995), 'Cultural Differences in Innovation Championing Strategies', *Journal of Management*, **21**(5): 931–52.

Shapiro, C. and H. Varian (1997), *Information Rules*, Boston MA: Harvard Business School Press.

7. The state at the crossroads: from welfare to the knowledge-based society

Isabel Salavisa

1 INTRODUCTION

This chapter is focused on the huge transformations concerning the role of the state in the knowledge-based society. Our main argument is that while invested with qualitatively different objectives the state cannot simply discard its old forms of social and economic intervention. For the state, the big challenge to be met is how to favour the rise of the knowledge-based society while also dealing with the old society, which remains. New and old problems appear intimately interlinked at a time when nation-states are under great strain due to the convergence of various phenomena: globalization of information, finance and commodities' markets; volatility of multinational companies' strategies; budgetary restrictions; adverse demographic trends, namely in the EU; and the inertia of the state itself as an institution, among others.

Within this framework, the emergence of the knowledge-based society requires a rapid improvement and enlargement of available skills in 'digital' areas; the increase of incentives to R&D activities; a high level of education and a strong aptitude for learning, life-long learning and re-skilling across the population; the provision of entirely new public goods, such as different sorts of non-material infrastructures; the implementation of transformations in diverse institutional and legal frameworks; and, last but not least, a strong commitment towards minimizing social exclusion due to the deep transformations under way.

Whereas the new tasks have come to the forefront, it is obvious that they do not simply substitute for the old ones: social security, education, health care provision, material infrastructures and many others. Therefore, the emerging 'neo-Schumpeterian Accord' (Petit, 2001) seems to overlap, at least partially, a large number of institutions created under the previous Fordist convention (Esping-Andersen, 1996; Boyer and Drache, 1996).

To address these questions the chapter draws on a body of stylized facts regarding state intervention, as well as on a number of different contributions on the welfare state and its transformation.

2 THE CHANGING ROLE OF THE STATE

The emergence of a new economic paradigm nowadays designated the knowledge-based economy or the knowledge-based society calls for a re-examination of the economic role of the state. The welfare state associated with Fordism in advanced countries has been put under great strain (Esping-Andersen, 1996, 2002a; Jessop, 2002) with some authors heralding its premature death since the 1970s, or even before. In fact, as early as 1953, Ludwig von Mises wrote, in an article with the telling title 'The Agony of the Welfare State': 'the world today has to face the agony of the much glorified policies of the Welfare States' (von Mises, 1953). Public choice economists theorized extensively against most of welfare state policies (see Buchanan, 1979, among others). Though our aim is not to assess those arguments, they will not be ignored hereafter.

Even among welfare state supporters a pessimistic view has emerged, related mostly to the challenges associated with globalization. This debate is certainly crucial. The question of whether globalization is undermining the welfare states must then be examined, bearing in mind that other important transformations are also under way and must be considered – such as demographic phenomena, attitudes toward labour and leisure and poor growth performances, just to mention a few. We will deal with these aspects assuming that: first, the welfare state is a major historical achievement and is a central institution in advanced countries; second, diversity of national configurations is the rule and is connected to diverse political solutions and compromises, labour market institutions and regimes, and macroeconomic policies, among others; and third, the transformation of the role of the state in the transition to the knowledge economy will take place in a context characterized by a complex of interlinked – but partly autonomous – societal and economic phenomena.

As to the impact of globalization on welfare states, arguments and figures will be examined in the next section, dedicated both to the examination of historical trends and to recent transformations. In both domains general shifts will emerge as well as distinct patterns across countries, which do not appear to converge. Hence diversity is a second aspect to be accounted for, looking for political, institutional and historical reasons behind it.

The recasting of welfare states is at the top of the political agenda in most advanced countries and constitutes a pillar of the European strategy towards the knowledge society. Notwithstanding the deep national diversity, the magnitude of the task should not be overlooked. In fact, the state is faced with the overlapping of distinct generations of phenomena, such as the past commitments and the inertia of the welfare state; the absorption of the negative impacts of the structural shift under way; the accommodation of negative demographic trends in most advanced countries; and the need to reformulate its intervention as a provider of an increasing amount of public goods, due to the emergence of a knowledge-driven networks economy. Although some authoritative academics present an optimistic and pragmatic view (see Barr, 2001), alternative political choices, criticism and difficulties are to be also taken into account. These issues are, however, beyond the scope of this chapter and so they will only be briefly referred to hereafter.

The new phase is characterized by deep transformations in growth regimes associated with the replacement of Fordism by a new regime based on the intensive use of information technologies and knowledge. It seems that transition is tentative, in spite of the American performance in the 1990s. Other national experiments also deserve to be taken into account since they present high levels of achievement combined with different social compromises and choices. Hence there is no one-way road to the knowledge-based society or to the reconfiguration of welfare, albeit most countries face a common challenge regarding the new drivers of growth. Section 4 is concerned with presenting the major issues at stake.

Finally, Section 5 attempts to outline the emerging aspects of the welfare state in the knowledge society, focusing on its new attributes associated with the new features of the economy and society. This constitutes an exercise of synthesis that is necessarily speculative in part, due to the complexity and nature of the subject matter.

3   THE CHALLENGE OF GLOBALIZATION

Taking the title from a recent paper (Navarro et al., 2004), is globalization undermining the welfare state? Is it responsible for a reversal of the historical pattern of state intervention in advanced nations? Have national patterns of intervention converged in a significant way in recent times? These are some of the main questions addressed hereafter, through relevant contributions on the matter and simple stylized facts.

According to Mishra, the vast literature on globalization has almost completely omitted the impact on the welfare state, an omission he intends to put right (Mishra, 1999). Having contributed previous studies on the decline of welfare state (Mishra, 1990), the author argues that the opening up of economies has curtailed the autonomy of nation-states in the area of policies aiming at sustaining growth and full employment. Consequently, the first line of defence – a well-paid full-time job for everybody or, admittedly, primarily for males – against poverty and dependence on public assistance has been undermined. The second line of defence – the systems of social protection in advanced nations – albeit somehow weakened, performed better (mostly for electoral reasons) in democratic regimes.

But globalization is not the only explanation for the difficulties of the new economic, political and ideological context of the welfare state. Two other elements must be considered: the collapse of the socialist alternative and the relative decline of the nation-state (Mishra, 1999: 1). After reviewing the main shifts undergone by developed nations, namely greater openness, increasing competition, pressures on deregulation, commodification and privatization, globalization of production led by MNCs, financial globalization – which is entirely new and of utmost importance – and the loss of autonomy of governments to conduct policies aimed at full employment and growth, the author examines the situation in labour markets with growing inequality and social polarization.

In his own words, a paradoxical conclusion is to be drawn:

> Increasing globalisation and competitiveness create economic conditions which require the state or the public sector to play a *more*, not less, important role in social protection. In diminishing the capacity of non-state sectors, especially employers, to provide welfare and at the same time destabilizing and shrinking the income base of a substantial section of the population, a globalised economy leaves the state, whether national or supranational, as the only stable and legitimate organisation able to assume responsibility for adequate social protection. (Mishra, 1999: 33)

This conclusion is interesting at two different levels. First, because it implicitly assumes that the state is the main institution that is able to accommodate the by-products of the functioning of markets and economic institutions; and second, because it contributes to an explanation of the continuity of huge government outlays, namely for social protection, notwithstanding the strengthening of neo-liberal conceptions in a significant part of the developed world since the 1980s.

As to the first aspect, an examination of the data over the last century corroborates the existence of a consistent trend towards increasing the share of GDP allocated by the state in most advanced countries. It is quite surprising that this phenomenon, a major aspect in contemporary economies, has attracted so little attention among economists until recently. The focus has been mainly on choice procedures involved in public allocation, efficiency, redistribution impact and so on (Le Grand et al., 1992;

Le Grand, 2003; Buchanan and the public choice school; and, more indirectly, the quoted von Mises, Hayek and the Austrian school) and not on the place and role of the state in economy and society. This subject has been left to sociologists, political scientists and others (Mishra, 1990 and 1999; Esping-Andersen, 1990, 1996 and 2002a, b; and Luhmann, 1999), with only a few exceptions (for example, Delorme and André, 1983).

In fact, in the long run, the history of capitalism is closely connected to changes in the economic role of the state. In the classical era of competitive capitalism, roughly covering the nineteenth century in advanced countries, the state was mainly focused on general functions, such as the production and enforcement of law, defence and security, although its intervention in other domains was already important (the spread of mass primary education, the building of transport and communication infrastructures, such as roads, railways and telegraph and the provision of basic public health). However, the size of the budget in relation to GDP remained small.

According to Maddison (1995), by the end of the nineteenth century, total government outlays were around 10 per cent of GDP in France, Germany, the United Kingdom and Japan (see Table 7.1). The same empirical evidence shows that there was a long-lasting tendency throughout the twentieth century towards increasing the share of GDP allocated by the state across advanced countries, although the figures vary significantly by the end of the century: around 50 per cent in 1992 in France, Netherlands, the UK and Germany, with Japan and the USA lower, at 34 per cent and 39 per cent, respectively (Table 7.1).

Excluding the immediate pre-war period for the main belligerent nations, it was only after World War II that a clear increase in public outlays took

Table 7.1   *Total government expenditure as a percentage of GDP,
1880–1992 (at market prices)*

	1880	1913	1938	1950	1973	1992
France	11.2	8.9	23.2	27.6	38.8	51.0[d]
Germany	10.0[a]	17.7	42.4	30.4	42.0	46.1[d]
Japan	9.0[b]	14.2	30.3	19.8	22.9	33.5
Netherlands	n.a.	8.2[c]	21.7	26.8	45.5	54.1
United Kingdom	9.9	13.3	28.8	34.2	41.5	51.2
United States	n.a.	8.0	19.8	21.4	31.1	38.5
Average	10.0	11.7	27.7	26.7	37.0	45.7

Notes: a. 1881; b. 1885; c. 1910; d. 1990.

Source: Maddison (1995: 67).

place. In fact, Keynesian macro policy and a new social compromise brought about a Beveridge welfare state, at least in Europe. Public spending expanded to unprecedented levels, with the state beginning to assure the supply of a large set of collective goods in three primary areas: the spread of school enrolment, including mass higher education; the provision of public health facilities; and a general system of social security.

During the 1970s and the 1980s the role of the state underwent major changes that can be summarized as follows: austerity and rationalization policies; relevant privatization in several countries; and reorganization and slimming down of welfare systems (Boyer and Drache, 1996). The structural crisis associated with the break-down of the Fordist growth regime appeared to be the main driving force behind these transformations. The state should withdraw at least partially from the economy and its role should be reconsidered. It was the era of the triumph of neo-conservative governments and policies in the US and the UK.

That period, as is recognized nowadays, corresponds to the transition between two different phases or paradigms, Fordism and the information and communication technologies paradigm, the latter calling for new domains of public intervention (see Freeman and Soete, 1997). At the same time, however, globalization has emerged as a major restriction on the autonomy of nation-states.

Hence the question is whether globalization has in fact entailed the reversal of the trend regarding public expenditures. It appears that deregulation of international capital flows and trade will narrow the scope of expansionist and redistributive policies and provoke cuts in social public expenditures and the deregulation of labour markets in the name of competitiveness.

The same line of argument would imply shifting away taxation from mobile factors towards less mobile ones. The question is addressed by Navarro et al. (2004) and involves the test of two competing hypothesis: the 'convergence' theory, which assumes that globalization is a great equaliser of welfare states, forcing cutbacks and the retrenchment of welfare domains; and the alternative and opposite one, according to which internal political forces are the principal determinants of the evolution of welfare states. This second hypothesis is labelled 'politics still matters'.

The test has involved the analysis of a number of welfare indicators at country level over the period 1980–2000. The main conclusion is that the 'convergence' hypothesis does not get empirical corroboration, since welfare patterns have continued to diverge across countries, keeping their pre-globalization characteristics, which draw on distinct political trajectories. Moreover, changes in each pattern are to be assigned to domestic political changes rather than to external conditions. The data are summarized in

Table 7.2 Social public expenditure and employment, 1980–97

Group of countries* (average)	Social public expenditures (% GDP)			Government employment (% total employment)		
	1980	1997**	Change	1974	1997**	Change
Social democratic	24.2	29.3	5.2	13.5	20.0	6.5
Christian democratic/ conservative	23.1	27.1	4.0	8.5	10.5	2.0
Liberal	14.7	17.6	2.9	9.8	8.8	−0.9
Ex-dictatorships	13.1	20.7	7.6	5.9	9.4	3.5

Notes:
* Social democratic: Austria, Denmark, Finland, Norway, Sweden; Christian democratic/conservative: Belgium, France, Germany, Italy, Netherlands, Switzerland; Liberal: Canada, United Kingdom, Ireland, Japan, US; Ex-dictatorships: Greece, Portugal, Spain.
** Data refer to1995 for Austria, Norway, the Netherlands, UK, Spain and Portugal.

Source: Adapted from Navarro et al. (2004).

Table 7.2, which displays the evolution of social public expenditure and government employment for European countries, Canada, Japan and the US. Countries are grouped according to the dominant political tradition in government parties.

Over the 1980s and 1990s, it appears that social public expenditures have increased in relation to GDP even in the group of countries with liberal traditions. The same occurred with government employment, with the exception of liberal countries, particularly the United Kingdom. The case of ex-dictatorships was expected since they have built a social protection system only recently. The case of social democratic countries is certainly dependent on political choices. The figures support the idea that the distinct patterns across countries have not converged. On the contrary, the distance between social democratic countries and liberal ones has increased, making their respective patterns even more contrasting, not only regarding the indicators presented but also those concerning social inequality, relative poverty rates and so on (Navarro et al., 2004: 138–42). These differences are to be explored later when considering the diversity of transition models toward the knowledge-based societies. Recently, a decrease in public expenditures took place as well as a slight convergence among countries (see Table 7.3 below).

In a way these conclusions are comparable to those of Esping-Andersen. In his classic book *The Three Worlds of Welfare Capitalism* (Esping-Andersen, 1990: 5) the author presents the welfare state as 'a principal institution in the construction of different models of post-war capitalism'.

The centrality of the state arises from its role in codifying and influencing the shaping of other institutional forms, rather than from the size of the public budget in relation to GDP. In fact, focusing on spending may be misleading, but ignoring major trends could be problematic as well. That is why detailed examination of long-run comparative basis data should be pursued.

Applying a set of indicators and analyses, Esping-Andersen identifies three highly diverse regime-types of welfare state 'each organized around its discrete logic of organization, stratification, and societal integration' (1990: 3–5). In the first type or cluster, the 'liberal' welfare state, modest social protection is the dominant feature. He writes: 'in this model, the progress of social reform has been severely circumscribed by traditional, liberal work-ethic norms' (idem: 26). The state encourages market solutions and guarantees are put at a minimum level. This cluster includes the United States, Canada and Australia.

A second type is characterized by a historical corporatist-statist legacy: social rights have been granted on condition that status differentials are preserved. This 'corporatist' state stands on a sound state edifice, capable of providing benefits directly, the market being attributed a marginal role. Continental European nations such as Austria, Germany, France and Italy are to be included in this cluster.

The 'social democratic' type constitutes the third cluster. Here the new middle classes were included as recipients of social benefits and the aim was to promote equality at the highest standard. Therefore, the system had to provide high quality services and benefits. Principles of universalism and de-commodification were applied to a much larger extent than in the previous types. Because it addresses individuals – instead of families – and aims at universalism, Esping-Andersen claims that the model is 'a peculiar fusion of liberalism and socialism' (idem: 28). Scandinavian nations are to be classified within this cluster.

A similar approach can be found in André (2000), who relies on a large set of quantitative data to examine the evolution of social protection in Europe over the 1980s and 1990s.

To summarize those aspects which should be remembered when dealing with this subject: first, the acceleration of government expenditure seems to have occurred during the inter-war period; second, there is a sharp contrast regarding the economic extension of the state sector between the United States on the one hand and most European countries on the other; third, even among European countries different realities emerge, with the Scandinavian countries as an extreme case and the Anglo-Saxon countries as the opposite case, France, Germany and Italy standing somewhere in the middle; fourth, in most countries a deceleration or even a decrease of public expenditure in GDP has taken place since the mid-1990s (see Table

Table 7.3   *Total government expenditure and social protection expenditure, 1995–2001 (% of GDP)*

	1995		2001	
	Total government expenditure	Social protection expenditure	Total government expenditure	Social protection expenditure
France	55.1	21.5	52.5	20.4
Germany	56.1	21.3	48.3	21.8
Italy	53.4	18.7	48.6	17.8
Belgium	52.8	18.6	49.5	17.2
Netherlands	56.4	20.7	46.6	17.5
UK	43.5	17.3	39.2	15.7
Ireland	41.5	13.6	33.9	9.5
Sweden	67.7	27.2	57.1	23.8
Denmark	60.3	26.8	55.3	24.0
Finland	59.6	26.0	49.2	20.6
Austria	57.3	22.6	51.8	21.5
Spain	–	–	39.4	13.4
Portugal	45.0	12.5	46.3	13.6
Greece	51.0	18.3	47.8	19.4
EU (15)	–	–	46.9	18.7

Source: Eurostat.

7.3), but the picture appears less pronounced regarding social expenditures.

The approaches presented so far come from supporters of the welfare state and not from its critics. Although we certainly have to pay attention to the latter's views and arguments it is not the purpose of this paper to proceed to that task (for a summary of those positions see Merkel, 2002; Chang, 2002; Le Grand, 2003; Evans, 1995; for a presentation by public choice authors themselves see Buchanan, 1979; Buchanan and Tullock, 1999). However, even among the former it is now clear that the recasting of the welfare state has come to the top of the political agenda.

This is quite explicitly accepted by Esping-Andersen when he assumes that there is a trade-off between egalitarianism and employment, that globalization affects the range of political choices and that ageing is a problem, after summarizing most of the diagnoses of the welfare state crisis (1996: 2).

But sharing at least part of the diagnoses does not mean coming up with the same remedies, as becomes obvious in the recent work of Esping-Andersen (2002b), Le Grand (2003) or Barr (2001), just to mention a few.

These contributions are also important at a different level: they suggest, if not systematically, some features of the 'new' welfare states able to favour the transition to the knowledge society as will be seen below.

4 FROM FORDISM TO THE KNOWLEDGE SOCIETY

In the previous section it has become clear that the new constraints set by globalization, combined with the rise of criticism toward the welfare state and the claims for its partial dismantling have not been able so far to induce its significant retrenchment. Arguments were also presented to support the urgent need of recasting the welfare state and of making it more compatible with the new economic, social and demographic realities.

In this section we will claim that the intervention of the state must also account for the new reality of the transition to the knowledge society, an issue that goes far beyond the welfare aims of the state. Although independent, the two aspects are certainly connected and interlinked.

Since the 1990s, the emerging ICT era has entailed the building of information highways and digital networks. Life-long education and training have emerged as new domains of state intervention. Likewise, its role as a supplier of informational and communicational public goods and as a ruler of the externalities arising from the semi-public nature of knowledge appears as much more significant than in the past. Finally, the awareness of the increased importance of innovation to competitiveness implies a new compromise for the nation-states or for supra-national institutions such as the EU to support countries' science and engineering bases. But is that all? Is it possible to recast state intervention, in welfare as well, without accounting for the changing nature of the growth regime, which is at the core of the transition to the knowledge-based economy itself?

Economic growth under Fordism was based on a cumulative causation pattern with the exploration of large economies of scale in manufacturing as the main driver. Productivity growth and the rise of real wages were then compatible with full employment – mostly for male workers – since high rates of GDP growth were the rule in advanced countries. This Kaldorian regime was led both by domestic demand within the context of nation-states and by incremental technological change along a few technological trajectories and grounded on sustained accumulation of physical capital. On the other hand domestic demand was fuelled by smooth rise in real wages and by the expansion of public expenditures associated with welfare states and increasing state intervention in a number of fields. The structural crisis and subsequent decline of Fordism was the subject of a plethora of studies (see Boyer, 1986 and Jessop, 2002, among many others).

The birth of the new era – initially faced with optimism due to the high potential of the new information and communication technologies – has become unexpectedly associated with the difficulty of substituting a new growth regime for the previous one. Although in the United States the 1990s seemed to start a 'new economy', with high rates of growth, low unemployment and smooth cycles, the beginning of this century has induced a much more moderate view.

Moreover, in the meantime, most European countries, particularly the larger countries, experienced serious difficulties in reducing unemployment, boosting growth and reforming markets and institutions. For the first time in decades European countries stopped converging to the US level of productivity and GDP per capita. On the contrary, they began diverging (Fagerberg et al., 1999; Fagerberg, 2001; Soete, 2001; EC, 2003). One of the principal causes for their meagre performance seems to be their insufficient investment in ICTs and knowledge – but this is certainly just a part of the problem since no mono-causal explanation appears as satisfactory.

Taking as a starting point the context described, we will address two principal questions in this section: first, the main traits of a viable substitute for Fordism; second, the diversity of forms under which the knowledge-based economy is making its way in different national contexts. These issues are central in regard to state intervention and have consequences on the new configurations of the welfare state.

As to the first issue, and according to Petit and Soete (2001: 179), the crucial question is 'whether innovation, driven by ICTs, can launch a cumulative mechanism based on services somewhat similar to the one experienced in the past in manufacturing'. This involves assessing the way innovation processes take place in services. In fact, such a cumulative growth pattern requires the increase of tradability of services in order to expand their markets. Together with innovation this expansion would entail a rise in efficiency in services, which would allow a new expansion of demand. However, since service goods are by nature sharply different from manufactured goods – according to a wide range of economic criteria – and also since they rely so heavily on innovation that takes place in manufacturing activities, this poses entirely new theoretical and practical problems.

Although the authors were mainly concerned with the impact of technological change on employment, their analysis has an unquestionable general scope. In fact, it has become clear that, with the honourable exception of high-tech industrial sectors, manufacturing as a whole is unable to create jobs and to continue sustaining overall growth as it used to do in a not so distant past in advanced countries. Of course globalization, de-localization, increased openness and competition, and the emergence of

NIEs (newly industrialised economies) also play an important role in this picture. But the problem of finding a substitute for Fordism remains and seems much more complex than promoting the creation and use of ICTs, sustaining learning routines, reforming a number of markets, institutions and organizations, and boosting knowledge accumulation – although all these tasks must be carried out.

Boyer explicitly assumes the complexity of the task. After presenting the presumed successors of the Fordist model that have been proposed since the 1970s he concludes that none of them has proved to be an adequate and feasible substitute, since each of them relies on a mono-causal explanation of the Fordist structural crisis (2002b: 75). In turn they shed light on a set of important aspects of the new era, they attained popularity among economists and policy-makers and they inspired strategies and policies. However, he claims, what is to be done is to analyse the effective transformations undergone by the American economy over the 1990s, trying to discover the new regularities and tendencies at work.

In doing that, Boyer proposes to distinguish between the aspects that are specific to the American economy – for example, deregulation of labour markets, the dividends from the reduction of military expenditures, the centrality and sophistication of financial markets in funding innovation, and the configuration of budgetary and monetary policies – from those that seem to have prevailed in all successful national experiences. In fact, when considering the whole set of countries that are succeeding in installing a knowledge-based economy, he finds that while deregulation of markets of goods appears as a necessary condition, the same does not hold to labour markets (2002b: 100–101).

Likewise, a large pool of venture capital and the existence of a sizeable and first-rate domestic industry of information and communication technologies do not seem to constitute necessary prerequisites or basic features of a knowledge-based economy, as shown by the cases of Denmark, Finland and Sweden – in the social democratic group – and Canada, Australia and New Zealand in the Anglo-Saxon one, Ireland presenting a singularity of its own.

In short, the adhesion to a growth regime led by technology is based on a set of aspects and conditions, which can briefly be described: an intensive and widespread use of ICTs by firms and households, which is strongly associated with low cost telecommunication services and a declining cost of equipment; important investment in R&D by firms; increased competition and deregulation of the markets of goods; high and improving levels of schooling across the population, which in turn has a high motivation to learn and a favourable attitude toward novelty. A growth regime based on these aspects will allow an increase of total factor productivity in relation to that of the 1980s, as well as a TFP performance above the average.

At this stage, some points are to be stressed, particularly regarding the role of the state. It is quite obvious that, in the countries belonging to the social democratic group, the state – and noticeably the institutions of the welfare state – has played an important and positive role in achieving success. As already pointed out a few years ago, 'a favourable institutional environment may be as capable as free markets of nurturing flexibility and efficiency' (Esping-Andersen, 1996: 6). The author was explicitly referring to 'strong consensus-building institutions', but those institutions certainly include the social democratic welfare state.

A similar assertion is made by Castells in his analysis of the Scandinavian societies (Castells, 2001) and by Aiginger (2002). After presenting his analysis of the most successful European countries regarding the knowledge-based economy, Aiginger notes the improvement of their incentive structures as one of the common elements of their policy strategies. These incentive structures refer both to firms and to workers. The latter 'have a high probability and true assistance if they look for a new job' (2002: 25). Hence, mobility is favoured by a high probability of getting a new job within a relatively short time-span but also by a reliable social protection net. This is an important distinctive feature of the European model in relation to that of the US. It is the new likely configuration of the welfare state, in the context of the recasting of the economic role of the state, which is dealt with in the final section.

5　A NEW WELFARE STATE?

As previously stated, the transformation of the place and role of the state appears to be inevitable. Actually, this transformation is already taking place in most industrialized countries due to the confluence of several phenomena: a poor growth performance combined with high levels of unemployment; the effects of a negative demographic trend on the sustainability of inherited social security benefits; the increase of life expectancy and its consequences on labour markets and on national health services; the need to provide an increasing amount of new public goods related to knowledge-intensive activities and skills; the globalization of markets and the resulting restrictions on national government action; the need to accommodate creative destruction in the form of the decline, restructuring and delocalization of industrial sectors.

The building of the welfare state was related to a specific era of capitalism in industrialized countries, characterized by a steady and regular path of GDP and productivity growth, supported by a particular accumulation regime and a specific mode of regulation (see Delorme and André, 1983; and Boyer, 1986).

State/society relations were not only a major Fordist institutional form. Due to the centrality of the state, it also played an essential role in the codification of the other institutional forms, such as the wage–labour nexus, the forms of competition and the monetary and international regimes. In short, welfare was only one of the aspects, albeit an important one, of the nature and role of the state under Fordism. Multidimensionality and complexity were already features of the Fordist state, an embedded state (see Delorme, 1991).

The search for new configurations of the state in the knowledge-based society is already under way. Within the framework of evolutionary economics, and after proceeding to a review of Schumpeter's points of view, Burlamaqui (2000: 45) suggests that the state (whose embedded autonomy is recognized) should be concentrated in three major areas:

> 1. *Entrepreneurial stimuli and investment coordination*, that is, uncertainty reduction by means of designing and negotiating investment strategies . . . ; 2. *Creative destruction management*, that is, buffering the problems associated with structural change . . . ; 3. *Institutional building and bridging*, that is, shaping both regulatory and developmental policy frameworks and building co-operative organizational capabilities . . .

From a different perspective, Petit (2001) and Boyer (2002a) analyse the viability and main characteristics of a neo-Schumpeterian accord or a Schumpeterian welfare state, capable of replacing the old Fordist state. In short, a new arbitrage is called for. This new vision emphasizes the role of the state as legislator and referee, side by side with its role as supplier of access to information and stimulator of knowledge creation. But as has been shown, the welfare state can mediate the transition to a new economy by providing a safety network able to reduce risk and favour labour mobility, as demonstrated in the Nordic countries (see Aiginger, 2002).

Taking these contributions into account, we will describe the major transformations concerning the role of the state in five different domains.

The first concerns support to the instalment of a growth regime led by ICTs and knowledge, based on a new cumulative causation, presenting the major characteristics analysed above and compatible with the specificity of national history and institutions. This involves particular attention to three aspects: the expansion of knowledge-intensive services and the strengthening of their mutual relation with ICT producers; the modernization of traditional services sectors through the dissemination of new technologies and forms of organization; and the creation of infrastructures to favour the development of sophisticated networks connecting firms, public agencies and academic institutions.

As in the recent past, government policies and incentives must continue promoting the creation, dissemination and access to knowledge. And public agencies must respond not only by the direct or indirect provision of knowledge for training and education. They must also intervene as legal providers of access through the implementation of interface and diffusion institutions and through legislation and law enforcement.

The second major transformation is related to the emergence of new types of markets. Soete (2001) speaks of new market rules, particularly concerning the exchange of pure information 'electronic' goods. In these markets three essential structural conditions do not apply: excludability, rivalry and transparency. This fact requires the strengthening and revision of property rights regime.

It seems that a new trade-off is emerging between a pervasive and rapid diffusion of knowledge and of new products, able to sustain a general and open access to the benefits of the new era, and the appropriate level of reward to the innovators. The tremendous success and dramatic expansion of the Internet relies on open access and on the fact that participants can also become creators and developers of products, that is, they are not simply users they have become participants (see Castells, 2001; and Dolfsma, 2005).

Nevertheless, there is a huge potential for litigation, and an increasing need for judicial regulation of economic transactions is likely to emerge. In other words, two aspects must be pointed out: the development of the regulatory functions and agencies of the state is under way; and the jurisdictional sphere is apparently expanding. A substantial share of exchanges will have to be dealt with as contracts, submitted to written procedures within a precise technical and legal framework. Legal procedures and the making of new laws will develop, while new areas of law will be created.

The third major transformation is related to the shifting organization of the economic system. Actually, an increase of externalities – an intrinsic feature of the networks economy – is taking place. The spread of networks is represented by the increasing density of interactions across the economic system. Empirical evidence can be found in the growing density of the I–O matrix running parallel with the increasing specialization of economic units, outsourcing being just the usual name of the game (see Barrios and Trionfetti, 2002; and Sakurai, 1995). While single economic units become increasingly specialized, the system becomes more and more integrated. In short, this calls for a new domain of state intervention in the provision, regulation and arbitrage of networks and corresponding externalities.

The fourth fundamental aspect refers to what Burlamaqui calls the creative destruction management, that is, the policies oriented towards accommodating the social consequences of the new techno-economic-institutional set-up. In fact, persistent high rates of unemployment, particularly in European countries, coexist with new forms of inequality spreading across professional categories and social strata. Fitoussi and Rosanvallon coined the term 'intra-category inequalities' (1996: 68), bearing in mind the French case in particular, opposite to the American model, mainly characterized by a vertical segmentation of the labour market ('the working poor' issue) and a sharp inequality of income distribution (see also Schienstock, 2001; Esping-Andersen, 2002a; Lindley, 2002).

Finally, the fifth major aspect concerning the role of the state regards the less developed countries, which face the two-fold task of catching up while preparing the transition to the knowledge-based economy. This is very demanding in technical and scientific capabilities and infrastructures, as well as in academic resources. New and old problems will then overlap, making the task particularly difficult. But even for developed countries most of the old functions of the state were not ruled out. That is why a significant decrease of public spending, if any, is not to be expected. Hence, although conventional recommendations have repeatedly pointed out the need for reducing the role of the state, the figures reveal the magnitude of the task.

It is clear that institutional rethinking and building is also needed, as Burlamaqui pointed out (2000). For that purpose we must adopt a more complex view of the state and of institutions in general, as presented by Evans (1995) and Chang (2002).

REFERENCES

Aiginger, K. (2002), 'The New European Model of the Reformed Welfare State', European Forum Working Paper, 2/2002, Stanford University.

André, C. (2000), 'Contemporary Evolutions of Social Protection in Europe: a Comparison', paper presented at the EAEPE Conference, Berlin, November 2000.

Barr, N. (2001), *The Welfare State as Piggy Bank*, Oxford: Oxford University Press.

Barrios, S. and F. Trionfetti (2002), 'Demand- and Supply-driven Externalities in OECD Countries: A Dynamic Panel Approach', paper presented at the XIII Congress of IEA, Lisbon, September 2002.

Boyer, R. (1986) (ed.), *Capitalismes fin de siècle*, Paris: Presses Universitaires de France.

Boyer, R. (2002a), 'Institutional Reforms for Growth, Employment and Social Cohesion: Elements for a European and National Agenda', in M.J. Rodrigues (ed.), *The New Knowledge Economy in Europe – A Strategy for International Competitiveness and Social Cohesion*, Cheltenham, UK, and Northampton, MA, USA: Edward Elgar, pp. 146–202.

Boyer, R. (2002b), *La croissance début de siècle – De l'octet au gène*, Paris: Albin Michel.

Boyer, R. and D. Drache (1996) (eds), *States against Markets*, London: Routledge.

Buchanan, J.M. (1979), *What Should Economists Do?*, Indianopolis: Liberty Press.

Buchanan, J.M. and G. Tullock (1999), *The Calculus of Consent – Logical Foundations of Constitutional Democracy*, Indianopolis: Liberty Fund (first published in 1962).

Burlamaqui, L. (2000), 'Evolutionary Economics and the Economic Role of the State', in L. Burlamaqui, A.L. Castro and H.J. Chang (eds), *Institutions and the Role of the State*, Cheltenham, UK, and Northampton, MA, USA: Edward Elgar, pp. 27–52.

Castells, M. (2001), *The Internet Galaxy – Reflections on the Internet, Business and Society*, Oxford: Oxford University Press.

Chang, H.J. (2002), 'Breaking the Mould: An Institutionalist Political Economy Alternative to the Neo-liberal Theory of the Market and the State', *Cambridge Journal of Economics*, **26**: 539–59.

Delorme, R. (1991), 'Etat et hétérogénéité: ERIC et le MPPE', *Cahiers de recherche sociologique*, **17**: 153–83.

Delorme, R. and C. André (1983), *L'Etat et l'économie*, Paris: Seuil.

Dolfsma, W. (2005), 'Towards a Dynamic (Schumpeterian) Welfare Economics', *Research Policy*, **34**(1): 69–82.

Esping-Andersen, G. (1990), *The Three Worlds of Welfare Capitalism*, Cambridge: Polity Press.

Esping-Andersen, G. (1996) (ed.), *Welfare States in Transition*, London: Sage Publications.

Esping-Andersen, G. (2002a), 'A New European Model for the Twenty-first Century?', in M.J. Rodrigues (ed.), *The New Knowledge Economy in Europe – A Strategy for International Competitiveness and Social Cohesion*, Cheltenham, UK, and Northampton, MA, USA: Edward Elgar, pp. 54–94.

Esping-Andersen, G. (2002b) (ed.), *Why We Need a New Welfare State*, Oxford: Oxford University Press.

Evans, P. (1995), *Embedded Autonomy – States and Industrial Transformation*, Princeton, NJ: Princeton University Press.

European Commission (2003), *European Competitiveness Report 2003*, Brussels.

Fagerberg, J. (2001), 'Europe at the Crossroads: The Challenge from Innovation-based Growth', in D. Archibugi and B.A. Lundvall (eds), *The Globalizing Learning Economy*, Oxford: Oxford University Press, pp. 45–60.

Fagerberg, J., P. Guerrieri and B. Verspagen (1999), 'Europe – A Long View', in J. Fagerberg, P. Guerrieri and B. Verspagen (eds), *The Economic Challenge for Europe – Adapting to Innovation Based Growth*, Cheltenham, UK and Northampton, MA, USA: Edward Elgar, pp. 1–20.

Fitoussi, J.P. and P. Rosanvallon (1996), *Le nouvel âge des inégalités*, Paris: Seuil.

Freeman, C. and L. Soete (1997), *The Economics of Industrial Innovation*, London: Pinter.

Jessop, B. (2002), *The Future of the Capitalist State*, Cambridge: Polity Press.

Le Grand, J. (2003), *Motivation, Agency and Public Policy – Of Knights & Knaves, Pawns & Queens*, Oxford: Oxford University Press.

Le Grand, J., C. Propper and R. Robinson (1992), *The Economics of Social Problems*, 3rd edn, Basingstoke: Macmillan.

Lindley, R.M. (2002), 'Knowledge-based Economies: The European Employment

Debate in a New Context', in M.J. Rodrigues (ed.), *The New Knowledge Economy in Europe – A Strategy for International Competitiveness and Social Cohesion*, Cheltenham, UK, and Northampton, MA, USA: Edward Elgar, pp. 95–145.

Luhmann, N. (1999), *Politique et complexité*, Paris: Les Éditions du Cerf.

Maddison, A. (1995), *L'économie mondiale, 1820–1992*, Paris: OECD.

Matzner, E. (2002), 'The Welfare State in the Twenty-first Century', Working Paper, 2/2002, IFIP – TU, Vienna.

Merkel, W. (2002), 'Social Justice and the Three Worlds of Welfare Capitalism', *European Journal of Sociology*, **43**: 59–91.

Mishra, R. (1990), *The Welfare State in Capitalist Society*, London: Harvester Wheatsheaf.

Mishra, R. (1999), *Globalization and the Welfare State*, Cheltenham, UK, and Northampton, MA, USA: Edward Elgar.

Navarro, V., J. Schmitt and J. Astudillo (2004), 'Is Globalisation Undermining the Welfare State?', *Cambridge Journal of Economics*, **28**, 133–52.

Petit, P. (2001), 'Distribution and Growth: Can the New Left deal with the Neo-Schumpeterian "Accord"?', Cepremap, no. 2001–07.

Petit, P. and L. Soete (2001), 'Technical Change and Employment Growth in Services: Analytical and Policy Challenges', in P. Petit and L. Soete (eds), *Technology and the Future of European Employment*, Cheltenham, UK, and Northampton, MA, USA: Edward Elgar, pp. 166–203.

Sakurai, N. (1995), 'Structural Change and Employment: Empirical Evidence for 8 OECD Countries', *STI Review*, **15**: 133–75.

Schienstock, G. (2001), 'Social Exclusion in the Learning Economy', in D. Archibugi and B.A. Lundvall (eds), *The Globalizing Learning Economy*, Oxford: Oxford University Press, pp. 163–76.

Soete, L. (2001), 'The New Economy: A European Perspective', in D. Archibugi and B.A. Lundvall (eds), *The Globalizing Learning Economy*, Oxford: Oxford University Press, pp. 21–44.

Von Mises, L. (1953), 'The Agony of the Welfare State', *The Freeman*, May 4.

8. Knowledge, the knowledge economy and welfare theory[1]

Wilfred Dolfsma

In this chapter I argue that the emerging realization that our economies are knowledge economies (OECD, 1996) entails that economists should study much more closely than hitherto what knowledge is, and how it accumulates and dwindles away. A further consequence is, as I argue in this chapter, that developments in the economy may also need to be evaluated differently than before. A different welfare theory might be required.

Baumol (2002) claims that over 60 per cent of the labour force in the United States, for instance, are knowledge workers. This reality of the knowledge economy is recognized in diverse strands of thought in the economics discipline after the puzzling findings in the growth accounting literature (for example, Denison, 1967). Romer (1986, 1993) has been developing ideas about how knowledge impacts on economic growth, better known as new growth theory. Studying a dynamic, knowledge-based economy requires that a conceptual understanding of knowledge and its role in society is developed and used in economics. The first section discusses this in some measure. My main argument in this chapter is, however, that the knowledge-based economy requires a different, partly complementary welfare theory that would allow one to evaluate developments in society or government policy. A dynamic welfare theory is needed. A second section will give a brief and admittedly incomplete outline of the welfare economic perspective that is now mostly adhered to, following Pareto. A dynamic, Schumpeterian welfare economics would emphasize the development of knowledge and its use in the economy. The third section suggests some elements for a welfare economic perspective. In the present environment, many tend to forget that knowledge is necessarily social, that innovation cannot occur in a social communication vacuum, and that, for instance, emphasizing appropriability as can be witnessed in recent developments in IPR isolates the knowledge sought to protect, thereby hampering the dynamics of a knowledge economy. Developments in a much debated policy domain that is very relevant for the knowledge-based economy (IPRs) are evaluated from the perspective of a dynamic welfare theory.

1 KNOWLEDGE AND THE DYNAMICS OF AN ECONOMY

In recent years it has come to be acknowledged that development of new knowledge is an important source of dynamics for an economy. Knowledge is, however, a very much heterogeneous entity and thus difficult to come to grips with (Dolfsma, 2001). Knowledge has distinct features that are worth discussing in light of this chapter. To paraphrase Isaac Newton, knowledge is developed by people who could see further because they stand on the shoulders of giants. This, of course, is a well-established observation about the cumulative nature of the development of knowledge, but at the same time was a derisive remark against Newton's opponent in a discussion about the nature of gravity in Newton's letter in 1776 to Robert Hooke. Hooke was a short, hunchbacked man on whose shoulders one would not want to stand. Even if one did stand on his shoulders, one would not see far. Knowledge develops as much in a social context as it is cumulative. The literature on the sociology of science has made this clear (Mäki, 1993). There are at least two other characteristics of knowledge that entail that in assessing welfare effects, one needs a perspective that takes dynamic processes by which knowledge develops into account. The development of knowledge involves tacit dimensions, and requires coding and decoding. These four characteristics are at work at the individual, the organizational,[2] the regional[3] as well as at a societal level (Mokyr, 2002; Leydesdorff et al., 2005).

Knowledge differs from information (data) in that it needs to be interpreted to be understood. Polanyi (1983) has developed a theory of knowledge acquisition that should be of interest to economists (Scitovsky, 1977) as well as to social psychologists (Bandura, 1986). Polanyi (1983: 7) argues that (tacit) knowledge is acquired in a process he calls 'subception'. Any piece of information to be transplanted from one person to somebody else is 'recepted' (ibid.: 5) by this other person and integrated or 'subsumed' into a larger framework of knowledge in which meaning is given to this new piece of information (ibid.: 19). To the extent that information is subsumed (and it has to be subsumed if it is to have any meaning) into a larger framework of knowledge, it is interiorized (ibid.: 29), as it were, to become a part of the body (Douglas, 1986: 13). From this it follows that man cannot always accurately state what it is that he knows about a certain topic. Such knowledge is typically 'fraught with further intimations of an indeterminate range' (Polanyi, 1983: 23), constituting what might be called a 'mountain of experience' (Dolfsma, 2002a). Where knowledge relevant to the particular subject becomes irrelevant is difficult to ascertain; there is a difficulty of separating relevant from irrelevant knowledge. Veblen

(1961: 74) goes even farther than this in asserting that man *is* 'a coherent structure of propensities and habits' (compare Dolfsma, 2002a). Prior knowledge is thus needed to acquire knowledge, but additional information does not necessarily increase one's knowledge: there are costs involved in storing knowledge. Knowledge building is not automatic, but involves being able to discern patterns. Despite having the same information, people might hold different views of the world, which can make communication difficult (costly) as decoding needs to occur. In addition to any decoding that might be necessary, communication (transfer of knowledge) is also costly in itself. Separating the knowledge one needs to communicate can be costly, while the means used to communicate can also involve costs for the sender. Such a view of knowledge and information differs from the one generally subscribed to in economics. Here, the idea is that additional knowledge will reduce noise (Denzau and North, 1994). Persistently diverging learning paths are excluded. The analogy between the view of the process by which an individual learns that would allow for persistently diverging learning paths and the view on the development of technological paradigms (Dosi, 1982; Van de Poel et al., 2002) is striking.

Mokyr (2002, and Chapter 1 in this volume) argues that the industrial revolutions need to be explained by the development, but mostly by the diffusion and use, of new knowledge. There are a number of noteworthy observations Mokyr makes about the role of knowledge for economic development. A first one is that there were striking macro inventions before the first Industrial Revolution in England. None of these inventions gave rise to sustained economic growth, however. Another observation is about the way in which bodies of knowledge relate to one another. Propositional knowledge is knowledge about 'how to manipulate nature' and includes more than what we would now call academic knowledge. *Savants* possess this type of knowledge. Prescriptive knowledge contains concrete directions about how to solve a particular problem; it is useful knowledge possessed by *fabricants*. Developments in both types of knowledge may stimulate one another. Simply adding to what is known in a field will not result in a 'tightening' of the knowledge base. Thus it can be considered a coincidence, in a way, that the first Industrial Revolution started in England around 1780. England was by no means the most technologically advanced country, and indeed it made extensive use of knowledge developed in countries such as France. Mokyr points to the institutions of English society that lowered the costs of communication about new knowledge. The result was that knowledge was much more readily exchanged. Communication both broadens and tightens the knowledge base and stimulates the development of techniques that find an immediate application in society and promote economic activity.

Knowledge can be recognized as immaterial assets in a firm's financial accounts, acknowledging its importance as a productive factor. Introducing knowledge into a firm's financial accounts allows it to be used as collateral in capital markets (Lev, 2001). Intellectual property (knowledge made exclusive) also plays an increasingly important role in strategic manoeuvring between firms (Lev, 2001; Shapiro and Varian, 1999; Granstrand, 1999). IPRs may make a firm an inevitable player in a network, and may allow a firm to exclude others from a network. This does not only hold for IPRs, but also for trade secrets and tacit knowledge, as long as access or use of such knowledge can be restricted. Economists have argued that agents need incentives to be persuaded to develop new knowledge. If such incentives – primarily in the case of a system of intellectual property right (IPR) laws – do not exist, there will be an under-supply of new knowledge and basic knowledge in particular (Nelson, 1959). This argument is made both in the case of patents and in the case of copyright (Landes and Posner, 1989). Without incentives, agents would not develop new knowledge, or would not make it publicly available. Nevertheless, it is known that firms do engage in fundamental research and have good reasons for doing so (Rosenberg, 1990), even when they know they cannot receive a patent to legally prevent others from commercially exploiting the knowledge. In addition, not all firms find it worthwhile to apply for a patent (Arundel, 2001; Levin et al., 1987). Increasingly the arguments legitimizing a system of IPRs have shifted to emphasizing the need for these institutions to offer protection so that investments in production facilities can be recouped before copycats who had to spend less in developing a product than the innovator enter the market (Hettinger, 1989). The discussion is a heated one, both in academia and beyond. Economists approach this discussion using Paretian welfare theory.

2 PARETIAN WELFARE ECONOMICS

Blaug (2001: 39) on several occasions lamented the 'replacement of the process conception of competition by an end-state conception [which] drained the idea of competition of all behavioural content', where not the existence of an equilibrium but rather the stability of that equilibrium state is analysed (compare Vickers, 1995).

Every first-year student of economics is presented with the picture of perfect competition between large groups of suppliers and consumers of homogeneous products. The Pareto optimum welfare conditions to attain a first-best situation are well known and need not be reproduced here. The thinking about welfare economics from the 1930s to the 1950s moved from discussing cardinal utility functions, to the Hicks–Kaldor compensation criteria, to the Lipsey and Lancaster second-best theorem, and to Arrow and Debreu's impossibility theorem (Cowen, 2000).

Paretian welfare economics has three main postulates: 'consumer sovereignty, individualism in social choice, and unanimity' (Blaug, 1980: 148). Every individual (agent) is the best judge of his own welfare, the welfare of individuals may not be compared but simply needs to be aggregated (by the market), and social welfare is defined only in terms of the welfare of individuals. These, together with assumptions about parties' objective functions and motivation (profit and utility maximization) allow one, for the analysis for instance of a world where two goods (A and B) are offered, to determine the optimum situation at the point of tangency, T, in Figure 8.1, where marginal costs of production equals marginal utility. At the same time, the relative price ratio between the two goods equals marginal utility, constituting a Pareto-optimal situation. Changes in either the supply or the demand curve in Figure 8.2, for whatever reason, will be evaluated in terms of welfare triangles. In the figure, a movement of the supply curve is shown (from S to S'), leading to a 'deadweight welfare loss' of the size of triangle abc.

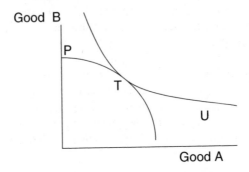

Figure 8.1   Utility maximization

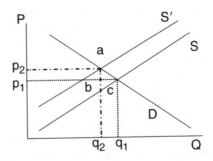

Figure 8.2   Welfare triangles

To date, Paretian welfare theory dominates, while a characterization made in a 1960 survey of welfare economics also still holds (Mishan, 1960: 198):

> No growth or innovation takes place, no uncertainty exists and individual tastes remain unaltered. In addition, the working population is fixed and is, in some sense, fully employed. Within this framework it is further assumed that individual behaviour is consistent, and . . . that the individual is the best judge of his own wants.

For my purposes, the first part of the quote is especially noteworthy. As Romer (1994) argues, the conditions that are here placed under the *ceteris paribus* clause are far from rare conditions. The kind of analysis that needs to posit these assumptions may thus not be as relevant as one might assume: 'to keep things simple, set aside the niggling disputes about consumer surplus as a welfare measure' is what he suggests (Romer, 1994: 15; compare Blaug, 2001: 47).

3   A DYNAMIC WELFARE PERSPECTIVE

A more appropriate (additional) welfare theory would acknowledge the dynamics in today's knowledge economies. The comparative static foundations of a Paretian approach seem less appropriate in such circumstances. Indeed, as Cowen (2000) has argued, there have been more attempts at suggesting different theories to the established welfare economics of Pareto. Cowen (2000, xiii) distinguishes 'three dominant yet incompatible strands': ordinalist Paretian welfare theory, applied cost–benefit analysis used in practical policy, and cardinalism, of which Amartya Sen is a representative.

The public interest in the creation of new knowledge has been long established, mainly due in more recent decades to Nelson (1959, 1990). In a dynamic economy, a static approach to welfare, emphasizing the end-state kind of competition, does not seem to be very appropriate. Thus, 'welfare loss triangles are admitted and downplayed' as Nelson (1981: 106) has expressed it, following Schumpeter (1943). A welfare perspective emphasizing the dynamics in an economy will need to combine insights from a diverse set of related fields, as such a perspective has not been developed to date (compare Mokyr, 2002: 21–7).

Schumpeter (1943) indicates that the effects of choices made by private or public parties should (also) be evaluated in terms of their long-term effects: which alternative leads to the most attractive outcome in the future? Schumpeter seems to indicate that measurable effects in the market as well as more immeasurable effects inside and outside of the market should be taken into consideration, although he is not very clear about how to develop these ideas into more operational terms. In line with Schumpeter's work, and prompted by a number of other scholars, I would suggest that 'communication' between agents plays an important role in shaping the processes through which an economy evolves from one stage to the next. To be more concrete, it would seem that there is a positive association between the ease with which communication may occur and economic development (see Dudley, 1999; Mokyr, 2002).

A main starting point in this chapter will be to use a Cobb–Douglas type function for the production of knowledge. The use of this kind of function to model the production of knowledge is far from unique (Audretsch, 1998; Dudley, 1999), despite the use of production functions being questioned in general (Shaikh, 1990), in part due to the failure of the efforts at growth accounting (Denison, 1967). I start from the idea that communication between parties can be more or less difficult, and that these difficulties can be translated into costs. The extent to which communication is difficult (costly) relates directly to the technology used, as well as to the established (cultural) mores about communication (compare Mokyr, 2002; Nelson, 1990), and to more formal institutions. The costs can be direct or more mediated, and the effects are both on levels of welfare and on the ways organizations take shape (Milgrom and Roberts, 1988).

In line with what Dudley (1999) suggests, three kinds of costs are related to communication – the level of the costs involved determines the kind of communication that one may expect.[4] One may distinguish storage (s), decoding (d) and transmission (tr) costs of communication. Communication is an input that would lead to the 'output' of newly used and created knowledge. As it can often only be determined ex post if the knowledge involved signifies an incremental or a radical development, the discussion here applies to both these situations.[5] When all of these costs are high, no communication occurs.[6] When transmission costs are low but the others remain high, communication will be centralized, much as shown in Figure 8.3a presents. As storage costs decrease, as in Figure 8.3b, a decentralized communication structure emerges. When, finally, decoding costs are low, a distributed kind of communication will be observed (Figure 8.3c). It would seem that these three different communication costs capture what Nelson (2004) calls 'the communitarianism of scientific knowledge'. The suggested sequence for decreases in these communication costs seems to match what may be observed when one considers developments in the use of techniques involved in communication. Table 8.1 summarizes this discussion. Communication that is distributed is to be preferred from the position of the public interest, as knowledge and information is exchanged most readily and conditions for economic and societal development are most conducive.

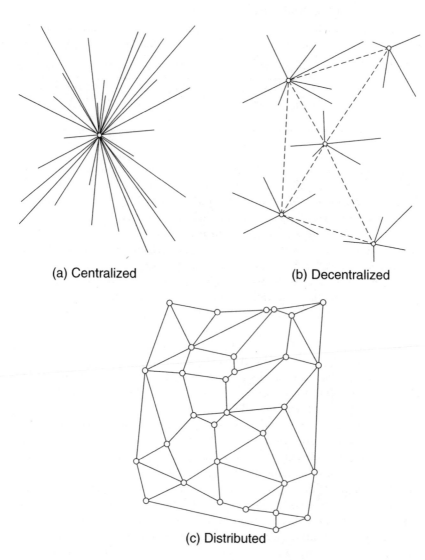

(a) Centralized   (b) Decentralized

(c) Distributed

Source: Dudley (1999).

Figure 8.3   Communication structures

Table 8.1 Communication and communication costs

Costs of	Type of communication			
	None	Centralized (a)	Decentralized (b)	Distributed (c)
Transmission (tr)	High	Low	Low	Low
Storage (s)	High	High	Low	Low
Decoding (d)	High	High	High	Low

The basic insight that centralization of communication raises costs, which is not beneficial for society, was also argued for by Nelson (1981: 101): 'the argument that centralization imposes high information and calculation costs carries considerable weight in a dynamic context'. Indeed, for him it is a central argument for favouring capitalism over socialism, as it was for Hayek. This view contrasts with 'the standard theoretical analysis [which] implies that only zero spillovers [of knowledge] are compatible with optimality in innovative activity' (Baumol, 2002: 121). Rather, extensive dissemination of new knowledge benefits society, and it is of course this argument that is fundamental for the system of intellectual property rights. In exchange for a temporary exclusive right to use of newly developed knowledge, a party is to make this knowledge publicly available in order for others to build on it. Many firms, however, even consider it directly beneficial for themselves to disseminate their newly developed knowledge (Baumol, 2002: 73), for instance because network effects can kick in more readily (Shapiro and Varian, 1999). Knowledge might also transfer inadvertently between firms, and it is for this reason that firms cluster geographically (Saxenian, 1994). Indeed, for firms in high-tech sectors there is reason to assume the existence of a *causal* link between the decision by a firm to set up shop in a particular location and the knowledge infrastructure already present in that vicinity (Van der Panne and Dolfsma, 2003).

Pace Dudley (1999) one could include the three different communication costs in a Cobb–Douglas production function in order to assess the effects of changes in communication costs for economic welfare (equation 8.1). The main purpose of this production function is to evaluate *changes* in communication costs in terms of their effect on social welfare, and less so to study the effect of the absolute size of these costs. For my discussion here issues of returns to scale are irrelevant. A Cobb–Douglas production function makes most sense when the analysis is at an aggregate level, while there is also support for the use of this function at a disaggregate level (for example, Gurbaxani et al., 2000). Given the nature of the exogenous variables involved, there is no point in assuming constant elasticities of substitution and hence adopting a CES production function. The Cobb–Douglas production function is the most readily interpretable production function and is used most often in the literature (compare Audretsch, 1998). The suggested Cobb–Douglas production function primarily provides a heuristic tool here, certainly in light of Rosenberg's (1994: 53–4, italics added) assertion that '[i]nnovation is the creation of knowledge that cannot, and therefore should not, be "anticipated" by the theorist in a *purely* formal manner'. Nonetheless, it seems plausible to assume that a community of size $(n)^7$ will, in period $(t+1)$, experience a social welfare (q) generated by communication in period (t) that can be represented as:

$$q_{t+1} = A \left(\frac{n_t}{s_t}\right)^\alpha \left(\frac{1}{tr_t}\right)^\beta \left(\frac{n_t - 1}{d_t}\right)^\lambda \qquad (8.1)$$

where:
$0 < \alpha, \beta,$ and $\gamma < 1,$
$n \gg 1,$ and
$s_t, tr_t,$ and $d_t > 0.^8$

In this function (A) is the efficiency parameter. The concrete shape of the production function makes economic sense. A rise in any of the communication costs will hamper economic activity and thus economic welfare – for this reason communication costs enter the denominator in the equation. Decoding communicated messages is proportional to the size of a population, but needs only to be done by the receiver of a message. On this Dudley (1999: 602) further remarks that 'the efficiency of markets depends on people's ability to negotiate and enforce contracts, output is decreasing in the cost, d, of decoding a unit of information. Owing to network effects, this transaction cost is offset by increases in the number of other people, $n_t - 1$, with whom each individual can communicate.' Due to the impact of knowledge on productivity, output (q) increases with the amount of information stored. The relation between (q) and storage cost (s) is inverse under competitive market conditions in particular. There is, furthermore, a direct link between the size of a population and the storage costs that need to be incurred. Transmission costs (tr) are not directly related to the size of a population; depending on circumstances (costs), a population of a given size can transmit knowledge extensively. If there are scale economies to joint production, for example because (co-) workers or partners need to be coordinated, however, increases in transmission costs will decrease (q). Usually, in reality, any development that affects one type of communication cost is likely also to affect other communication costs.

A dynamic welfare perspective, for which some suggestions are brought forward in these pages, might favour policy measures that violate the Pareto criterion. This would then be for different reasons than possible violations of the Pareto criterion that Pigou, for example, suggests. Pigou (1924: 78) suggests that an income redistribution from rich to the poor would be justifiable because that would allow 'more intense wants to be satisfied'. Indeed, for the dynamic welfare perspective suggested here utilitarian considerations play a less prominent role than for the Paretian view to which Pigou also subscribes in large measure. How the suggested dynamic Schumpeterian welfare perspective suggested here fits in Cowen's classification introduced at the start of this section is not clear. In any case, I would not present this approach as necessarily incompatible with the other three kinds.

4 CHANGES IN THE SYSTEM OF IPRS AND WELFARE

Intellectual Property Rights (IPRs) are central institutions in a knowledge economy. The relevant legal and technological changes are easily identified, even though not all of their effects are clear. Evaluating developments in IPRs from a perspective of their effects on the dynamics of an economy is entirely appropriate given the objectives for this part of the system of law. Indeed, the purpose of establishing IPRs is two-fold: first to stimulate the creation of new (useful) knowledge, and, second, to stimulate its dissemination. As Levin et al. (1987) observed, among others, however, the positive effects of the presence and extension of IPRs is often assumed to be self-evident. IPRs are believed to be beneficial for both the firm that has obtained them and for society as a whole. There is, of course, some discussion in academic circles about the effects of IPRs and how to evaluate these (Towse and Holzhauer, 2002), but these are mostly in comparative-static Paretian terms. The duration and scope of patents is one such topic. A disregard for IPRs need not hurt the innovating firm. Other means to protect one's innovations might be preferred (Levin et al., 1987), or network effects might better kick in if the innovating firm strengthens or enforces its IPR position less rigorously (Takeyama, 1994). In what follows I will discuss a number of changes in patent law and copyright law in terms of their effects on communications costs. The changes I discuss are not exhaustive, although they do include the most significant ones. Each of the changes in IPRs discussed will have effects on all of the three communication costs.

The span of the IPR system has grown over time. In the US, a law protecting legal rights in databases has been introduced, while the protection under patent law of software or business models is now allowed. In addition, the (statutory) limitations on the commercial exploitation of the knowledge developed have decreased in number. This is no mixed picture: IPRs have grown stronger over time. Especially in the past decade a number of noteworthy developments can be mentioned. Often, the development in the United States is followed by changes in Europe. In this chapter, the differences between the two legal systems (US and Europe) are emphasized less than the similarities between the two. The purpose of the discussion here is thus to evaluate the potential effects of *changes* to the system of IPRs rather than to offer an analysis of the systems as they exist in a way that is relevant for economists.[9] A more standard welfare approach has also noted the undesirable effects of changes in IPRs in general and patents in particular. It is argued, for instance, that such developments may distort the direction of technological change (Adams and Encauoua, 1994), possibly slow down technological progress (Takalo and Kanniainen, 2000), or reduce incentives to compete in R&D or in downstream product markets (Encaoua and Hollander, 2002).

Following the US, Europe has now decided that software can be protected under patent law in addition to copyright law, under which it would have been protected previously. The protection patent law offers is shorter than copyright law, but is more powerful. Copyright law protects the particular expression of an idea, while patent law protects the idea itself irrespective of the way in which it is expressed. As ideas can usually be expressed in more than one way, copyrights offer a weaker kind of protection than patents do. Copyrights do not need to be registered in most countries, albeit that registration may facilitate enforcement in some cases, and is in force immediately after publication of the material, while an application for a patent needs to be filed and approved, involving a variety of expenses.[10] Several criteria need to be met before a patent can be granted: an inventive step needs to be involved, one that is non-obvious to someone skilled in the prior art. There needs to be an industrial application, and, in addition, at least until recently, a physical component has to be part of the application.

The scope of patent law is most hotly debated at the moment, both in the US and in Europe, in relation to the question of whether business models and software should also be patentable. Does Amazon.com's patent for 'one-click shopping' not violate the requirement that a patent should involve a physical component and must involve an inventive step? It is true that software is often not clearly distinguishable from hardware, and the demand that a patent application needs to constitute an inventive step might be difficult to sustain. Reneging on these requirements too easily might, however, give rise to rent-seeking behaviour on the part of the producing firms. In this case, only software is involved, while the software ('cookies') had already been developed prior to the application by Amazon. The particular business model is a useful invention, to be sure, but does the patent on this model not unduly raise communications costs? Certainly it does for other firms who would like to use this method and now have to license it. In addition, the model also allows firms to increase the extent to which they may differentiate their products and discriminate their prices. The net result of the latter is likely to be that consumers suffer (compare Dolfsma, 2004). The decision to extend the scope of patents to include living tissue is contested as well. Besides the moral aspects of the debate, there is the issue that the distinction between discovering and inventing, never entirely clear, is blurred to the extent that it no longer exists. The latter (invention) used to be a precondition for a patent to be granted. Patentability on living tissue might, but need not, have speeded up the discovery of the exact shape of the human genome, for instance, but it will severely restrict the use to which that knowledge can be put in the coming years.

The duration of patents has increased too, most recently (1998) from 18 to 20 years in the US. The lengthening of the patent for pharmaceutical products is probably less problematic in this light, given the requirements these face before they are allowed on the market, although it does fit the general picture. Fisher (2001) provides a more extended discussion of the development in patent law and its effects on innovative activity.

Copyright equally has extended in scope and duration; legal scholar Lessig (1999, 2001) is among the more prominent people to lament this development.[11] Most recently, the duration of copyright in the US was lengthened from the life of the author plus 50 years to the life of the author plus 70 years, effective retrospectively. Several years ago both the US and Europe started protecting databases as part of copyright laws. In the past a collection of 'brute facts' would not constitute a creative act and would thus not warrant protection, however, a database is now protected (Maurer et al., 2001). The American Digital Millennium Copyright Act (DMCA, which came into force in 1998) as well as the European Directive on Copyright (2001) prohibit agents from making available technical measures that might be used to circumvent measures taken to protect copyrighted work (Koelman, 2000). As these means can often also be used for other, legitimate purposes, this element of the new copyright law is much debated. It is also unclear what 'making available' means: does a scientist in the field of, for example, cryptology, presenting his work to fellow scientists make available a means to circumvent the technical protection (encryption) on copyrighted work? Encryption technology is also used to prevent consumers from making copies of work to be used in different regions of the world than their own. The world is divided into regions with different hardware specifications, which prevent software from one region being recognized in one of the other five regions (Dunt et al., 2002). The cost to society seems evident as consumers are restricted in the consumption of something they have legally obtained (Dunt et al., 2002). Encryption may also be used to prevent consumers from playing a CD on a personal computer, making a copy for personal use, to share with family and close friends, or as a back-up. This especially increases storage costs.

The tendency to strengthen the protection offered by copyright law is also clear in the way in which it is enforced. A law can never spell out how exactly it should be applied, and perhaps it should not as a matter of principle. Therefore, judges when applying the law have room for their own interpretation, certainly in a Roman Law system but even in a Common Law system where leeway for a judge looking at a specific case is more limited by need to consider to a larger degree the rulings given in other, similar cases. Considerations about the effect of enforcing copyright for competition in a market are rarely aired – the fields of IPR and anti-trust law are quite separate even when one sees them conflict in reality (Encaoua and Hollander, 2002; Dolfsma, 2002b). An example is the ruling on Napster, where what is called in legal terms 'normal exploitation' of a work is extended to the full exploitation, covering the publication of a work in ways that were not foreseen at the time of the creation. Walt Disney could not have foreseen that his creation Mickey Mouse (formerly Steamboat Willie) would be published digitally and distributed over the Internet. This creation would not formerly have been protected under copyright law from publication by others on the Internet, as this means of exploitation would not be included under 'normal' exploitation at the time of the creation. Now this existing work is also protected, retrospectively, under copyright law, from distribution over the Internet. In actual fact, there is another catch to this court case against Napster. The court decided that existing players should first be allowed to develop a means by which to make music available in digital form legally, without limiting the time they could take.[12] The use of copyright law as an entry barrier has become stronger.

The developments listed above restrict the use of a legally acquired work by a consumer. Either directly or indirectly the limitation built into copyright law of 'fair use' is restricted by a combination of legal and technical means.[13] At present, legal and technical developments are thus under way to make a 'strong' system of digital rights management possible under copyright law. In addition to a strict enforcement of a strengthened copyright law, techniques such as encryption are required. The circumvention of the latter then needs to be prohibited by law as well. These developments have clearly been informed by a desire to strengthen the economic position of the owner of the intellectual rights (Koelman, 2004). For their effects on the dynamics in the economy to be appreciated one would have to assess their impact on communication costs, either directly or indirectly.

Relating the discussion about the development of IPRs to the different kinds of communications costs introduced in Section 3 is quite straightforward. It is also useful to suggest the translation of some of these developments into communication costs. Certainly, communication costs increase in relative terms as a result of the full-scale application of IPRs to the knowledge economy (Stiglitz, 1999), a result further shored up by the developments in the system of IPR itself. Decoding costs rise as a result of the technical measures to prevent copyrighted works from being copied, used in certain electronic equipment, or outside certain geographical boundaries. More information carriers are needed than would otherwise be the case, or a higher price would have to be paid for the carrier that can be used in the different regions. Using available knowledge for new acts of creation will become more expensive when the scope and duration of IPRs expand – this basically relates to direct transmission costs (licences), but also to costs that need to be borne in inquiring whether an action would be violating another party's legal rights (Lessig, 2001). As the development of knowledge is necessarily cumulative, such costs may be high, and having to incur such costs will not be a stimulus for innovation. Storage costs rise as a consequence. The fact that transmission costs rise seems clear, certainly when discussing developments in the area of copyright. For copyright law two central notions come into play: publishing and copying. Transmitting knowledge, either using an existing channel or using a new way of publishing material, becomes more expensive as a result of the developments discussed, as the rights holders' position has become stronger over the years. A rights holder can refuse to publish a work through a new means of communication. More kinds of works are protected, while the number of limitations to a legal position has been restricted, thus increasing transmission costs. This holds for transmission of knowledge protected under patent law as well, as circumstances under which a party would need to take a licence proliferate. Unless the authorities impose a compulsory licence when the public interest would seem to demand it, the rights holder can prevent the use of a particular piece of knowledge by others, implying a steep increase in transmission costs.

5   IPR, COMPETITION AND SOCIAL WELFARE

How may one evaluate the developments in IPRs, which may be considered among the more important institutions for a knowledge economy, from the perspective of a dynamic (Schumpeterian) welfare theory? As knowledge is often communicated as information, the characteristics of information goods are important to note. The well-known characteristics of such goods and the markets they are exchanged on (Dolfsma, 1998) entail that a full-scale application of IPRs in a knowledge economy is itself a de facto strengthening of IPRs, and certainly to the extent that the knowledge economy is a digital one (Stiglitz, 1999), irrespective of the developments in IPRs that may be witnessed. Stiglitz (1999: 10) holds that information goods generate more positive externalities than physical goods. While the social returns to innovation are much bigger than the private ones in general anyway (Jones and Williams, 1998), the creation of new information goods (knowledge) would in this line of reasoning serve the public interest even more. Further restricting the diffusion of such information and knowledge would generate high opportunity costs.

Considering this discussion of the development of IPRs in light of the proposed dynamic welfare perspective developed earlier, one could claim with Stiglitz (1999: 9) that 'it is possible that an excessively "strong" intellectual property regime may actually inhibit the pace of innovation', and slow the pace of economic development. Such a conclusion hinges, of course, on the effects of developments in IPRs in terms of communication costs on innovative activity.

Economists would be interested in the effects of such developments on competition in a market too (Boldrin and Levine, 2002; Romer, 2002). Some of these effects are not always clear, and can perhaps be illustrated best by referring to the case of the music industry and the role copyright plays. The existing business model of firms in the music industry is strongly predicated on the existence of copyrights (Huygens et al., 2001; Dolfsma, 2000). At least until a complete harmonization on all legal issues of law is realized across the globe, a legal system's geographical boundaries are important to keep in mind. The geographical basis of copyright law is a de facto restriction of the relevant market, allowing firms to monitor each other's behaviour closely – indeed a game theoretic analysis shows that collusion is likely to occur (Klaes, 1997). In the oligopolistic market such as this one, the outcome is an absence of competition on price (compare Selten, 1973).

It is Baumol (2002) who has argued forcefully that competition in a free market is to be regarded as the main cause for economic growth. His explanation is that it is not only the creation, but *most importantly* the diffusion of knowledge that is best facilitated by the free market (see also Mokyr, 2002). According to calculations by Baumol (2002), 80 per cent of the economic benefits generated by innovations do *not* accrue to the parties directly or indirectly involved with the innovation. Extending the scope and duration of IPRs should decrease that percentage. The conviction that the creation of new knowledge is thus stimulated is premised on a number of beliefs that need not be true – instead, their validity needs to be established empirically. These (possibly incorrect or incomplete) views include:

- Innovators are motivated by monetary/material rewards (only);[14]
- Creative individuals possess the rights in their creations and will thus receive the reward;
- IPRs are the best means to reward creative individuals materially;[15]
- It is always, or at least in most cases, in the best interest of rights holders to diffuse the knowledge (or the products which embody them) as much as possible once they have obtained IPR protection.[16]

The last point, concerning the inclination to diffuse newly developed knowledge, stimulated by the system of IPRs, relates to the question of which circumstances stimulate economic growth. Does allowing innovators a larger share of the economic pie stimulate innovation and economic growth such that in absolute (even if not in relative) terms everybody's pie is larger, or is it a zero-sum game? The matter relates directly to a government's goal of the public good and whether that is best served by enforcing IPRs. The argument as suggested in Section 3 particularly is that the dynamic effects are at least as important in such considerations as the static, distributive ones, and that the effects of developments in IPRs in these terms may well have to be judged as detrimental.

6 CONCLUSION

A knowledge-based economy needs a welfare theory that is able to grasp and evaluate its dynamics. In this chapter, I have taken suggestions from Schumpeter in developing some ideas for a dynamic welfare economics. These ideas acknowledge the role of knowledge for an economy. As knowledge develops cumulatively in direct interactions between people, and is not simply available off the shelf or indeed like manna from heaven to be put to use freely, the cost of communication has a strong impact on the diffusion of knowledge and the social welfare of a country. I distinguish storage, decoding and transmission costs related to communication of knowledge, to indicate that changes in these costs will affect (future) social welfare. Recent developments in intellectual property rights (IPRs) in the terms of their effect on communication costs, suggests that the current strengthening of IPRs is debatable. Changes in IPRs increase the costs of communication and could therefore be a potential impediment for the dynamics of the economy, and thus for future social welfare. The conclusion drawn by Romer (1993: 66) that an economics of ideas requires 'a policy of openness with few distortions' would thus find support (compare Nelson, 2004).

NOTES

1. This chapter builds on earlier work (Dolfsma, 2005).
2. See Hansen (1999), Aalbers et al. (2005), van der Eijk et al. (2005).
3. See Saxenian (1994), and Van der Panne and Dolfsma (2003) and references therein.
4. Casson (1997: 279) argues that transaction costs are a special case of communication costs. His is a plausible argument that needs to be pursued further, but that will not be undertaken here.
5. In addition, a technology (knowledge) may be introduced from one context into another, where it may be perceived as radically new while in the former context it had been developing incrementally (Levinthal, 1998).
6. For the sake of clarity, I assume that communication cost is a binary variable; it is either 'high' or 'low'.
7. A community need not be a country, and is perceived here as relatively homogeneous in terms of the cognitive distance (Nooteboom, 2000) of its members towards each other and in terms of the knowledge that is tacit.
8. Therefore, this production function is strictly quasi-concave, while its isoquants are negatively sloped and strictly convex.
9. See Raskind (1998) and Kitch (1998). For a broad overview, see Towse and Holzhauer (2002). For a theoretical economic justification for copyrights, see Landes and Posner (1989). Hettinger (1989) provides a broader discussion of the rationale for copyrights.
10. OECD (1997) discusses some of the differences in the way in which patents are administered in the US and Europe, as well as their implications.
11. See also Netanel (1996); and among economists see Towse and Holzhauer (2002) and Stiglitz (1999).
12. Court of Appeals for the Ninth Circuit, A&M records, INC. vs. Napster, INC; see also Dolfsma (2002b).
13. For a discussion of the US 'fair use' principle (fair dealing in the UK), and its relation to similar limitations in Continental European law – in the Roman Law tradition – see Alberdingk Thijm (1998). In brief, in Continental Europe an exhaustive list of uses that copyright does not prohibit is drawn up, while the US uses a procedure to establish if the use of copyright protected material is fair. How computer code (software) can restrict uses that are in fact legal is discussed by Lessig (1999). Guibault (2002) discusses how contract law is used to obviate the limitations to exclusive exploitation by the copyright owner present in copyright so as to allow for an extended legal protection.
14. See Hui and Png (2002), or Frey (1997) and Le Grand (2003) for a more general argument.
15. However, see Shavell and van Ypersele (2001).
16. Compare Jaffe and Lerner (2004).

REFERENCES

Aalbers, R., W. Dolfsma and O. Koppius (2005), 'On and Off the Beaten Path: How Individuals Broker Knowledge through Formal and Informal Networks', mimeo, Erasmus University Rotterdam.

Adams, W.J. and D. Encaoua (1994), 'Distorting the Direction of Technological Change', *European Economic Review*, **38**: 663–73.

Alberdingk Thijm, C. (1998), 'Fair Use', *Informatierecht/AMI*, **9**: 145–54.

Arundel, A. (2001), 'The Relative Effectiveness of Patents and Secrecy for Appropriation', *Research Policy*, **30**: 611–24.

Audretsch, D.B. (1998), 'Agglomeration and the Location of Innovative Activity', *Oxford Review of Economic Policy*, **14**: 18–29.

Bandura, A. (1986), *Social Foundations of Thought and Action – A Social Cognitive Theory*, Englewood Cliffs, NJ: Prentice-Hall.

Baumol, W.J. (2002), 'The Free-market Innovation Machine: Analyzing the Growth Miracle of Capitalism', Princeton, NJ: Princeton University Press.

Blaug, M. (1980), *The Methodology of Economics*, Cambridge: Cambridge University Press.

Blaug, M. (2001), 'Is Competition Such a Good Thing? Static versus Dynamic Efficiency', *Review of Industrial Organization*, **19**: 37–48.

Boldrin, M. and D. Levine (2002), 'The Case against Intellectual Property', *American Economic Review*, **92**: 209–12.

Casson, M. (1997), *Information and Organization – A New Perspective on the Theory of the Firm*, Oxford: Clarendon Press.

Cowan, R., P. David and D. Foray (2000), 'The Explicit Economics of Knowledge Codification and Tacitness', *Industrial and Corporate Change*, **9**: 211–53.

Cowen, T. (2000), 'Introduction', in T. Cowen, (ed.), *Economic Welfare*, Cheltenham, UK, and Northampton, MA, USA: Edward Elgar, pp. xiii–xviii.

Denison, E.F. (1967), The Brookings Institution, Washington, DC: Why Growth Rates Differ.

Denzau, A.T. and D.C. North (1994), 'Shared Mental Models: Ideologies and Institutions' *Kyklos*, **47**: 3–31.

Dolfsma, W. (1998), 'Internet: An Economist's Utopia?' *Review of International Political Economy*, **5**: 712–20.

Dolfsma, W. (2000), 'How Will the Music Industry Weather the Globalization Storm?', *Firstmonday*, **5** (May), www.firstmonday.org.

Dolfsma, W. (2001), 'Metaphors of Knowledge in Economics', *Review of Social Economy*, **59**: 71–91.

Dolfsma, W. (2002a), 'The Mountain of Experience: How People Learn in a Complex, Evolving Environment', *International Journal of Social Economics*, **29**: 675–84.

Dolfsma, W. (2002b), 'Napster & KaZaA: Copyright & Competion, IER – Intellectueel Eigendom en Reclamerecht', **18**: 178–80.

Dolfsma, W. (2004), 'The Logic of Collective Consuming: Consumers as Subcontractors on Electronic Markets', *International Journal of Social Economics*, **31**: 832–9.

Dolfsma, W. (2005), 'Towards a Dynamic (Schumpeterian) Welfare Theory', *Research Policy*, **34**(1): 69–82.

Dosi, G. (1982), 'Technological Paradigms and Technological Trajectories: A Suggested Interpretation of the Determinants and Directions of Technical Change', *Research Policy*, **11**: 147–62.

Douglas, M. (1986), *How Institutions Think*, London: Routledge & Kegan Paul.

Dudley, L. (1999), 'Communication and Economic Growth', *European Economic Review*, **43**: 595–619.

Dunt, E., J.S. Gans and S.P. King (2002), 'The Economic Consequences of DVD Regional Restrictions', *Economic Papers*, **21**: 32–45.

Encaoua, D. and A. Hollander (2002), 'Competition Policy and Innovation', *Oxford Review of Economic Policy*, **18**: 63–79.

Fisher, W. (2001), 'Intellectual Property and Innovation: Theoretical, Empirical, and Historical Perspectives', in *Industrial Property, Innovation, and the Knowledge-based Economy*, Beleidsstudies Technologie Economie, Vol. 37.

Frey, B.S. (1997), *Not Just for the Money – An Economic Theory of Personal Motivation*, Cheltenham, UK, and Northampton, MA,USA: Edward Elgar.

Granstrand, O. (1999), *The Economics and Management of Intellectual Property*, Chetenham, UK, and Northampton, MA, USA: Edward Elgar.

Guibault, L. (2002), 'Copyright Limitations and Contract', PhD thesis, Institute for Information Law, Amsterdam.

Gurbaxani, V., N. Melville and K. Kraemer (2000), 'The Production of Information Services: A Firm-level Analysis of Information Systems Budgets', *Information Systems Research*, **11**: 159–76.

Hansen, M. (1999), 'The Search-Transfer Problem: The Role of Weak Ties in Sharing Knowledge Across Organizational Subunits', *Administrative Science Quarterly*, **44**: 82–111.

Hettinger, E.C. (1989), 'Justifying Intellectual Property', *Philosophy and Public Affairs*, **18**: 31–52.

Hui, K.-L. and I.P.L. Png (2002), 'On the Supply of Creative Work: Evidence from the Movies', *American Economic Review*, **92**: 217–20.

Huygens, M., C. Baden-Fuller, F.A.J. Van Den Bosch and H.W. Volberda (2001), 'Co-evolution of Firm Capabilities and Industry Competition: Investigating the Music Industry, 1877–1997', *Organisation Studies*, **22**: 971–1011.

Jaffe, A. and J. Lerner, (2004), *'Innovation and its Discontents'*, Princeton, NJ: Princeton University Press.

Jones, C. and J. Williams (1998), 'Measuring the Social Returns to R&D', *Quarterly Journal of Economics*, **113**: 1119–35.

Kitch, E.W. (1998), 'Patents', in P. Newman (ed.), *The New Palgrave Dictionary of Economics and Law*, Vol. 3, London: Macmillan, pp. 13–17.

Klaes, M. (1997), 'Sociotechnical Constituencies, Game Theory and the Diffusion of the Compact Disc', *Research Policy*, **25**: 1221–34.

Koelman, K. (2000), 'A Hard Nut to Crack: The Protection of Technological Measures', *European Intellectual Property Review*, **22**: 272–88.

Koelman, K. (2004), 'Copyright Law & Economics in the EU Copyright Directive: Is the Droit d'Auteur Passé?', *International Review of Intellectual Property and Competition Law*, **35**: 603–38.

Landes, W.M. and R.A. Posner (1989), 'An Economic Analysis of Copyright Law', *Journal of Legal Studies*, **18**: 325–63.

Le Grand, J. (2003), *Motivation, Agency, and Public Policy*, New York: Oxford University Press.

Lessig, L. (1999), *Code and other Laws of Cyberspace*, New York: Basic Books.

Lessig, L. (2001), *The Future of Ideas – The Fate of the Commons in a Connected World*, New York: Basic Books.

Lev, B. (2001), *Intangibles – Management, Measurement and Reporting*, Washington, DC: Brookings Istitution Press.

Levin, R., A. Klevorick, R. Nelson and S. Winter (1987), 'Appropriating the Returns from Industrial Research and Development', *Brookings Papers on Economic Activity*, **3**: 783–831.

Levinthal, D.A. (1998), 'The Slow Pace of Rapid Technological Change. Gradualism and Punctuation in Technological Change', *Industrial and Corporate Change*, **7**: 217–47.

Leydesdorff, L., W. Dolfsma and G. van der Panne (2006), 'Measuring the Knowledge Base of an Economy in terms of Triple-helix Relations among "Technology, Organization, and Territory"', *Research Policy*, **35**(2).

Mäki, U. (1993), 'Social Theories of Science and the Fate of Institutionalism in Economics', in: U. Mäki, B. Gustafsson and C. Knudsen (eds), *Rationality, Institutions and Economic Methodology*, New York: Routledge, pp. 76–109.

Maurer, S.M., B. Hugenholz and H.J. Onsrud (2001), 'Europe's Database Experiment', *Science*, **294**: 789–90.

Milgrom, P. and J. Roberts (1988), Communication and Inventory as Substitutes in Organizing Production', *Scandinavian Journal of Economics*, **90**: 275–89.

Mishan, E.J. (1960), 'A Survey of Welfare Economics', *Economic Journal*, **70**: 197–265.

Mokyr, J. (2002), *The Gifts of Athena – Historical Origins of the Knowledge Economy*, Princeton, NJ: Princeton University Press.

Nelson, R.R. (1959), 'The Simple Economics of Basic Scientific Research', *Journal of Political Economy*, **67**: 297–306.

Nelson, R.R. (1981), 'Assessing Private Enterprise: An Exegesis of Tangled Doctrine', *Bell Journal of Economics*, **12**: 93–111.

Nelson, R.R. (1990), 'Capitalism as an Engine of Growth', *Research Policy*, **19**: 193–214.

Nelson, R.R. (2004), 'The Market Economy, and the Scientific Commons', *Research Policy*, **33**: 455–71.

Netanel, N.W. (1996), 'Copyright and a Democratic Civil Society', *Yale Law Review*, **106**: 283–387.

Nooteboom, B. (2000), *Learning and Innovation in Organizations and Economies*, Oxford: Oxford University Press.

Organisation for Economic Cooperation and Development (1996), *Employment and Growth in the Knowledge-based Economy*, Paris: OECD.

Organisation for Economic Cooperation and Development, (1997), *Patents and Innovation in the International Context*, Paris: OECD.

Pigou, A.C. (1924), *The Economics of Welfare*, 2nd edn, London: Macmillan.

Polanyi, M. (1983) [1966], *The Tacit Dimension*, Gloucester, Massachusetts: Peter Smith.

Raskind, L.J. (1998), 'Copyright', in: P. Newman (ed.), *The New Palgrave Dictionary of Economics and Law*, London: Macmillan, pp. 478–83.

Romer, P. (1986), 'Increasing Returns and Long-run Growth', *Journal of Political Economy*, **94**: 1002–37.

Romer, P. (1993), 'Two Strategies for Economic Development: Using Ideas and Producing Ideas', Proceedings of the World Bank Annual Conference on Development Economics 1992, IBRD/World Bank.

Romer, P. (1994), 'New Goods, Old Theory, and the Welfare Costs of Trade Restrictions', *Journal of Development Economics*, **43**: 5–38.

Romer, P. (2002), 'When Should We Use Intellectual Property Rights?', *American Economic Review*, **92**: 213–16.

Rosenberg, N. (1990), 'Why Do Firms Do Basic Research (with their Own Money)?', *Research Policy*, **19**: 165–74.

Rosenberg, N. (1994), *Exploring the Black Box: Technology, Economics and History*, Cambridge: Cambridge University Press.

Saxenian, A. (1994), *Regional Advantage*, Cambridge, MA: Harvard University Press.

Schumpeter, J. (1943) [1952], *Capitalism, Socialism and Democracy*, London: Allen & Unwin.

Scitovsky, T. (1977), *The Joyless Economy*, Oxford: Oxford University Press.

Selten, R. (1973), 'A Simple Model of Imperfect Competition where Four are Few and Six are Many', *International Journal of Game Theory*, **2**: 141–201.

Shaikh, A. (1990), 'Humbug Production Function', in: J. Eatwell, M. Milgate and P. Newman (eds), *The New Palgrave: A Dictionary of Economic Theory and Doctrine*, London: Macmillan, pp. 191–4.

Shapiro, C. and H. Varian (1999), *Information Rules*, Boston, MA: Harvard Business Review Press.

Shavell, S. and T. van Ypersele (2001), 'Rewards versus Intellectual Property Rights', *Journal of Law and Economics*, **44**: 525–47.

Stiglitz, J. (1999), 'Public Policy for a Knowledge Economy', Department for Trade and Industry & Centre for Economic Policy Research, London.

Takalo, T. and V. Kanniainen (2000), 'Do Patents Slow Down Technological Progress? Real Options in Research, Patenting, and Market Introduction', *International Journal of Industrial Organization*, **18**: 1105–27.

Takeyama, L.N. (1994), 'The Welfare Implications of Unauthorized Reproduction of Intellectual Property in the Presence of Demand Network Externalities', *Journal of Industrial Economics*, **42**: 155–66.

Towse, R. and R. Holzhauer (eds) (2002), *The Economics of Intellectual Property*, 4 vols, Cheltenham, UK, and Northampton, MA, USA: Edward Elgar.

van de Poel, I., M. Fransen and W. Dolfsma (2002), 'Technological Regimes: Taking Stock, Looking Ahead', *International Journal of Technology, Policy and Management*, **2**: 482–95.

van der Eijk, R., W. Dolfsma and A. Jolink (2005), 'Black Box and Black Hole: Social Capital, Gifts and Culture', paper presented at the EGOS conference, Berlin, Germany.

van der Panne, G. and W. Dolfsma, (2003), 'The Odd Role of Proximity in Knowledge Relations – High-tech in the Netherlands', *Journal of Economic and Social Geography*, **94**: 453–62.

Veblen, T. (1961), 'Why is Economics not an Evolutionary Science?', in T. Veblen, *The Place of Science in Modern Civilisation and Other Essays*. New York: Russell & Russell, pp. 56–81.

Vickers, J. (1995), 'Concepts of Competition', *Oxford Economic Papers*, **47**: 1–23.

9. Beyond the codification debate: a 'Naturalist' view of knowledge

Jorge Bateira

1 INTRODUCTION[1]

A lack of theoretical discussion in economics on concepts such as *knowledge* and *information*, particularly in science and technology literature and in the broader field of innovation, has been recently acknowledged (Metcalfe and Ramlogan, 2005; Smith, 2002). This situation may be due to a defensive attitude adopted by a large number of economists who refrain from interdisciplinary dialogue, or even admit that the discipline should 'economise' this kind of speculation. An illustration of this lack of interdisciplinary curiosity is the uncritical adoption, mostly in evolutionary economics, of ideas imported from artificial intelligence (AI) and the cognitivist psychology diffused by Herbert Simon since the 1950s. The problem is that those theories are framed within a mechanistic understanding of knowledge that flagrantly contradicts the evolutionary affiliation invoked by that same literature. Acknowledging the above-mentioned inconsistency, this chapter would like to show, firstly, that there is an evolutionary alternative to cognitivism and, secondly, what kind of implications we might expect from its adoption in economics.

The neoclassical growth models of the 1980s (Lucas, 1988; Romer, 1986), and their subsequent refinements, continue to be an important field of diffusion by mainstream economics of a peculiar understanding of knowledge, a kind of disembodied capital good. However, the 1980s also saw the emergence of a rival stream of research. Integrating the concept of 'tacit knowledge' from Michael Polanyi within Herbert Simon's theoretical framework, Nelson and Winter (1982) provided a strong critique of neoclassical economics and laid what has been called the foundational work for most contemporary evolutionary thinking in the discipline (Cantner and Hanusch, 2002).

While mainstream economists continue to apply neoclassical analysis to the production, transmission and management of knowledge, a 'new economics of science' appeared in the 1990s (Dasgupta and

David, 1994; David and Foray, 1995; Cowan and Foray, 1997). This strand combines neoclassical analysis with contributions of new institutionalism, and identifies information with codified knowledge, which can be treated as a commodity. Despite these innovations, knowledge is still conceptualized as a personal stock that determines the so-called collective knowledge of organizations and the 'general level' of a society's knowledge.

Acknowledging this intellectual background, the present chapter takes as its point of departure the current debate about knowledge codification and the importance of 'tacit knowledge' (Ancori et al., 2000; Cowan et al., 2000; Nightingale, 2003), in order to argue for an understanding of knowledge that goes beyond the opposing stances. Adopting an interdisciplinary approach, the chapter attempts to present a new understanding for information and knowledge that bridges the current gap between economics and natural sciences. At the same time, it aims to bring into discussion a broad (and hopefully consistent) framework that could be useful for those economists who are not content with current approaches to knowledge (Dolfsma, 2001; Nooteboom, 2001).

The chapter proceeds as follows. In the second section, we contrast the positions in the 'codification debate' with Michael Polanyi's texts. The third section argues for an evolutionary understanding of the mind, which points to a 'Naturalist' worldview in line with forerunning intuitions of Polanyi. The fourth section presents basic ideas about the interactivist-constructivist (I-C) model of cognition, which fits the Naturalist stance outlined in the previous section. The fifth section reviews the above-mentioned debate in light of the I-C model proposed, and discusses some implications. A brief conclusion summarizes the basic tenets of the argument and suggests its usefulness for evolutionary economics.

2   DISENTANGLING A DEBATE

2.1   Back to Polanyi

Since Lündvall and Johnson's (1994) arguments on the emergence of a 'knowledge economy', economists have shown increasing difficulties in dealing with this fuzzy reality we call knowledge. Despite such difficulties, and with a few exceptions, most economics literature has not used recent research results of other disciplines in order to build on a warranted understanding of knowledge. A possible reason for this may reside on the pivotal work of Nelson and Winter (1982) (from now on N&W), which exerted a strong influence in the evolutionary stream of economics by combining the conceptual contributions of two great promoters of interdisciplinary research, Michael Polanyi and Herbert Simon.

Taking N&W as the foundational reference, most non-mainstream economists and other social scientists quickly adopted the concept of 'tacit knowledge', mostly identified with non-articulated knowledge underlying a skill, and left behind both the original texts of Polanyi and his epistemological framework. Although this movement has been important for the revitalization of an alternative to the neoclassical school, the close association of N&W's interpretation of Polanyi with the cognitivist conception of a 'rule-based' mind[2] had the consequence of diverting attention from the evolution of cognitive science beyond cognitivism during the last decades (Overton, 1994).

In fact, N&W made their interpretation of Polanyi's tacit knowledge through the cognitivist concept of 'rules'. The fact that Polanyi said – in a earlier work developed during the 1950s – 'that the aim of a skilful performance is achieved by the *observance of a set of rules* which are not known as such to the person following them' (Polanyi, 1962: 49; emphasis mine) has been particularly useful for N&W's reading of Polanyi's ideas within the cognitivist framework. Setting aside the fact that a rule-based concept of mind is absent from Polanyi's thinking, we want to highlight that this work corresponds to an intermediate step in his research, which led to reformulations that he explicitly acknowledged in the Introduction to Polanyi (1966: x).

This mediated reception of the concept of 'tacit knowledge' may be exemplified by the definitions used in the texts chosen for the present discussion. Following Ancori et al.'s (2000) definition, 'basically, explicit knowledge refers to knowledge that is transmittable in formal, systematic language, while tacit knowledge has a personal quality which makes it hard to formalize and communicate' (p. 273). On the other hand, Cowan et al. (2000) present a particular tripartite typology of knowledge including *articulated*, *unarticulated*, and *unarticulable* knowledge, the latter being a residual type to put aside 'as not very interesting for the social sciences' (p. 230). About the tacitness of knowledge associated with a skilful performance, Cowan et al. (2000: 219) claim that N&W 'accept Polanyi's (1967) account of such situations as being contextual, rather than absolute', and conclude that costs matter in the process of converting tacit into codified knowledge: 'Rather, the question is whether the costs associated with the obstacles to articulation are sufficiently high so that the knowledge *in fact* remains tacit' (p. 82).

Reading N&W, Cowan et al. (2000) found enough material to consolidate the idea (supposedly subscribed by Polanyi) that a skilful performance needs two types of knowledge – *articulated* knowledge in correspondence with *focal awareness*, and *tacit* knowledge in correspondence with *subsidiary awareness* – and that there exists a boundary between these two types of knowledge that is not absolute but contextual. However, when we read Polanyi's texts we do not find this dichotomy. On the contrary, what Polanyi discusses is *a unitary process of knowing based on two kinds of awareness*. Already in the Introduction to Polanyi (1966: p. x) we can read:

> all thought contains components of which we are subsidiarily aware in the focal content of our thinking, and that all thought dwells in its subsidiaries, as if they were parts of our body. Hence thinking is not only necessarily intentional, as Brentano has taught: it is also necessarily fraught with the roots that it embodies. It has a from–to structure.

As we can see across his texts, Polanyi names 'tacit knowing' the overall process by which we integrate a subsidiary awareness into the focal awareness when we attend to something. Polanyi does not identify 'subsidiary' awareness with the unconscious, which is a frequent misunderstanding of his ideas. In a late text that summarizes his arguments, Polanyi (1975: 39) stated: 'Focal awareness is, of course, always fully conscious, but subsidiary awareness, or from-awareness, can exist at any level of consciousness, ranging from the subliminal to the fully conscious. What makes awareness subsidiary is its functional character.'

Further, Polanyi (1975: 41) clearly emphasized that the integration of these subsidiaries is a skill that we acquire by training, which 'cannot be replaced by any explicit mechanical procedure'. Therefore, after having analysed how even natural sciences must rely on some personal skill and personal judgement, Polanyi (1975: 31) concludes: 'Personal, tacit assessments and evaluations, we see, are required at every step in the acquisition of knowledge – even "scientific" knowledge'.

As a medical scientist and chemist Michael Polanyi has been attentive to research in other disciplines. A careful study of the results in different fields of science authorized him to stress the embodiment of knowing, the core of his concerns: 'I said that by elucidating the way our bodily processes participate in our perceptions we will throw light on *the bodily roots of all thought*, including man's highest creative powers' (Polanyi, 1966: 15; emphasis mine).

This brief overview sharply contrasts with much diffused ideas on a supposed dichotomy of 'tacit *versus* codified' knowledge in Polanyi's thinking. Instead of the tacit dimension of all knowledge insistently argued by Polanyi, 'tacit knowledge' became a specific type of knowledge that appears in variable combinations with 'explicit knowledge'. Moreover, depending on the costs involved, the former could be converted into the latter

(Nelson and Winter, 1982: 78, 82). In fact, this is just the opposite of Polanyi's ideas: 'even though one can paraphrase the cognitive content of an integration [of the subsidiaries], *the sensory quality which conveys this content cannot be made explicit*. It can only be lived, can only be dwelt in' (Polanyi, 1975: 41; emphasis mine). In other words, knowledge is always 'personal' knowledge.[3]

2.2   The Computer Metaphor

The authors of the 'new economics of science' recur, in a more or less explicit way, to the cognitivist psychology and the vocabulary of AI. Cowan et al. (2000: 217) accept a moderate version of the 'algorithmic model' of knowledge production, which means that they distinguish between information ('structured data', codified knowledge) and knowledge ('the state of the agent's entire cognitive context'). Concerning the latter, the authors recognize that humans have the capacity to 'create new categories for the classification of information, and learn to assign meanings to (sensory) data inputs' (p. 217); unfortunately, they do not discuss how that knowledge is created. Less explicitly, the same influence underlies Ancori et al. (2000) as we can see by the vocabulary used (examples: *pieces* of knowledge, *retrieval* property of knowledge, knowledge *codification*), and by their model of the cognitive process structured in different layers that interact with each other according to cybernetic principles.

In opposition to behaviourist theory, which focused on observed stimulus-response on the individual, ignoring crucial factors going on in the mind, the cognitivist theory became dominant in the 1960s in close articulation with the development of cybernetics. The cognitive functions of the individual and the individual's interactivity with the environment were integrated by recurring to the 'feedback' concept (Rizzello, 1999). The brain was considered as a symbolic rule-based system (the hardware) operating through a mind (the software) comprising two levels: (i) *data* – symbols directly representing specific objects or concepts; (ii) *programme* – a set of logical relationships (rules) between symbols. This set of rules is supposed to be governed by a centralized control composed by meta-rules (Cilliers, 1998).

Dating from the 1950s this intellectual source became the core of mainstream AI studies and psychology. One of its tenets is a particular concept of representation, which plays a crucial role by establishing a correspondence between systems' states (brain states) and conceptual meaning (mind states). Fodor's (1975) theory of representation, which states that we are born with a 'inner language' built into our neural structure, a language-like symbol system that shares with spoken language a formal syntax, is well known.[4]

This theory was seriously criticized in the 1980s by the connectionist stream of AI, which argues for the relevance of interactions through networks in the explanation of complex systems. Against the 'rule-based' model of representation, basically inspired by the idea that reason is disembodied and language obeys a formal logic, connectionists argued from a different point of view (Cilliers, 1998):

- *Meaning is produced internally* by the relationships between the structural components of the system following an external activation. Therefore, meaning comes out of a process involving internal and external as well as historical elements of the system.
- *Representation is distributed;* no element of the system has meaning per se. The elements of the system only have patterns of relationships with many others. Indeed, 'relationship' is the core concept of the paradigm, not the elements (neurones) or the nodes (synapses) of the network.
- *Information* is not 'stored' (or represented) in any specific symbol, which could be recalled when necessary. On the contrary, building on previous patterns of relationships, information is reconstructed each time the network (or part of it) is activated.

This new computational metaphor is now widely used by neurologists and points to an understanding that sees the *mind as an emergent level* based on multiple interactions involving the neural system and other parts of the body. Despite its limitations (see Section 4), connectionism succeeded in questioning the trivial assumption that 'mind runs on the brain', although the latter does not play any decisive role in the functioning of the mind. Further questioning of cognitivism developed during the 1990s from a dialogue between the connectionist strand of AI, neurobiology research, and new empirical studies in cognitive linguistics. The outcome of these intellectual interactions is a second generation of cognitive science, which sees cognitivism as the modern version of Cartesian dualism (Lakoff and Johnson, 1999). The qualification of 'dualism' comes from the cognitivist understanding that mental processes are identical with *functional* states of the brain, which are viewed in abstract/disembodied terms. Using Jacobson's (1995: 26) definition:

> Functionalism is the view that behaviour and the mind are not explained by the physical composition of the brain but by its functions, that is, by its operational programs. Those imply causes, goals, and purposes (teleofunctionalism) . . . Functionalists accept that there are 'bridge rules' relating mental events to neural events and claim that mental events could be deduced from neural events if the rules were known. They like to represent nervous systems as black

boxes connected by functional rules like 'store', 'retrieve', 'compare', 'execute', and so on.

It is known how Simon's critique of neoclassical rational choice theory has been important for non-mainstream economics. However, its acceptance had an inevitable consequence: the discourse of mind's computational limits ('bounded rationality') carried into economics a (modern) machine-like understanding of the mind and its foundational metaphor.[5]

2.3   Ambiguities of an Eclectic Stance

Recently, Nightingale (2003) made a contribution to the so-called 'codification debate' arguing that tacit knowledge and articulated words and symbols 'are complements rather than alternatives', and that 'the binary distinction between tacit and codified knowledge is confused' (p. 153). Accounting for three levels of explanation of knowledge – the empirical *hardware* (neurological basis), the abstract *programme* level (Simon's information processing), and the subjective *knowledge* level (Polanyi's phenomenology) – he shows how neurobiology research 'supports Polanyi's phenomenology and the idea that knowledge is an embodied process and that all our conscious attention is dependent on a whole range of unconscious, tacit processes' (p. 162). Moreover, drawing on the philosophy of John Searle, he argues against programme-level explanations. However, and despite (or because of) the abundant literature of neurosciences reviewed, which he linked to a much-criticized philosophy,[6] Nightingale (2003) still rests at the surface of Polanyi's thinking and ultimately falls into a problematic eclectism.

An example of misunderstanding of Polanyi is Nightingale's (2003) identification of tacit knowledge with 'unattended neural images' (p. 156) or 'unconscious, tacit processes' (p. 162). Polanyi (1966: 95–6) argued vehemently: 'it is a mistake to identify subsidiary awareness with unconscious or preconscious awareness, or with the Jamesian fringe of awareness. What makes an awareness subsidiary is the *function it fulfils*; it can have any degree of consciousness, so long as it functions as a clue to the object of our focal attention.' More recently, a multi-level understanding of consciousness has been extensively discussed in Donald (2001), who also argues against the very common error of identifying the automaticity of a skilled behaviour with unconsciousness:[7]

> the automaticity of learned motor skills constitutes one of the principal *benefits* of conscious processing . . . Conscious processing is needed to establish and maintain our own internal cognitive habits. It is also needed to alter them. And it is needed as well to use them in any complex situation. Automaticity is not the

antithesis of consciousness. It is a necessary complement to it. Moreover, it is one of its by-products. (p. 57)

Most importantly, a deep ambiguity underlies Nightingale's (2003) contribution. The author reviewed vast neurological research that establishes knowledge as an embodied acquisition in the evolutionary process of life. Yet, after validating the third level of explanation related to Polanyi, and having criticized programme-level theories for lacking any explanatory power, it is somehow surprising that Nightingale goes on using the hardware/software vocabulary, and closes his arguments saying that 'even though Polanyi and Simon are incompatible when talking about knowledge, there is no need to choose which is correct as they are being used at different levels in the causal hierarchy' (p. 178).

On very different grounds, both Polanyi and John Searle would certainly reject this compromise. On the one hand, in Polanyi's emergentist thinking the mind has an ontological autonomy established by a complex interdependence with the human body and the environment. Thus, cognition is a first-person phenomenon that cannot be explained in terms of abstract, computation models. On the other hand, although rejecting an eliminativist stance, Searle argues for a moderate reductionism that is still incompatible with the computer metaphor (Searle, 1999: 51–2):[8]

> I do not think we are forced to either dualism or materialism. The point to remember is that consciousness is a biological phenomenon like any other. It is true that it has special features, most notably the feature of subjectivity, as we have seen, but that does not prevent consciousness from being a higher-level feature of the brain in the same way that digestion is a higher-level feature of the stomach.

Nightingale acknowledges the incompatibility of programme-level explanations with Searle's reductionism (p. 177), but maintains 'that program-level explanations can be very useful as they help specify operational principles at the organizational level. Problems only emerge when one assumes that the abstract program level is real and can be used *instead* of causal, hardware level' (p. 177). Thus, his final stance may be summarized in two points: programme-level explanations that rely on information processing lack neurological evidence and ignore real processes of causality; but, for common-sense reasons related to its generalized use and its intuitive explanations, we should keep programme-level theories as a useful descriptive tool.

Having explored our best neurological science, Nightingale (2003) fails to extract all the implications of his argument, thereby coming to an inconsistency.[9] From my point of view, it is inappropriate to pick up the idea of different levels of explanation from Newell (one of the fathers of cognitivism), then align arguments from neurobiology against cognitivism, and finally still retain cognitivism 'because it is so convenient to talk in program-level terms' (p. 177). It is certainly valid to warn about this kind of procedure that it is 'not enough to pile up levels of explanation; they have to be integrated into a single hierarchized explanatory framework that demonstrates their mutual compatibility' (Roy et al., 1999: 45).

In brief, this is the flaw in Nightingale's eclectic stance: he wants to save the autonomy of the mind, the level of Simon's historical contribution, and at the same time accept recent advances in neurobiology, which establish the mind as an embodied phenomenon, in line with Searle's reductionism. In the midst, Polanyi appears somewhat misunderstood taking account that his concept of 'emergence' (Polanyi, 1966: Chap. 2) gives the clue for a way out of both Simon's Cartesian dualism and Searle's reductionist philosophy. Unfortunately, Nightingale failed to capture the richness of Polanyi's thinking.

3 PHILOSOPHICAL AND SCIENTIFIC BACKGROUND

3.1 Evolutionary Perspective

As discussed in the previous section, Polanyi's analysis of 'tacit knowing' put in evidence 'the bodily roots of all thought'. This conclusion shows evident connections with the ideas of the French philosopher Merleau-Ponty (1945) who developed a phenomenology centred on our human experience as 'flesh in the world', in the sense that we feel the world by bodily experiencing it (Lakoff and Johnson, 1999). In Mingers's words (2001: 112):

> [Merleau-Ponty] argued that human behaviour could neither be explained in a behaviourist way in terms of external causes, nor internally in terms of conscious intentionality. Rather, it had to be explained structurally in terms of the physical structures of the body and nervous system as they develop in circular interplay within the world. The world does not determine our perception, nor does our perception constitute the world.

Such a view of human perception suggests the rejection of a split meta-theory that sees antinomies everywhere: the subject opposed to the world, perception distinct from action, mind separated from the body (Overton, 2004). In order to overcome the negative effects of fragmentary understandings of human nature, we adopt in this chapter a view based on the complex interdependency of the three poles – 'mind–body–world' – and on their overall unity under an emergent and cohesive new level, the 'person': 'the locus of evolution of persons is *human activity* in the bio-physical and sociocultural world. It is not in the evolving brain or in his-torically developing culture except as these are linked through human activity' (Martin, 2003: 95; emphasis mine). A similar understanding is presented in Bickhard (2004), who argues that only an *action-centred approach* to cognitive processes is able to account for the social ontology of persons.

This relational perspective gains its full meaning when we place man in the evolutionary process of Nature, as did Polanyi. He felt it plausible to assume that the structure of man's way of knowing corresponds to the structure of the entities that are the object of knowing. At both levels (the epistemological and the ontological), there is a comprehensive entity controlled by principles that 'rely for their operations on laws governing the particulars' and, at the same time, those laws 'would never account for the organizing principles of a higher entity which they form' (Polanyi, 1966: 34). In this passage, as in many others in the book, Polanyi referred to the concept of 'emergence' and assumed that human cognition emerged according to the same processes that govern the evolution of the rest of the universe.[10]

Polanyi did not accept the Darwinian theory of his time (Polanyi, 1966: 46–7), which he accused of ignoring the self-organizing processes at work in the emergence of new and ever more complex levels of life. However, it seems reasonable to suggest that he would have been open to a recon-sideration of his ideas about Darwinism had he seen the debates that have occurred since the end of the 1980s. The recent convergence between physics and biology, which is giving rise to an 'expanded' Darwinism (Depew and Weber, 1989; Kauffman, 2001), is in fact an attempt to over-come the warranted critique of the so-called 'modern synthesis' (gene-centred Darwinism) addressed by researchers of different disciplines such as the physics of thermodynamic open systems, developmental biology, and the science of ecological systems. As put by Griffiths and Gray (2001: 215),

> Neo-Darwinism was the result of the union of Darwin's theory of natural selec-tion with a particular view of heredity . . . In rejecting the narrowly gene-centred view of heredity and bringing developmental processes back into our account of evolution, we are not rejecting the theory of natural selection but are attempt-ing to unite it with the developmental systems account of heredity and thus to reveal new and promising research agendas.

Therefore, by adequately revising the traditional 'variation–selection–retention' scheme, a third-wave Darwinism may provide a unifying scien-tific framework that integrates developmental processes and accepts an ecological view of selection, both mechanisms being part of a co-evolutionary process between the individual and his environment (Weber and Depew, 2001).[11]

3.2   Mind as Process

An evolutionary understanding of the human being and its cognitive capabilities, as framed within expanded Darwinism, should provide an original formulation going beyond the traditional oppositions in the debate of the so-called 'mind–body problem'. Different authors who reject both Cartesian dualism and physicalism have discussed this new approach; despite the differences, they share an ontology of mind based on the concept of emergence, which includes some kind of 'downward causation' as a property of the mind (Bickhard with Campbell, 2000; Emmeche et al., 2000; O'Connor, 2000).

According to the evolutionary perspective, the human mind (in its aspects of intentionality, reflexivity, and qualia) is an integral part of the universe, which appears organized in emergent strata with specific properties that are not present in lower levels. Thus, the outcome of evolution is a diversified universe: 'Within the order of the world, however, there may be different categories of things, including fundamentally different kinds of properties' (Smith, 1999: 107). This includes both the mind, with its *subjective* properties, and the immense variety of things from stones to quarks, with their *objective* properties. About this point, a word of caution is in order: accepting an ontological pluralism of properties does not mean accepting the dualist stance of Eccles and Popper (1977) who argue for an interaction of mental and physical 'substances'. Certainly, mental and physical properties are different; however, both their (deep) nature and that of the universe in general are not accounted for by substance categories, as discussed below.

The references we have made to a 'world of things' need qualification. Twentieth-century quantum physics put forward a picture of the world that makes a rupture with our common sense. Although reality appears to our senses in discontinuous forms (things), its inner nature is continuous and made up of quantum waves, which eventually may collapse into particle-states following an observation. Thus, quantum fields are processes and (ultimately) 'things' are patterns of those processes (Omnès, 1999). In fact, quantum physics invites us to abandon traditional metaphysics of things (or substance), and adopt a metaphysics that is consistent with our current knowledge of microscopic reality. This means that *everything in the world is organization out of a natural process, which obviously includes the mind* (Bickhard with Campbell, 2000).

3.3 Naturalist Worldview

Quantum physics tells us that the ultimate nature of the world is a veiled reality (D'Espagnat, 1995); it is best understood as a process, which continuously self-organizes at different levels in the (still running) evolutionary process (Emmeche et al., 1997). This makes it plausible to accept that the different properties of mind and body are both grounded in the same *originary and unitary process*, a higher-order totality in ontological terms, which encompasses multiple domains – the physical/inanimate, the living, the human, the social – all of them coming from, expressing, and constituting that totality.[12] In this sense, the ontological plurality of the world has its roots in *the foundational process we call Nature*.

This Naturalist stance is based on process metaphysics, which in different ways underlies the philosophies of Peirce, James, Whitehead, and Bergson. More recently, the Spanish scholar Pedro Laín Entralgo (1992) made an important contribution to this stream by building on the process metaphysics of Zubiri (1968).[13] Entralgo claimed that *reality is in itself dynamics*: ceaselessly from the Big Bang on, reality's mode of being is 'giving-from-itself' new structures. In the human being, reality – Nature qua *natura naturans* – gave-from-itself a higher level structure that includes the precedent ones. In this sense, the anthropology of Entralgo is also an emergentist attempt to overcome the traditional dichotomy of 'physicalism versus dualism'. His stance could be labelled *Naturalist ontology*: against all kinds of reductionism, the human being evolved a singular mind with powerful causal properties of its own, which made of humans an intrinsically relational species; but, against dualism, the human being became an emergent level of reality out of biological and cultural processes that manifest the evolutionary dynamics of Nature.

Linking the different steps of the argument, we conclude with a brief statement about the so-called 'mind–body problem': it is intelligible to argue for a non-reductionist stance, and still reject dualism, in so far as we adopt both *process metaphysics* that sees reality organized in clusters of processes (Rescher, 2000) and *a concept of Nature* that grounds and gives unity to the ontological diversity of the world (Entralgo, 1992).

4 NATURALLY KNOWING THE WORLD

The approach to knowledge summarized in the next paragraphs follows the ontological choices outlined in the previous section, and draws extensively on the contributions of a particular stream of cognitive science, which argues for an interactivist-constructivist (I-C) model of cognition.[14]

The latter understands mental representations and higher-level cognition as evolutionary realities in *dynamical situated agents*. In order to present an outline of this alternative to the view in use by the large majority of economists, we concentrate on three critical aspects of the I-C model.

Evolutionary epistemology

The I-C model is consistent with an evolutionary explanation of mind. Largely beyond the capacities of other mammals, human beings have developed a particular type of intelligence: a self-directed adaptive capacity that includes mental representations of a complex kind, and smooth higher order integration of internal with external processes, which includes linguistic interactions. According to Christensen and Hooker (2000: 14), intelligence is 'the capacity for fluid, adaptable, context-sensitive (in some cases "insightful") action' of a living system in order to maintain its autonomy (survival, identity). With continued interactions, intelligent systems are able to anticipate and evaluate the results that are most convenient for their maintenance. Moreover, in the process of directing action they are able to improve their capacity for interaction management. They construct learning skills to face complex environments.

The I-C model is incompatible with algorithmic ideas about cognition, as proposed by cognitivists (Newell and Simon, 1972). The latter do not recognize that most problems we face are vague, poorly specified in the beginning; they are not tractable by computational information processing designed to find the optimal solution for an explicitly defined problem. As discussed above (Section 2.2), cognitivist models are 'mind-centred' and leave outside the embodied and interactive dimensions of cognition, which are crucial in learning processes that autonomous agents develop. More realistically, the I-C model points to an evolutionary epistemology: cognitive structures emerge and are involved in 'variation–selection–retention' processes that make them progressively more complex, and more effective for the individual's adaptiveness (Christensen and Hooker, 1999).[15]

To sum up, the I-C model argues that cognition is internally constructed and validated through the individual's interactive experience; it argues for an action-based evolutionary epistemology.

Self-organizing agents

If mental images are internally constructed, as stated by Damasio (1994), how are they related to the environment? How can we say that our knowledge is true? Standard answers to this question, both cognitivist and connectionist, assume that mental representations have an encoding nature based on an *informational relationship* with the world. For example, the optic tract would encode the colour of light that impinges on the retina.

However, colours *are not* properties of the light encoded by our minds; they are a qualitative experience of the subject produced by a complex of environmental and internal conditions (Thompson, 1995). In fact, the assumption that our mental images stand in correspondence with the world by encoding external information has been subject to strong criticism (Maturana and Varela, 1980; Bickhard and Terveen, 1995). In the following we synthesize two arguments against this meta-theory taking the I-C framework as reference (Bickhard and Terveen, 1995; Bickhard, 2000).

Codification ideas accept that we represent something in the world by encoding sensorial 'information' about it, which in fact is no more than factual correspondence. The proper act of encoding can only be based on the *explicit* identification of its content. To represent (give meaning to) anything by an encoding we would need to have epistemic access to that 'something' in the world in the first place, in order to give content to the encoding. This is not possible: we cannot step out of our bodies to have an independent access to the world. Certainly, we make encodings of other types of encodings; but we cannot fall into an infinite regress by which mental encodings always carry previously provided contents. If we consider a bottom level, the codification theory faces fatal problems. Either it assumes that the bottom-level encoding gives itself its content, which is equivalent to assuming that there is no representation at all; or it assumes that without any more encoded contents it is unable to provide a genuine (non-encoding) representational content, and then the theory reveals its failure to give account of the emergence of mental representations. Ultimately, the codification theory is incoherent.

But there is another major objection to the codification theory: the intrinsic absence of error in mental representations as encodings. We must recall that in this kind of representation there is *a correspondence between the mental encoding and its content in the external world*. The concept provides only two possibilities: either the correspondence exists and there is no error in representation, or the correspondence does not exist, and the mind has failed to build a representation. The problem with this formulation is that we cannot have a representation that has the wrong content. With representations as encodings of reality, the latter cannot be taken as an autonomous referent against which to confront representational contents and identify possible errors; in this sense, the concept lacks a normative dimension. Therefore, the concept does not provide the possibility of learning from errors, which is a flaw that makes the codificationist stance unsuitable for a realist approach to cognition.

Rather than presuming that representations are impressed on a passive mind, the I-C model understands cognition as self-directive processes of intelligent beings concerned with the modulation of forward-looking interactions with the environment. In human beings, higher-order cognitive structures are built upon more fundamental representations, which also have an interaction-based nature. According to the I-C perspective, a *representation* about an environment is an indication for future interaction based on anticipated outcomes that are desirable. Possibly, this anticipated outcome is not reached and, in this case, representation is considered in error. However, the living system is able to functionally detect the error by confrontating of actual and anticipated outcomes.

In this understanding, representations have a content that is not external information about the environment; information is only implicit and comes from (internal) indicative relationships based on presuppositions about environmental conditions. Thus, representations that have the right content are those that get support from the environment for the anticipated outcomes. Certainly, sensorial processing mediates the relation between the mental outcome and the environmental conditions; however, 'this is information in the strict sense of covariation, not semantics' (Bickhard, 2000: 71). In fact, meanings only emerge in the future use of the differentiations about the environment that these 'sense data' provide. Therefore, information relationships with the world 'are crucial to the functioning of interactive systems, including the representational functioning, but they are not in themselves *constitutive* of representation' (Bickhard, 2000: 72).[16]

As mentioned above, the model distinguishes between microgenetic processes – the constituting of internal differentiations about the environment as outcomes of particular interactions – and the continuous process of construction of relations involving mental representations. The latter is a macrogenetic process: with time, self-directed agents build more complex forms of representations upon the foundational ones by (internally) differentiating properties of indications for action that proved adequate. As already argued by Piaget (1970), we construct 'schemes' that are useful for future interactions with the environment. Those schemes are in themselves cognitive realities, which are as well subject to an evolutionary process. In fact, when we use the concept of *knowledge*, we actually refer to those 'mental structures' taken as clusters of processes in continuous mutual adjustments and bearing interactive cognitive properties.

From this point of view, *learning* is also constructive and occurs when we build a new cognitive scheme that succeeds in new interaction situations, for example in solving a new problem. However, it may be the case that the latter is too complex or too far away from the competencies already acquired. Vygotsky (1934) addressed this problem and for the first time called attention to the importance of developmental 'scaffolding':[17] the educational tasks that support learning within a 'zone of proximal distance' of the child's experience. The I-C model shares some aspects of Vygotsky's (1934) approach but does not accept his notion of 'internalization' of constructions supplied by another agent (Bickhard, 1995). Despite external stimulation, the learning process is always an internal construction that functionally links something already learned to that to-be-learned by recurring to the microgenetic process that supported previous knowledge. As proposed by Bickhard and Campbell (1996: 144), 'Development and learning, then, must involve changes in those topology inducing microgenetic processes, in order to get access to old successes and change the way that new microgenetic constructions will proceed.'[18]

Christensen and Hooker (2000: 6–7) synthesize the nature of the model in the following terms: 'This framework brings to the fore what searching for algorithms suppresses, namely, the ways in which the ongoing interaction process itself generates information for the interacting system which it can use to further modify subsequent interaction.'

Language: social operator not codified knowledge

For logical positivism we have a non-problematic relationship with the world; our encoded representations are like mirroring the world. Further, codificationism extended this view to a 'transmission model' of language: mental structures (themselves encodings) are codified into language, which is suitable for transmission of information bearing meanings that are independent of the context.

In the I-C approach, linguistic communication does not create any 'intersubjective' realm between individuals for the simple reason that our inner life is not encoded into language to be transmitted. In linguistic communication participants must always make their own interpretation, in the I-C sense that mind makes non-encoding representations of utterances *as it does for any other particular aspect of the environment*.[19] In our approach, rather than assuming a cognitive and individualistic understanding of language, we see it as a powerful 'social resource for the creation, maintenance, and transformation of social realities' (Bickhard and Terveen, 1995: 237), which includes the transformation of mental processes in so far as they emerge through social interactions. In this sense, a transformative view of language integrates a dimension of 'thought expression' without compromising with on encoding assumptions.

Human interactions are a source of complex contingencies. Facing another person we do not know what will be his/her next action, what is his/her definition of the situation, and the same occurs on the other side. As knowledge is forward looking, we tend to reduce that range of possible interactions in order to manage the situation. Language is the most important tool we use to coordinate multiple understandings of social situations.

It is 'a conventional system for the production of utterances which operate on situation conventions' (Bickhard, 1987: 49). Therefore, despite its cognitive connection, the *direct* object of language is intrinsically social as it aims to transform a situation convention; the latter is a common understanding (not necessarily explicit) of a social situation.

The social and transformative nature of language carries important implications. One is that utterances operate on social relations; their result depends both on the utterance itself and on the initial context, which makes language intrinsically *context dependent*. Certainly, sometimes we try to reduce this dependency but, in fact, we can never get rid of it, even when using formalized logic. Another implication is that the meaning of an utterance resides in its *operative power* over a situation, not in the correspondence between the utterance and a propositional (encoded) meaning. Finally, as a consequence of being a conventional system that operates on social conventions, language is both *recursive* (language operates on its results), and *reflexive* (language operates on itself). These characteristics make language a complex and powerful tool for individual and social development: language supports the emergence of a person after the birth of the infant; language underlies the increasing complexity of social conventions during the history of humanity (Bickhard, 2004).

A consequence of the I-C approach to knowledge now appears obvious: instead of an individualistic, computational information processing view of mind, evolutionary economics should adopt an interactivist and constructivist understanding of cognitive processes, which provides a Naturalized, embodied and embedded account of meaning. From this vantage point, knowledge is not a *thing* to be transferred and stocked (either in the mind or in artifacts); rather, it is a *process of evolutionary change* that involves the whole situated person. The theoretical and methodological implications of this view are so vast that we can hardly touch them in the next section.

5 THEORETICAL AND MANAGEMENT IMPLICATIONS

A Naturalist approach undermines the idea of 'codebooks' (Cowan et al., 2000) that establish meanings and support codification once knowledge is articulated. Consequently, it also undermines the explanation of Cowan et al. (2000: 232) of the existence of communities of practice (Brown and Duguid, 2001) by recurring to the concept of 'codified yet non-articulated' knowledge. From our point of view, this is a natural process of socialization: members of the group develop (do not receive) knowledge through common learning histories, and/or through shared practice and intense interaction. Interactions within a group produce a relative convergence in individuals' cognitive structures that leads to the emergence of normative understandings about what a given situation is, and how to achieve co-ordination. Instead of evoking shared codebooks, we should see communities of practice as an illustration of our action-based sociality, which develops and adapts according to particular contexts and stages of life. As Bickhard (2004: 128) emphasized, 'human beings are socially open as infants, but their sociality is not genetically fixed. . . . It develops as a culture sensitive ontological emergent over many years.'

Despite the attempt to present a 'reasonable position' in the debate about tacit knowledge, Ancori et al. (2000) share with the 'absolutist position on codification' a common conceptual basis. In fundamental assumptions their discourse is codificationist; they stick to the idea of representation as correspondence to the world by means of incoming information. This understanding is clear in their concept of 'crude knowledge', 'information as an event without meaning' (p. 266). Therefore, they accept that knowledge may be codified although not necessarily commodified (p. 258). An encoding and transmission model of language logically follows: 'knowing how to transmit knowledge implies obviously the mastery of codes and/or languages' (p. 267). Thus, when viewed from our vantage point, both stances in the debate are deeply undermined by a Naturalist view of information and knowledge.

Combining an ontological realism with an epistemological interactionist constructivism, so far we have provided a theoretical framework that overcomes the problematic assumptions of opposing stances in the tacit-codified debate and a better foundation for an economics approach to cognitive processes and their articulation with the social realm. We further suggest that a Naturalist approach points to new research perspectives for economics, and provides new insights for management practice. In the following paragraphs we attempt to illustrate these claims.

Understanding organizations

An interactivist-constructivist understanding argues that knowledge and learning concepts should not be applied to the social realm, which is an ontologically distinct level of reality; 'collective knowledge' (Daft and Weick, 1984; Spender, 1996; Tsoukas, 1996) is an erroneous metaphor for the analysis of organizations' nature and functioning. Empiricism in economics and management literature claims that organizational knowledge is the sum of knowledge 'stored' by the members of the organization plus knowledge 'stored' in technological artifacts. This perspective has been strongly criticized by process-based approaches, which see collective knowledge as shared knowledge, sometimes giving origin to a so-called 'group mind' (Weick and Roberts, 1993). Despite the insightful critique of the empiricist and mechanistic view of organizations, the process-based perspective still fails to establish a true autonomy for the social level. An example of ambiguity is the following statement: 'Managers may not agree fully about their perceptions, but the thread of coherence among managers is what characterizes organizational interpretations. Reaching convergence among members characterizes the act of organizing and enables the organization to *interpret as a system*' (Daft and Weick, 1984: 285; emphasis mine).

The conflation of the organizational level with an intermediate 'social-practice level' is a hallmark of process-based theories and is well illustrated in the recent contribution by Tsoukas (2003). Inspired by Wittgenstein's *Philosophical Investigations* the author refers to a social reality that attributes meanings, which are captured by individuals in the use of language. Tsoukas (2003) underlines that those meanings 'are not just in the minds of the individuals involved but in the practices themselves; the meanings are the common property of the practice at hand – they are inter-subjective' (p. 612). Therefore, the concept of *inter-subjectivity* provides the basis for 'a "collective subject" without thinking of it as a contradiction in terms' (Tsoukas, 2003: 613).

As argued in the previous section, there is no such *public* (inter-) subjectivity because meanings are inherently private, and language is not a system of encodings that convey meanings; rather, language is an institution we use to operate on social situations through others' understandings about them. Hence, language solves the coordination problem that emerges when epistemic agents interact, a subject central to the work of Talcott Parsons (Vanderstraeten, 2003). On this point the Naturalist view connects with the tradition of the sociological research and argues that *relations between individuals are not properties of the individuals themselves*. As put by Meijers (2003: 181; emphasis mine), 'the bonds between these [related] individuals are the social relations formed in their speaking and acting. *Agreeing is an act that creates such social relations* as claim and obligation between the participants.' Therefore, our view argues that despite persons' intrinsic openness to social relations this should not authorize the transfer of cognitive concepts into the social realm, as is the case in process-based theories of organizations.

Tsoukas (2003) conflates in a middle-level defined by 'social practices' both the organization and individuals' agency, which is certainly inspired by Giddens's structuration theory. For the Naturalist view of knowledge, which is rooted in a multi-level evolutionary ontology, social structures belong to a new level of reality, distinct from individual agency.[20] Further, as argued by Hodgson (2002), certain types of social structures (institutions) have the power of not only enabling and constraining human agency but also of changing their purposes, preferences and behaviour; institutions are a truly emergent level of reality endowed with the property of 'reconstitutive downward causation' over the individuals on which they depend. Therefore, a Naturalist view supports the critique of 'conflationary' theorizing in any of its different forms (Archer, 1995): Upwards conflation of empiricist realism, which reduces the organization to an epiphenomenal effect of human interactions in specific contexts; Downwards conflation of social constructionism, which through society's conversation reduces agency to an instantiation of organizational structures, and downplays individuals' powers, creativity and aspirations; and Central conflationism, which despite rejecting both Up and Downward reductionisms sees agency and structures as inseparable and mutually constituting, thus rejecting the reality of an organization external to human practices and memory.

In brief, circumscribing the use of cognitive concepts to the individual level, the Naturalist view connects with a critical realist understanding of 'organizations' that preserves both the autonomy and the interdependence of the epistemic and the social realms (Archer, 2000; Reed, 2003).[21]

ICTs as scaffolds
Steinmueller (2000: 361) claims that 'information and communication technologies (ICTs) most often are defined in terms of their capacities to acquire, store, process and transmit information . . . Under what circumstances is it possible to reproduce knowledge by exchanging information and under what circumstances is it not possible?'

In this quotation there is a problematic assumption taken for granted: ICTs can transfer information. According to the I-C model, and regardless of the medium used for linguistic communication, the above-mentioned question is ill formulated because utterances do not carry information, which is an action-based embodied outcome. In a convergent stance, Mingers (2001) showed how an embodied view of knowledge highlights crucial dimensions that are ignored in the so-called 'knowledge management' (KM) projects mostly inspired by the cognitivist framework. Failure in a large number of those projects (Desouza, 2003), and evidence of their limitations (Butler, 2003; Orlikowski, 2002), strongly suggest that a Naturalist view of knowledge, and a renewed understanding of organizations, should guide ICT investments (Bartlett and Ghoshal, 2002).

Even so, it is necessary to point out other dimensions of new ICTs that are seldom discussed in the 'embodied knowledge' literature (Mingers, 2001). We need to remember that the wide diffusion of symbolic technologies (written language in different media) enabled human beings to build a cultural universe on the basis of two crucial aspects of cognition: interaction with a symbolic technology enables the individual to focus awareness and achieve more clarity in his thoughts through the scaffolding mechanism of variation and selection operating within the epistemic function;[22] the same scaffolding mechanism gains enlarged horizons with the access to an expanded variety of symbolic technologies, taking account of the limited and rather unreliable long-term memory of human beings (Donald, 2001). Therefore, when viewed from the perspective of an action-based model of cognition, ICTs have a potential that is not fully appreciated in the embodied-cognition literature. Emphasizing the role of the body against cognitivism, in a certain sense that literature puts the mind in the background and, hence, gives less importance to scaffolding processes supported by ICTs as scaffolds. If, as we argue, knowledge comes from human interaction in multiple forms – with other agents, physical environment, and also symbolic technologies – developmental processes supported by those technologies certainly deserve a positive reference in our assessment of ICTs (Bruun and Langlais, 2003).

A broader appreciation of what is at stake in the evolution of our societies led Brier (2001) to formulate a crucial choice: either we develop technologies that take over human activities and attempt to substitute them with mechanical operations, therefore setting the frame for poor interactions; or we develop technologies that support and enhance human capabilities for doing things, learning and making judgements. Priority should be given to the use of ICTs in promoting personal interaction at all levels, sustaining communication processes leading to 'generative dialogue', and improving skills and competencies. This seems to be a more interesting programme than one of attempting to 'codify tacit knowledge', an ambition ultimately led by a machine-like understanding of knowledge (Cilliers, 2000; Stacey, 2000).

5   CONCLUSION

This chapter argues for the adoption of a Naturalist view of knowledge and information in economics, and proposes an expanded Darwinian way of dealing with epistemic and ontological issues. Our view about knowledge could be summed up in a phrase: human beings are constituted as persons by *interacting* with the (natural and social) world, which enables them to *construct* implicit information of the latter, to *generate* meanings, and to *develop* knowledge and skills in order to manage their life as members of a society they co-create.

This view is built upon the following philosophical claims: reality is the originary process of Nature that appears organized by levels, emergent clusters of processes; physical objects, biological life, human beings, institutions are emergent levels of that kind; we have no access to reality other than by interacting with it through our body. Such a philosophical stance points to current research in cognitive science that connects with American pragmatists' process metaphysics, and early Piaget's psychology. In economics, our approach shares with new-Austrian economics the core idea of 'subjective knowledge'[23] and partially connects with contributions of Nooteboom (2001). Further, by making a clear distinction between knowledge and social relations, the Naturalist view supports a critical realist approach to the study of economic institutions such as firms, or markets (Lawson, 1997, 2003b). As a social science open to interdisciplinary dialogue, economics should focus on the *study of co-evolutionary interactions* between agents (either individuals or organizations) and the social structures involved in production, distribution, and consumption of goods and services, rather than making experimental research in the neurobiology of economic decisions as recently proposed by Dopfer (2004).

A Naturalist understanding of knowledge undermines neoclassical economics both in the traditional version and in the modern one of new growth theory; but it also challenges taken-for-granted assumptions in the evolutionary stream of economics. Those who cling to equilibrium conditions, methodological individualism, and calculatory rationality certainly will find it difficult to follow. This should not be the case of evolutionary economics, on the condition of abandoning a few auxiliary theories such as cognitivist psychology and gene-based Darwinism.[24] Then, an interactionist-constructivist epistemology, coupled with an evolutionary multi-level ontology, could provide new insights to understand economic processes and, which is more important, a basis for inter-disciplinary dialogue in order to generate creative variation in the process of evolutionary economics development.

NOTES

1. This text is a substantially revised version of a paper presented to the EAEPE 2003 Conference held at Maastricht. The author is much grateful to Mark Bickhard for very useful and supportive comments on previous versions of the paper, and to Richard Nelson for comments on a previous draft. I am also grateful to Stan Metcalfe and Mark Harvey for helpful suggestions and friendly discussions at CRIC, and to Pedro Teixeira for improvements in my writing. Last but not least, comments of Wilfred Dolfsma have been of enormous help and motivation in my attempt to be clear. The usual disclaimer applies.
2. Nelson and Winter (1982: 74, footnote) explicitly recognize the rising influence of cybernetic theory and computer modelling on the cognitive science of that time, and on the

authors they quote. However, it is important to acknowledge that Richard Nelson is now distant from cognitivism and much closer to the interactivist, developmental perspective argued here. See for example Nelson and Nelson (2002).

3.   This quotation from Polanyi contradicts Cowan et al. (2000: 220; emphasis mine) when they say that N&W 'do not insist, *any more than did Polanyi*, that tacitness implied "inarticulability"'.

4.   This model is associated with Chomsky's idea that humans have a 'language module' in the brain. For a discussion about the issue, see Stjernfelt (2000).

5.   See Nelson and Winter (1982: 74): 'The following features of computer programs are analogous to, and instructive regarding, corresponding features of human skills.'

6.   Searle's philosophy is problematic on different grounds: his theory of intentionality has been strongly criticized (Meijers, 2000); his 'background' seems a dubious concept (Viskovatoff, 2002); his theory of language is framed by analytic philosophy, which is opposed by the embodied-linguistics camp (Lakoff and Johnson, 1999: Chap. 21).

7.   Nelson and Winter (1982) themselves do not refer to the unconscious: 'skilled human performance is automatic in the sense that most of the details are executed without conscious volition' (p. 75).

8.   Searle's view actually corresponds to 'epiphenomenalism' in the sense that 'neural processes are the cause of consciousness and other mental phenomena, but the latter can have no causal effects on the neural processes' (Jacobson, 1995: 120). Despite rejecting epiphenomenalism, Searle (1999: 57–62) remains silent about the literature accounting for mind's 'downward causation' (Martin, 1999).

9.   Eventually, this led Nightingale (2003: 177, footnote 50) to state that Simon, 'by anyone's standards, is one of the most influential social scientists of the 20th century.' However, this should not be an obstacle to the acknowledgement of current advances in cognitive science that undermine cognitivism.

10. For an overview of the concept of 'emergence' see O'Connor and Wong (2002). For a deep discussion of the concept, see Emmeche et al. (1997, 2000).

11. A devastating critique of gene-centred Darwinism under multiple perspectives is Oyama et al. (2001).

12. The idea connects with Barbaras (1999) for whom the essence of each living being 'resides in a totality, an originary unity with the environment it actualises in each experience and falls short of inasmuch as it actualises this unity' (p. 534).

13. To my knowledge, Entralgo (1992) is not available in English.

14. In broad lines the I-C model connects with the pragmatist philosophy of Peirce and James, some ideas of Dewey, and the action-based psychology of Piaget.

15. The model acknowledges the important contribution of Campbell (1974), but also recognizes that his thinking was framed within the traditional 'population perspective' of Darwinism. The latter overlooks the internal self-organization of the being, which undermines a fitness-based understanding of selection. See Christensen and Hooker (1999) for a critique of D.T. Campbell's evolutionary epistemology from the point of view of an expanded Darwinism.

16. There is an important difference between epistemic *contact with* the world and epistemic *knowledge of* the world. About this distinction see Bickhard (2001: 233).

17. In fact, the concept of (developmental) 'scaffolding' was formulated later by Bruner (1975), although in relation to Vygotsky's model. I thank Mark Bickhard for this precision.

18. The model attributes a great importance to *self-scaffolding* processes such as breaking down a problem into sub-problems, first exploring analogies, or recurring to provisional resources. Despite being an important skill for personal development, self-scaffolding is not even conceivable within the passive-agent, encoding framework (Bickhard, 2001).

19. Note, 'if the *direct* object of an utterance were the mind of the hearer (or audience), then the successful completion of an utterance would be dependent on the effect it had on the mind of the hearer – a command would not be a command unless it were obeyed, nor an assertion an assertion unless it were believed' (Bickhard and Terveen, 1995: 237).

20. See Lawson's (2003a: 181) definitions: '*I take social reality to be the realm of all phenomena that, for their existence, depend, at least in part, on us. And by asserting that the social realm is structured I claim, in particular, that it consists in far more than actualities such as (actual) human behavior including its observable patterns. It also consists in features such as social rules, relations, positions, processes . . . that do not reduce to human behavior. Nor (I shall argue) do features such as these exist just in their instantiation or manifestation in behavior . . . Such features which do not reduce to behavior can be termed* social structures, *constituting, in their entirety,* social structure.'

21. Nelson and Winter (1982: 105) also argue for a concept of 'collective memory'. This is a good example of how a cognitivist approach based on encoding assumptions impedes the identification of an autonomous social level (the organization) emerging from individuals' interactions. Obviously, the latter are linked to the cognitive life of the participants, as recognized by Archer (2003).

22. See Lorenz (2001: 322; emphasis mine) in a convergent intuition: 'For this reason, language and verbal texts, rather than being thought of as instances of codified knowledge, are better thought of as *coordinating tools* used in task performance.' See also Clark (1997: Chap. 10) in a broad convergence despite the codification assumptions.

23. In line with new-Austrian thinking, Metcalfe and Ramlogan (2005) argue for 'the distinction between private knowledge and the institution of social understanding . . . as an emergent phenomenon arising from the interaction between individuals in specific contexts' (p. 16). Here it is important to note the idea of *emergence of a social reality*. Moreover, if by 'social understanding' is meant the establishment of a language-based social convention, despite the codification framework of the paper the formulation would resemble our separation of the epistemic from the social level.

24. See Hodgson's (2003) gene-centred discussion of Nelson and Winter's (1982) concept of routine. However, it must be said that Richard Nelson's current reflection does not subscribe to the adoption by social sciences of gene-based Darwinism, even in the context of firms' interactions in the market (personal e-mail communication, December 2004).

REFERENCES

Ancori, B., A. Bureth and P. Cohendet (2000), 'The Economics of Knowledge: The Debate about Codification and Tacit Knowledge', *Industrial and Corporate Change*, **9**(2): 255–87.

Archer, M.S. (1995), *Realist Social Theory: The Morphogenetic Approach*, Cambridge: Cambridge University Press.

Archer, M.S. (2000), *Being Human: The Problem of Agency*, Cambridge: Cambridge University Press.

Archer, M.S. (2003), *Structure, Agency, and the Internal Conversation*, Cambridge: Cambridge University Press.

Barbaras, R. (1999), 'The Movement of the Living as the Originary Foundation of Perceptual Intentionality', in J. Petitot, F.J. Varela, B. Pachoud and J.-M. Roy (eds), *Naturalizing Phenomenology*, Stanford: Stanford University Press.

Bartlett, A. and S. Ghoshal (2002), 'Building Competitive Advantage Through People', *MIT Sloan Management Review*, Winter: 34–41.

Bickhard, M.H. (1987), 'The Social Nature of the Functional Nature of Language', in M. Hickmann (ed.), *Social and Functional Approaches to Language and Thought*, London: Academic Press.

Bickhard, M.H. (1995), 'World Mirroring versus World Making: There's Gotta Be a Better Way', in L.P. Steffe and J. Gale (eds), *Constructivism in Education*, Hillsdale, NJ: Erlbaum.

Bickhard, M.H. (2000), 'Information and Representation in Autonomous Agents', *Journal of Cognitive Systems Research*, **1**: 65–75.

Bickhard, M.H. (2001), 'Why Children Don't Have to Solve the Frame Problems: Cognitive Representations Are Not Encodings', *Developmental Review*, **21**: 224–62.

Bickhard, M.H. (2004), 'The Social Ontology of Persons', in J.I.M. Carpendale and U. Muller (eds), *Social Interaction and the Development of Knowledge*, Mahwah, NJ: Erlbaum.

Bickhard, M.H. and R.L. Campbell (1996), 'Topologies of Learning and Development', *New Ideas in Psychology*, **14**(2): 111–56.

Bickhard, M.H. with D.T. Campbell (2000), 'Emergence', in P.B. Andersen, C. Emmeche, N.O. Finnemann and P.V. Christensen (eds), *Downward Causation: Minds, Bodies, and Matter*, Aarhus: University of Aarhus Press.

Bickhard, M.H. and L. Terveen (1995), *Foundational Issues in Artificial Intelligence and Cognitive Science*, Amsterdam and New York: Elsevier.

Brier, S. (2001), 'The Necessity of Trans-Scientific Frameworks for doing Interdisciplinary Research': http://www.flec.kvl.dk/personalprofile.asp?id=sbr&p=engelsk.

Brown, J.S. and P. Duguid (2001), 'Knowledge and Organization: A Social-Practice Perspective', *Organization Science*, **12**(2): 198–213.

Bruner, J.S. (1975), 'From Communication to Language – A Psychological Perspective', *Cognition*, **3**(3): 255–87.

Bruun, H. and R. Langlais (2003), 'On the Embodied Nature of Action', *Acta Sociologica*, **46**(1): 31–49.

Butler, T. (2003), 'From Data to Knowledge and Back Again: Understanding the Limitations of KMS', *Knowledge and Process Management*, **10**(3): 144–55.

Campbell, D.T. (1974), 'Evolutionary Epistemology', in P.A. Schilpp (ed.), *The Philosophy of Karl Popper* (Book I), LaSalle, IL: Open Court.

Cantner, U. and H. Hanusch (2002), 'Evolutionary Economics, its Basic Concepts and Methods', in H. Lim et al. (eds), *Editing Economics: Essays in Honour of Mark Perlman*, London and New York: Routledge.

Christensen, W.D. and C.A. Hooker (1999), 'The Organization of Knowledge: Beyond Campbell's Evolutionary Epistemology', *Philosophy of Science*, 66, *Proceedings of the 1998 Biennial Meetings of the Philosophy of Science Association*, S237–S249.

Christensen, W.D. and C.A. Hooker (2000), 'An Interactivist–Constructivist Approach to Intelligence: Self-directed Anticipative Learning', *Philosophical Psychology*, **13**(1): 5–45.

Cilliers, P. (1998), *Complexity and Postmodernism*, London and New York: Routledge.

Cilliers, P. (2000), 'Knowledge, Complexity and Understanding', *Emergence*, **2**(4): 7–13.

Clark, A. (1997), *Being There: Putting Brain, Body, and World Together Again*, Cambridge, MA and London: The MIT Press.

Cowan, R., P.A. David and D. Foray (2000), 'The Explicit Economics of Knowledge Codification and Tacitness', *Industrial and Corporate Change*, **9**(2): 211–53.

Cowan, R. and D. Foray (1997), 'The Economics of Codification and the Diffusion of Knowledge', *Industrial and Corporate Change*, **6**(3): 595–622.

Daft, R.L. and K.E. Weick (1984), 'Toward a Model of Organizations as Interpretation Systems', *Academy of Management Review*, **9**(2): 284–95.

Damasio, A. (1994), *Descartes' Error: Emotion, Reason and the Human Brain*, New York: Putnam's Suns.

Dasgupta, P. and P.A. David (1994), 'Towards a New Economics of Science', *Research Policy*, **23**: 487–521.

David, P.A. and D. Foray (1995), 'Accessing and Expanding the Science and Technology Knowledge Base', *STI Review of OECD*, **16**: 13–68.

Depew, D.J. and B.H. Weber (1989), 'The Evolution of the Darwinian Research Tradition', *Systems Research*, **6**(3): 255–263.

Desouza, K.C. (2003), 'Knowledge Management: Why the Technology Imperative Seldom Works', *Business Horizons*, January–February: 25–9.

D'Espagnat, B. (1995), *Une incertaine réalité*, Paris: Bordas.

Dolfsma, W. (2001), 'Metaphors of Knowledge in Economics', *Review of Social Economy*, **LIX**(1): 71–91.

Donald, M. (2001), *A Mind so Rare: The Evolution of Human Consciousness*, New York: Norton.

Dopfer, K. (2004), 'The Economic Agent as Rule Maker and Rule User: *Homo Sapiens Oeconomicus*', *Journal of Evolutionary Economics*, **14**: 177–95.

Eccles, J.C. and K.R. Popper (1977), *The Self and its Brain. An Argument for Interactionism*, Berlin: Springer International.

Emmeche, C., S. Koppe and F. Stjernfelt (1997), 'Explaining Emergence: Towards an Ontology of Levels', *Journal of General Philosophy of Science*, **28**: 83–119.

Emmeche, C., S. Koppe and F. Stjernfelt (2000), 'Levels, Emergence, and Three Versions of Downward Causation', in P.B. Andersen, C. Emmeche, N.O. Finnemann and P.V. Christensen (eds), *Downward Causation: Minds, Bodies, and Matter*, Aarhus: University of Aarhus Press.

Entralgo, P.L. (1992/2003), *Corpo e Alma*, Coimbra, Portugal: Livraria Almedina; Portuguese translation of 1992 Spanish edition, *Cuerpo y Alma*, Madrid: Editorial Espasa Calpe.

Fodor, J.A. (1975), *The Language of Thought*, Cambridge, MA: Harvard University Press.

Griffiths, P.E. and R.D. Gray (2001), 'Darwinism and Developmental Systems', in S. Oyama, P.E. Griffiths and R.D. Gray (eds), *Cycles of Contingency: Developmental Systems and Evolution*, Cambridge, MA and London: The MIT Press.

Hodgson, G.M. (2002), 'Reconstitutive Downward Causation', in E. Fullbrook (ed.), *Intersubjectivity in Economics: Agents and Structures*, London and New York: Routledge.

Hodgson, G.M. (2003), 'The Mystery of the Routine: The Darwinian Destiny of *An Evolutionary Theory of Economic Change*', *Revue économique*, **54**(2): 355–84.

Jacobson, M. (1995), *Foundations of Neuroscience*, New York and London: Plenum Press.

Kauffman, S.A. (2001), 'Prolegomenon to a General Biology', in A.R. Damasio, A. Harrington, J. Kagan, B.S. McEwen, H. Moss and R. Shaikh (eds), *Unity of Knowledge: The Convergence of Natural and Human Science*, Annals of the New York Academy of Sciences, v. 935.

Lakoff, G. and M. Johnson (1999), *Philosophy in the Flesh: The Embodied Mind and its Challenge to Western Thought*, New York: Basic Books.

Lawson, T. (1997), *Economics and Reality*, London: Routledge.

Lawson, T. (2003a), 'Institutionalism: On the Need to Firm up Notions of Social Structure and the Human Subject', *Journal of Economic Issues*, **XXXVII**(1): 175–207.

Lawson, T. (2003b), *Reorienting Economics*, London and New York: Routledge.

Lorenz, E. (2001), 'Models of Cognition, the Contextualisation of Knowledge and Organisational Theory', *Journal of Management and Governance*, **5**: 307–30.

Lucas, R. (1988), 'On the Mechanics of Economic Development', *Journal of Monetary Economics*, **22**: 3–42.

Lündvall, B.-A. and B. Johnson (1994), 'The Learning Economy', *Journal of Industry Studies*, **1**(2), 23–42.

Martin, J. (2003), 'Emergent Persons', *New Ideas in Psychology*, **21**: 85–99.

Martin, P. (1999), *The Healing Mind: The Vital Links between Brain and Behavior, Immunity and Disease*, New York: St Martin's Press.

Maturana, H. and F. Varela (1980), *Autopoiesis and Cognition: The Realization of the Living*, Dordrecht: Reidel.

Meijers, A.W. M. (2000), 'Mental Causation and Searle's Impossible Conception of Unconscious Intentionality', *International Journal of Philosophical Studies*, **8**(2): 155–70.

Meijers, A.W.M. (2003), 'Can Collective Intentionality be Individualized?', *American Journal of Economics and Sociology*, **62**(1): 167–83.

Merleau-Ponty, M. (1945/1962), *Phenomenology of Perception*, translated by C. Smith, London: Routledge & Kegan Paul. Original edition of 1945, Paris: Gallimard.

Metcalfe, J.S. and R. Ramlogan (2005), 'Limits to the Economy of Knowledge and Knowledge of the Economy', *Futures*, **37**(7): 655–74.

Mingers, J. (2001), 'Embodying Information Systems: The Contribution of Phenomenology', *Information and Organization*, **11**: 103–28.

Nelson, K. and Nelson, R.R. (2002), 'On the Nature and Evolution of Human Know-how', *Research Policy*, **31**: 719–33.

Nelson, R.R. and S.G. Winter (1982), *An Evolutionary Theory of Economic Change*, Cambridge, MA: The Belknap Press.

Newell, A. and H.A. Simon (1972), *Human Problem Solving*, Englewood Cliffs, NJ: Prentice-Hall.

Nightingale, P. (2003), 'If Nelson and Winter are Only Half Right about Tacit Knowledge, Which Half? A Searlean Critique of "Codification"', *Industrial and Corporate Change*, **12**(2): 149–83.

Nooteboom, B. (2001), 'From Evolution to Language and Learning', in J. Foster and J.S. Metcalfe (eds), *Frontiers of Evolutionary Economics: Competition, Self-Organization and Innovation Policy*, Cheltenham, UK, and Northampton, MA, USA: Edward Elgar, pp. 41–69.

O'Connor, T. (2000), 'Causality, Mind, and Free Will', *Philosophical Perspectives*, **14**: 105–17.

O'Connor, T. and H.Y. Wong (2002), 'Emergent Properties', in E.N. Zalta (ed.), *Stanford Encyclopedia of Philosophy*, Stanford: The Metaphysics Research Lab, Stanford University: http://plato.stanford.edu/contents.html.

Omnès, R. (1999), *Quantum Philosophy: Understanding and Interpreting Contemporary Science*, Princeton, NJ: Princeton University Press.

Orlikowski, W.J. (2002), 'Knowing in Practice: Enacting a Collective Capability in Distributed Organizing', *Organization Science*, **13**(3): 249–73.

Overton, W.F. (1994), 'The Arrow of Time and the Cycle of Time: Concepts of Change, Cognition, and Embodiment', *Psychological Inquiry*, **5**(3): 215–37.

Overton, W.F. (2004), 'A Relational and Embodied Perspective on Resolving Psychology's Antinomies', in J.I.M. Carpendale and U. Muller (eds), *Social Interaction and the Development of Knowledge*, Mahwah, NJ: Erlbaum.

Oyama, S., P.E. Griffiths and R.D. Gray (eds) (2001), *Cycles of Contingency: Developmental Systems and Evolution*, Cambridge, MA and London: The MIT Press.

Piaget, J. (1970), *Genetic Epistemology*, New York: Columbia University Press.

Polanyi, M. (1962), *Personal Knowledge: Towards a Post-critical Philosophy*, Chicago: University of Chicago Press.

Polanyi, M. (1966/1983), *The Tacit Dimension*, Gloucester, MA: Peter Smith.

Polanyi, M. (1975), 'Personal Knowledge', in M. Polanyi and H. Prosch, *Meaning*, Chicago and London: University of Chicago Press.

Reed, M. (2003), 'The Agency/Structure Dilemma in Organization Theory – Open Doors and Brick Walls', in H. Tsoukas and C. Knudsen (eds), *The Oxford Handbook of Organization Theory*, Oxford: Oxford University Press.

Rescher, N. (2000), *Process Philosophy. A Survey of Basic Issues*, Pittsburgh: University of Pittsburgh Press.

Rizzello, S. (1999), *The Economics of the Mind*, Cheltenham, UK, and Northampton, MA, USA: Edward Elgar.

Romer, P. (1986), 'Increasing Returns and Long-run Growth', *Journal of Political Economy*, **94**(5): 1002–37.

Roy, J.-M., J. Petitot, B. Pachoud and F.J. Varela (1999), 'Beyond the Gap: An Introduction to Naturalizing Phenomenology', in J. Petitot, F.J. Varela, B. Pachoud and J.-M. Roy (eds), *Naturalizing Phenomenology*, Stanford: Stanford University Press.

Searle, J. (1999), *Mind, Language and Society*, London: Phoenix.

Smith, D.W. (1999), 'Intentionality Naturalized?', in J. Petitot, F.J. Varela, B. Pachoud and J.-M. Roy (eds), *Naturalizing Phenomenology*, Stanford: Stanford University Press.

Smith, K. (2002), 'What is the "Knowledge Economy"? Knowledge Intensity and Distributed Knowledge Bases', Discussion Paper Series no. 2002–6, INTECH– The United Nations University, Maastricht.

Spender, J.-C. (1996), 'Making Knowledge the Basis of a Dynamic Theory of the Firm', *Strategic Management Journal*, **17**: 45–62.

Stacey, R. (2000), 'The Emergence of Knowledge in Organization', *Emergence*, **2**(4): 23–39.

Steinmueller, W.E. (2000), 'Will New Information and Communication Technologies Improve the "Codification" of Knowledge?', *Industrial and Corporate Change*, **9**(2): 361–76.

Stjernfelt, F. (2000), 'The Idea that Changed the World', *Cybernetics and Human Knowing*, **17**(1): 77–82.

Thompson, E. (1995), *Colour Vision: A Study in Cognitive Science and the Philosophy of Perception*, London and New York: Routledge.

Tsoukas, H. (1996), 'The Firm as a Distributed Knowledge System: A Constructionist Approach', *Strategic Management Journal*, **17**: 11–25.

Tsoukas, H. (2003), 'New Times, Fresh Challenges – Reflections on the Past and the Future of Organization Theory', in H. Tsoukas and C. Knudsen (eds), *The Oxford Handbook of Organization Theory*, Oxford: Oxford University Press.

Vanderstraeten, R. (2003), 'Education and the *Condicio Socialis*: Double Contingency in Interaction', *Educational Theory*, **53**(1): 19–35.

Viskovatoff, A. (2002), 'Searle's Background: Comments on Runde and Faulkner', *Journal of Economic Methodology*, **9**(1): 65–80.

Vygotsky, L.S. (1934/1987), 'Thinking and Speech', in R.W. Rieber and A.S. Carton (eds), *The Collected Works of L.S. Vygotsky, Volume 1: Problems of General Psychology*, New York: Plenum.

Weber, B.H. and D.J. Depew (2001), 'Developmental Systems, Darwinian Evolution, and the Unity of Science', in S. Oyama, P.E. Griffiths and R.D. Gray (eds), *Cycles of Contingency: Developmental Systems and Evolution*, Cambridge, MA and London: The MIT Press.

Weick, K.E. and K.H. Roberts (1993), 'Collective Mind in Organizations: Heedful Interrelating on Flight Decks', *Administrative Science Quarterly*, **38**: 357–81.

Zubiri, X. (1968/2003), *Dynamic Structure of Reality*, Urbana and Chicago: The University of Illinois Press.

Index